CW00815831

The
Strangeness of Tragedy

The Strangeness of Tragedy

PAUL HAMMOND

OXFORD
UNIVERSITY PRESS

Great Clarendon Street, Oxford OX2 6DP
Oxford University Press is a department of the University of Oxford.
It furthers the University's objective of excellence in research, scholarship,
and education by publishing worldwide in

Oxford New York

Auckland Cape Town Dar es Salaam Hong Kong Karachi
Kuala Lumpur Madrid Melbourne Mexico City Nairobi
New Delhi Shanghai Taipei Toronto

With offices in

Argentina Austria Brazil Chile Czech Republic France Greece
Guatemala Hungary Italy Japan Poland Portugal Singapore
South Korea Switzerland Thailand Turkey Ukraine Vietnam

Oxford is a registered trade mark of Oxford University Press
in the UK and in certain other countries

Published in the United States
by Oxford University Press Inc., New York

First published 2009

British Library Cataloguing in Publication Data
Data available

Library of Congress Cataloging in Publication Data
Library of Congress Control Number: 2009928981

Typeset by SPI Publisher Services, Pondicherry, India
Printed in Great Britain by
the MPG Books Group, Bodmin and King's Lynn

ISBN 978-0-19-957260-1

1 3 5 7 9 10 8 6 4 2

πολλὰ τὰ δεινὰ κοὐδὲν ἀν-
θρώπου δεινότερον πέλει.

SOPHOCLES

CONTENTS

A NOTE ON TEXTS AND TRANSLATIONS

The plays are quoted from the following editions. Other editions which have been consulted are cited in the footnotes. Any unattributed translations are my own. Quotations from Greek texts are presented in Greek type, but citations of technical terms are transliterated for the convenience of the reader without Greek.

AESCHYLUS The Greek text is from Denys Page's Oxford Classical Texts edition, *Aeschyli Septem Quae Supersunt Tragoedias* (Oxford, 1972), though I have not followed his use of the lunate sigma and iota adscript; the English translations (unless otherwise stated) are from *Aeschylus: Oresteia*, translated by Hugh Lloyd-Jones (London, 1982).

SOPHOCLES The Greek text and English translation (unless otherwise stated) are from *Sophocles*, edited and translated by Hugh Lloyd-Jones, Loeb Classical Library, 2 vols. (Cambridge, Mass., 1994).

SENECA The Latin text and English translation are reprinted by permission of the publishers and the Trustees of the Loeb Classical Library from *Seneca: Tragedies*, Loeb Classical Library ® Volumes 62 and 78, translated by John G. Fitch, Cambridge, Mass.: Harvard University Press, Copyright © 2004 by the President and Fellows of Harvard College. The Loeb Classical Library® is a registered trademark of the President and Fellows of Harvard College.

SHAKESPEARE Shakespeare is quoted from *The Complete Works of William Shakespeare*, edited by Herbert Farjeon, The Nonesuch Shakespeare, 4 vols. (London, 1953), which reprints the First Folio text verbatim. This edition is used with the kind permission of the Nonesuch Press and Gerald Duckworth & Co Ltd. Since this edition does not give line numbers, these have been added from the most recent Arden editions.

RACINE *Phèdre* is quoted from the most recent Pléiade edition, Racine, *Œuvres complètes: I: Théâtre-Poésie*, edited by Georges Forestier (Paris, 1999), which calls the play *Phèdre et Hippolyte* following the first edition (1677); it was retitled *Phèdre* for the second edition in 1687. To avoid confusion I have used the customary, revised title.

ABBREVIATIONS

Chantraine	Pierre Chantraine, *Dictionnaire étymologique de la langue grecque* (Paris, 1968; second edition 1999)
LSJ	*A Greek—English Lexicon*, compiled by Henry George Liddell and Robert Scott, revised by Sir Henry Stuart Jones (Oxford, 1940, revised edition with supplement 1996)
OED	*The Oxford English Dictionary*, second edition on CD-ROM 2002
OLD	*The Oxford Latin Dictionary*, edited by P. G. W. Glare (Oxford, 1982, corrected reprint 1996)

Prologue

Quis hic locus, quae regio, quae mundi plaga?[1]

In Seneca's *Hercules*, the protagonist in his madness believes that he is making an assault upon the heavens; in fact, he is slaughtering his own wife and child. For this tragic moment he moves on a plane which he alone inhabits; others can only watch in horror. He lapses into sleep. When he awakes, unaware of what he has done, he fails to recognize the world into which he is returning, and asks what place this is:

> Quis hic locus, quae regio, quae mundi plaga?
> ubi sum? sub ortu solis, an sub cardine
> glacialis Ursae? numquid Hesperii maris
> extrema tellus hunc dat Oceano modum?
> quas trahimus auras? quod solum fesso subest?
> certe redimus: unde prostrata domo
> video cruenta corpora? an nondum exuit
> simulacra mens inferna? post reditus quoque
> oberrat oculis turba feralis meis?[2]

> What place is this, what region, what tract of the earth? Where am I? Beneath the sun's rising, or beneath the turning point of the icy Bear? Can this be the limit set to Ocean's waters by the farthest land on the western sea? What air do I breathe? What ground lies under my weary body? Certainly I have returned: why do I see blood-stained

[1] Seneca, *Hercules*, l. 1138: 'What place is this, what region, what tract of the earth?' The line was quoted redemptively by T. S. Eliot as the epigraph for *Marina* (1930).

[2] *Hercules*, ll. 1138–46.

> bodies in a ruined house? Has my mind not yet cast off images from the underworld? Even after my return does a throng of the dead wander before my eyes?

He sees both the house around him and the underworld, laminating one kind of space upon another. He sees both blood-stained bodies and the wandering shades of the dead. Theseus and Amphitryon hide their faces, and cannot bring themselves to answer Hercules' questions: *Tacita sic abeant mala* ('These troubles must just pass in silence').[3] Once he realizes what he has done, Hercules summons land, sea, and sky to punish him, before resolving to immolate himself in order to cleanse the earth and escape to the underworld. His father Amphitryon manages to dissuade him, and when Hercules asks what region can possibly tolerate him as an exile, Theseus offers his own land as a place of refuge and of cleansing:

> Nostra te tellus manet.
> . . . .
> illa te, Alcide, vocat,
> facere innocentes terra quae superos solet.[4]

> My land awaits you . . . That land summons you, Alcides, which customarily restores gods to innocence.

In his tragic dementia, Hercules has moved into a dimension of his own imagining; as he recognizes what he has done—and the recognition is no less tragic than the killing—he seeks oblivion, seeks a place of annihilation; finally, he is offered a place of healing. The tragic protagonist has been displaced into a form of space which no one else shares. His time is not their time, either, for his act endures impervious to the motions of change and decay which are the rhythms of the ordinary world:

> Arctoum licet
> Maeotis in me gelida transfundat mare
> et tota Tethys per meas currat manus,
> haerebit altum facinus.[5]

[3] *Hercules*, l. 1186. [4] *Hercules*, ll. 1341–4.
[5] *Hercules*, ll. 1326–9. For Shakespeare's echo of this idea in *Macbeth* see p. 140 below.

> Though chill Maeotis should pour its northern seas over me and all the Ocean stream across my hands, the deed will stay deeply ingrained.

Haerebit . . . facinus: the crime will stick fast; the verb combines the spatial (remain attached, adhere) and the temporal (abide, continue). He speaks a language which is not that of the bystanders, who shield themselves in silence.

The case of Hercules exemplifies a mode of estrangement which seems to be characteristic of tragedy, a movement of translation and of decomposition. The protagonist is translated out of his normal time and space into forms of these which others cannot inhabit. The space in which he stands is one which has been transformed by his imagination into a terrain contoured by guilt or ambition or desire; shaped by loyalty to the dead, to their realm and their laws; providing the ground on which fantastically imagined narratives unknown to others can be played out. The time in which he moves is not the time of his neighbours, but a dimension in which what they would call the past is urgently present to him, or in which the future seems already to have happened; laws of sequence, of cause and effect, no longer apply. Language no longer joins the protagonist to his social milieu: he speaks his own idiolect, uses the concepts of his homeland to build an alien world. As Jean-Pierre Vernant writes:

> Les mots échangés sur l'espace scénique ont moins alors pour fonction d'établir la communication entre les divers personnages que de marquer les blocages, les barrières, l'imperméabilité des esprits, de cerner les points de conflit. Pour chaque protagoniste, enfermé dans l'univers qui lui est propre, le vocabulaire utilisé reste dans sa plus grande partie opaque; il a un sens et un seul. A cette unilatéralité se heurte violemment une autre unilatéralité.[6]

[6] Jean-Pierre Vernant, 'Tensions et ambiguïtés dans la tragédie grecque', in Jean-Pierre Vernant and Pierre Vidal-Naquet, *Mythe et tragédie en Grèce ancienne*, 2 vols. (Paris, 1972–86; reprinted 2001), i 35: 'The function of the words used on stage is not so much to establish communication between the various characters as to indicate the blockages and barriers between them and the impermeability of their minds, to locate the points of conflict. For each protagonist, locked into his own particular world, the vocabulary that is used remains for the most part opaque. For him it has one, and only one meaning. This one-sidedness comes into violent collision with another.' (*Myth and Tragedy in Ancient Greece*, translated by Janet Lloyd (New York, 1988), p. 42.)

And yet these self-enclosed idiolects which combat one against the other are themselves fissile, and decompose.

Such tragic metamorphoses translate the central figure of the drama into new modes of being, and into new, only half-comprehensible languages, but this translation is not the carrying across (*translatio*) of an integral being: there is a decomposition of the self, a deformation which may sometimes render that figure sublimely heroic, but is also liable to make him estranged and fractured.[7]

The strangeness of such tragic transformations is a estrangement of the protagonist from his home territory, or from what had seemed to be home ground. Indeed, what tragedy takes apart is the very notion of the homely, of the self and its rootedness. In his essay *Das Unheimliche* (usually translated as 'The Uncanny'), published in 1919, Freud explains how in German the words *heimlich* (homely, familiar) and *unheimlich* (strange, uncanny) appear to be opposites, but actually have overlapping semantic fields, so that *heimlich* means both 'what is familiar and agreeable' and 'what is concealed and kept out of sight', and in this latter sense 'inaccessible to knowledge, hidden and dangerous'—and therefore *unheimlich*.[8] The *unheimlich* is also that which 'ought to have remained secret and hidden but has come to light'.[9] The private and intimate is made public and visible. These two terms—which are two keystones of the human world, two essential means through which we define ourselves and others—do not simply change places or cancel each other out; rather, they remain distinct and necessary terms, but now each is shown to have the potential to decompose into the other. Though Freud's *unheimlich*

[7] This combination of failed translation between key terms and the decomposition of an integral self and of unitary meaning might appropriately be termed 'deconstruction', had not that term been excessively and too loosely used. Nevertheless, I acknowledge a general debt to the work of Jacques Derrida in my approach to tragedy. Tragedy is, *par excellence*, a deconstructive medium.

[8] *The Standard Edition of the Complete Psychological Works of Sigmund Freud*, edited by James Strachey et al., 24 vols. (London, 1953–74), xvii 220–6; the German text is found in Sigmund Freud, *Gesammelte Werke*, edited by Anna Freud et al., 18 vols. (London and Frankfurt, 1940–68), xii 227–68.

[9] Freud, *Standard Edition*, xvii 225.

is normally translated as 'uncanny', that word has connotations of encounters with the supernatural which make it a potentially misleading term; 'unhomely' might be a better rendering. Freud's exploration of the *unheimlich* or unhomely also discusses the phenomenon of people seeing doubles, and in such encounters, he says,

> the subject identifies himself with someone else, so that he is in doubt as to which his self is, or substitutes the extraneous self for his own. In other words, there is a doubling, dividing and interchanging of the self. And finally there is the constant recurrence of the same thing—the repetition of the same features or character-traits or vicissitudes, of the same crimes, or even the same names through several consecutive generations.[10]

The *unheimlich* describes the condition of being displaced; one's grasp of 'home' (*Heimat*) is undone, as the distinction between home and foreign is elided; one becomes divided or multiplied, as events seem to be repeated and time no longer seems to follow its normal course: man is no longer at home in the world.[11]

It is in such a sense that this book will explore the strangeness which tragedy fashions. Through the estrangement and the decomposition of the tragic protagonist we are brought face to face with the fragility of our identity, and the fragility of the languages through which we make sense of that identity. The space which we think of as home—and by space here I mean both geographical space and conceptual space, both the literal hearth and that framework of familiar assumptions which holds our selves in place—such a space is labile; we discover that our home ground is *unheimlich*, that a foreignness haunts the familiar. Tragic protagonists are displaced from their *heimlich* spaces, and find their

[10] Freud, *Standard Edition*, xvii 234: 'so daß der eine das Wissen, Fühlen und Erleben des anderen mitbesitzt, die Identifizierung mit einer anderen Person, so daß man an seinem Ich irre wird oder das fremde Ich an die Stelle des eigenen versetzt, also Ich-Verdopplung, Ich-Teilung, Ich-Vertauschung—und endlich die beständige Wiederkehr des Gleichen, die Wiederholung der nämlichen Gesichtszüge, Charaktere, Schicksale, verbrecherischen Taten, ja der Namen durch mehrere aufeinanderfolgende Generationen.' (*Gesammelte Werke*, xii 246).

[11] There is a Heideggerian resonance to the idea of being 'at home in the world', to which we shall return in the Epilogue.

identities fissured or multiplied. 'Wir selbst Fremdsprachige sind', said Freud,[12] 'We ourselves speak a language that is foreign'; but if this is the common condition of all speakers, it is pre-eminently the tragic protagonist whose language becomes foreign, who speaks a *parole* which no longer quite meshes with the *langue* of those around him. Tragedy translates the protagonist into his own dimension, separated from the social world around him, and now inaccessible to others.

The space of tragedy is often liminal.[13] Characters such as Agamemnon or Oedipus stand on the threshold of something beyond the ordinary which is nevertheless already theirs; they are no longer grounded in the life of the everyday, but neither have they yet passed beyond into the grave or into some communion with the gods. One of the elements which makes the staged spaces of tragedy so unstable is that they seem to abut onto, or to open out into, other spaces which we cannot quite grasp: these are not contiguous places, but other kinds of space, other ways of inhabiting or perceiving. In *Oedipus the King* our attention is repeatedly drawn to those spaces which we do not see: to Mount Cithaeron where the baby was exposed, the crossroads where Laius was killed, the bed where Oedipus and Jocasta conceived their children, the inner house where Jocasta hangs herself and where Oedipus puts out his own eyes; and to the underworld where Oedipus knows that his parents await him. Such spaces haunt—that is, destroy the coherence of—the spaces which we do see. And because we are repeatedly made aware that actions in the present have their causes elsewhere, off-stage in a plane which we never touch (as Phèdre says, 'Mon mal vient de plus loin'[14]), these actions never exist solidly and squarely in the present space, in the space that is visible to the eye, following the normal logic of cause and effect, but decompose into events which stretch towards us from a space that is visible only to the

[12] Freud, *Gesammelte Werke*, xii 232; *Standard Edition*, xvii 221.

[13] A classic study of the symbolic spaces and structures with which tragedy engages is Jean-Pierre Vernant and Pierre Vidal-Naquet, *Mythe et tragédie en Grèce ancienne*. For the spaces of Greek tragedy see also André Bernard, *La Carte du tragique: La géographie dans la tragédie grecque* (Paris, 1985).

[14] 'My trouble [or 'evil'] comes from further back [or 'further away']': Racine, *Phèdre*, I iii 269.

mind's eye, a space whose contours and frontiers are as intermittent and ungraspable as those of a dream.

And so it is that the time of tragedy is also transformed.[15] It is an obvious characteristic of tragedy that its protagonist is not granted time to change, to repent, to restore. By contrast, the genre of comedy, however occasionally cruel, seems to be ultimately forgiving in allowing time for the characters to change, for events to be reversed, for entanglements to be sorted out. It inhabits a holiday time.[16] In the comic twin which haunts the tragedy of *Othello*, always subliminally suggesting an alternative outcome, Emilia would discover the significance of the handkerchief in time to tell Othello, Iago's lies would be exposed, and Othello enabled to ask Desdemona's forgiveness for aspersing her. Romeo would arrive at Juliet's tomb just as she wakes from her sleeping draught; Edmond would repent in time to prevent Cordelia from being hanged. But tragedy forces events to their conclusion, refusing time for reflection and repentance and recovery. The protagonist has moved, or has been moved by forces which we cannot quite name, into a new kind of time; as Iago says of Othello:

> Not Poppy, nor Mandragora,
> Nor all the drowsie Syrrups of the world
> Shall ever medicine thee to that sweete sleepe
> Which thou owd'st yesterday.[17]

It is not only a particular past time which is made irrecoverable, but the very mode of existence which had made those previous experiences possible. Iago prefaces the words just quoted by saying to the audience, 'Looke where he comes': Othello has already passed into another form of time and space, a place of the imagination which Iago can delineate and exhibit to us, but which he does not himself share.

But there is another way in which we might understand tragic time. Protagonists never quite inhabit their present: their time, like their

[15] For time in Greek tragedy see Jacqueline de Romilly, *Le Temps dans la tragédie grecque*, second edition (Paris, 1995).

[16] See Charles Barber, *Shakespeare's Festive Comedy* (Princeton, 1959).

[17] Shakespeare, *Othello*, III iii 333–6.

space, decomposes, for as we are aware that an event in the present has roots in the past, this past is brought into the present in a way which disturbs it, troubling it and undoing its coherence without ever making those causes and origins accessible for confrontation or repair. 'Mon mal vient de plus loin' is a temporal as well as a spatial reflection. The past is never quite past, never completed, but always alive in its potential to undermine the autonomy and integrity of the present. Freud cites the usage of *heimlich* to refer to a family: 'they are like a buried spring or a dried-up pond. One cannot walk over it without always having the feeling that water might come up there again.'[18] This could be a description of Argos or Thebes, Elsinore or Dunsinane.

The language of tragedy likewise slips from coherence. There is in all literary texts a troubling of linguistic and semantic order, a solicitation or shaking of the structures of meaning and thought.[19] When language is viewed as a system of traces, there is a continual movement away from the present towards another field (not necessarily a temporal past, and hardly ever an actual historical past) which is itself a fiction of coherence and stability, and as such beyond reach. Any literary text, by compelling our attention to the semantic play of its words, may surprise us into seeing the complexities of the linguistic field, the gaps and doublings of language. But tragedy does this most ruthlessly, for one of the tragedies which it holds out to us is that human language has no *signifié transcendantal*,[20] no ultimately fixed point, no ground. Linguistic signs beckon us into a world of receding traces, a world elsewhere, an ever-shifting mirage of coherence. In tragedy, rigorous coherence and full intelligibility are indeed a mirage: here 'nothing is, but what is not', as Macbeth says.[21]

[18] Freud, *Standard Edition*, xvii 223; *Gesammelte Werke*, xii 234: 'es kommt mir mit ihnen vor, wie mit einem zugegrabenen Brunnen oder einem ausgetrokneten Teich. Man kann nicht darüber gehen ohne daß es Einem immer ist, als könnte da wieder einmal Wasser zum Vorschein kommen.'

[19] I draw here on Jacques Derrida, especially *L'Écriture et la différance* (Paris, 1967, reprinted 1994) and *De la grammatologie* (Paris, 1967).

[20] Derrida, 'La Structure, le signe, et le jeu dans le discours des sciences humaines', in *L'Écriture et la différance*, p. 411.

[21] Shakespeare, *Macbeth*, I iii 142.

Though the great concepts which define us as human—God, Nature, Reason, Truth—are the currency of tragic speech, the work of tragedy is to place these concepts *sous rature*,[22] visible but cancelled, necessary but impossible, no longer guarantors that human thinking is coherent and viable, but relics now of a struggle in which these cherished terms have been irrecoverably damaged. They no longer match the actual grain of tragic experience. There is, then, a tragedy of language, as well as a tragedy of individuals and of societies. The shared language fractures, but so too does the linguistic bond which connects the tragic figure with his peers. The individual's idiolect separates the protagonist from those around him, becoming a form of prison, for signs no longer connect him with his hearers. His own semiotic system becomes self-enclosed, self-referential, and autistic, increasingly unintelligible to those who try to speak to him.

The individual is now not *individuus*, neither undivided in himself or inseparable from others,[23] for he loses his coherence, through fissuring and through doubling. This capacity of the tragic genre to estrange one from oneself is symbolized in the earliest forms of tragedy through the use of the mask[24] and the invocation of Dionysus the god of ecstasy (in Greek ἔκστασις: 'displacement', 'standing aside'). Nietzsche saw Apollo as the god of individuation, Dionysus as the god of union,[25] but if tragedy unites the subject it does so with a strange force, one which abolishes the Apollonian integrity of the rationally based, rationally intelligible human. Tragedy prevents a

[22] Derrida's typographical technique in *De la grammatologie*, which cancels a problematic term by placing a cross through it, so that it remains legible but is marked as a word which cannot be allowed to function normally in the sentence, or operate unchallenged in the conceptual structures which he is analysing.

[23] The word has two distinct meanings: *OED s.v.* individual *adj.* 1 ('forming an indivisible entity'); 2 ('inseparable', e.g. from a friend; the first example of this sense is from Shakespeare's *Timon of Athens*). The Latin *individuus* likewise has the two principal meanings 'indivisible' and 'inseparable' (*OLD* 1, 2).

[24] For a recent study of the tragic mask see David Wiles, *Mask and Performance in Greek Tragedy* (Cambridge, 2007), and for the mask in the wider context of Greek identities see Françoise Frontisi-Ducroux, *Du Masque au visage: Aspects de l'identité en Grèce ancienne* (Paris, 1995).

[25] In *Die Geburt der Tragödie aus dem Geiste der Musik* (1895).

gathering of the self, prevents an articulation of its components along the lines of a common syntax which others can recognize.[26] Sometimes the individual as an agent is compromised: in Greek thought, moments of extreme passion are often figured as the intervention of a deity, so that in the access of sexual desire one is overcome by Aphrodite, or in martial rage by Ares.[27] In tragedy this is forced to a new point, and we focus on the moment when the protagonist both is and is not himself. At such moments of extreme suffering, any explanation expressed simply in terms of how an individual acts seems inadequate. Oedipus says that his own hand blinded him, but also that Apollo did this.[28] Oedipus too is the classic example of a doubled self: both son and husband, both father and brother. The individual may also lose his selfhood by becoming mythologized: the Chorus in *Oedipus at Colonus* see only the monstrous, mythologized Oedipus, not the old man seeking rest and shelter; eventually they see another mythologized version of him, the bringer of blessings. Both Antony and Cleopatra in Shakespeare's play are translated into myth by those around them: Antony the great general, or the abject lover of Cleopatra; Cleopatra the queen of Egypt, or the lustful gypsy. In Dryden's version of the same story, *All for Love*, we see those characters struggling with their own past versions of themselves, seeking a way to free themselves from that form of history which is encapsulated in their mythologies.[29] All through tragedy there recurs an attempt to understand whether the individual has free will, what this notion might mean in particular cases, how he relates to those powers which we name the gods, or fate, or fortune when we try to

[26] Paradoxically, in the Greek play which actually brings Dionysus on stage, Euripides' *Bacchae*, it is the protagonist's refusal to be displaced from what he takes to be the common social modes of life which proves tragic, as Pentheus denies the *unheimlich* power of the god and is ultimately dismembered by the Bacchantes. See Euripides, *Bacchae*, edited by E. R. Dodds (Oxford, 1944, second edition 1960).

[27] See E. R. Dodds, *The Greeks and the Irrational* (Berkeley, 1951); Ruth Padel, *In and Out of the Mind: Greek Images of the Tragic Self* (Princeton, NJ, 1992).

[28] See p. 82 below.

[29] See Paul Hammond, 'Redescription in *All for Love*', *The Aligarh Critical Miscellany*, 13 (2000), 26–43.

chart the limits of the human. In translating the individual into something other than the human (be it corpse or myth) tragedy probes that very concept.

The book which follows is an essay—an essay only, and by no means intended as a definitive treatise—on the ways in which tragedy effects radical forms of estrangement by translating the protagonist into modes of time, space, and language which are alienated from those forms of time, space, and language which, in the different imaginations of different societies, constitute the human home. Tragedy makes the *heimlich* into the *unheimlich*, and in so doing fashions forms of the unhomely in which man is made to dwell. The individual and his conceptual space are transformed, but so too is the conceptual space of the audience, as we see how our own structures of thought may be grounded upon unstable foundations.

The distinctive method of this book is a close attention to the linguistic strangeness of these texts, to features which are often obscured by the paraphrases of translators, or the glosses of editors, who are tempted to normalize and domesticate the language of tragedy. The reading of local linguistic tensions, ambiguities, and ruptures will be a means of approaching the larger conceptual perplexity and fragmentation which tragedy brings about. As the tragic protagonist moves into reconfigured forms of time and space, it is language estranged from its common paths which fashions this new world: metaphor, tense, and syntax forget their habitual ways of establishing identity or likeness, the sequence of cause and effect, the distinction between agent and patient. And it is particularly when it comes to map the relations between the human and the divine that the language of tragedy becomes most uncertain, perplexed and perplexing. Greek tragic vocabulary evokes various named gods, and Fate, and avenging Erinyes, and an anonymous daimon which may haunt a family; there are also concepts such as fear and anger which may appear from time to time to take on personified form. The plays may attempt to say how these powers act, but their ways remain beyond definition. Agency, both divine and human, becomes a deeply troubled concept. Senecan drama translates some of these terms into Latin equivalents which do not inhabit quite the same conceptual space as that of Greek thought. And the language of Shakespeare fashions a world in which Christian and classical terms jostle. That which lies beyond the human is repeatedly evoked and repeatedly escapes understanding; and as this happens, the boundaries of the human world, and of the human self, become permeable: we cannot be sure that it is Oedipus who acts—or quite what it means now to say 'Oedipus'.

The plays chosen for discussion range from Aeschylus' *Agamemnon* to Racine's *Phèdre*, from classical Greek drama to its reworking in the sixteenth and seventeenth centuries. They are all works which lie within a classical tradition, in that they share and reconfigure myths, plot motifs, and philosophical problems, and use vocabularies which are transmitted and translated within a shared tradition: a transformation of its key concepts. To move beyond this already diverse selection (for example, into the estranged domesticities of Ibsen or Beckett) would require a move into yet more distant conceptual and theatrical languages. The question, *Quis hic locus, quae regio, quae mundi plaga*?—what is this terrain into which tragedy transforms our world?—is already hard enough to answer.

1

THE WORK OF TRAGEDY

Quis hic locus? The space delineated by tragedy often carries a mythic freight and temporal complexity: these are places which are inhabited not only by the creatures of the human and visible present, but by people of the past, by ancestors, giants, heroes, gods, witches, ghosts. And by abstract nouns which perhaps have their own autonomy and agency—Fate, Fear, Justice. At the opening of Aeschylus' *Agamemnon*, Sophocles' *Electra*, or Seneca's *Thyestes* we are made aware that the house is a richly-stored space of family lore; some form of narrative will uncoil from inside this store-house of myth, sacrifice, murder, generational resentments, blood grudges, and dishonoured gods. Something will spill out of these spaces to haunt the stage. Both presence and loss inflect these spaces.

In Seneca's *Troades* the site once occupied by Troy has been so thoroughly obliterated that there are no ruins left that stand sufficiently high to hide a child, so that Andromache has to conceal her son Astyanax from the Greeks in his own father's burial mound. The distracted mother begs the earth to split open and hide the treasure which she has entrusted to it, even to take Astyanax down into the underworld.[1] When Ulysses threatens to demolish Hector's tomb and scatter the ashes, an unspeakable violation which would also expose

[1] Seneca, *Troades*, ll. 498–521.

her son's hiding place, Andromache summons the ghost of her husband, and she sees his spirit though Ulysses cannot:

> rumpe fatorum moras,
> molire terras, Hector! ut Ulixem domes
> vel umbra satis es.—arma concussit manu,
> iaculatur ignes! cernitis, Danai, Hectorem?
> an sola video?[2]

> Break through death's barriers, force away the earth, Hector! Even as a ghost you are enough to master Ulysses. He brandished his weapons in his hands, he is hurling firebrands! Can you perceive Hector, you Danaans? Or do I alone see him?

Here the arid site is filled with ghostly presences: with Hector who appears to Andromache's distracted mind; with the tomb which not only shelters the remains of Hector but stands by synecdoche for the lost civilization of Troy itself, its lost prowess but also its abiding care for the dead. Memories and values are stored along with Hector's ashes in the mound which provides *unheimlich* shelter to Astyanax, and Andomache cannot bear to imagine these memories and these ashes scattered on the waves. She calls Astyanax from his hiding place, and the child is taken off by Ulysses to be put to death by being hurled from Troy's one remaining tower. The boy, refusing to be a victim, *sponte desiluit sua | in media Priami regna* ('leapt down of his own accord, into the midst of Priam's kingdom').[3] *Priami regna*: a kingdom which is now only a lost way of life, a set of values which are momentarily recovered by the boy's heroism. The etymology of the lad's name is made horribly ironic: 'Astyanax' combines *ἄστυ* ('city') and *ἄναξ* ('lord'): he is lord of the city. But the heir to these ruins and fragments becomes himself another set of broken pieces. Who will consign his body to the tomb?, asks Andromache. There is no body left to bury, replies the messenger. These characters exist among the traces of a kingdom. The space which Seneca's characters inhabit is both geographical—the ruined buildings, the burial mound—and conceptual: Trojan ways, Priam's kingdom, Andromache's maternal

[2] *Troades*, ll. 681–5. [3] *Troades*, ll. 1102–3.

and uxorial compassion, Astyanax's heroism, values which are contrasted with the deviousness of Ulysses and the callousness (*nefas*, the messenger calls it, a transgression of divine law) of the Greek spectator who sat on top of Hector's tomb in order to have a better view of the boy's death.

At moments of extreme passion, the world around the protagonists dissolves, turns into a world elsewhere in which they find themselves or into which they wish themselves.[4] Senecan heroes often seek some other world. In his *Oedipus* the protagonist wishes to find a place separated from both the living and the dead: *quaeratur via | qua nec sepultis mixtus et vivis tamen | exemptus erres* ('Search for a way to wander without mixing with the dead, and yet removed from the living').[5] At the beginning of the *Phoenissae* Oedipus rejects guiding hands and seeks to return to his own place, which calls to him:

> Est alius istis noster in silvis locus,
> qui me reposcit: hunc petam cursu incito;
> non haesitabit gressus, huc omni duce
> spoliatus ibo. quid moror sedes meas?
> mortem, Cithaeron, redde et hospitium mihi
> illud meum restitue, ut expirem senex
> ubi debui infans.[6]

> There is another place, my place, in those forests, that calls me back. I shall make for it in urgent haste, my steps will not falter, I shall go there bereft of any guide. Why keep my own abode waiting? Give me back my death, Cithaeron; restore to me that lodging place of mine, so that I may die in old age where I should have died in infancy.

This *locus* is more than another geographical place: Mount Cithaeron, where he was exposed as a baby, is his place, his *sedes*, which means 'dwelling place' but also 'burial place'.[7] Partly personified, it calls him

[4] It is Shakespeare's Coriolanus who exclaims 'There is a world elsewhere' (III iii 135): he refuses to conform to the political ritual whereby candidates for office expose to public view the wounds which they have received in their country's service; forced to leave Rome, he joins Rome's enemies, but never finds a home with them; nor can he return to Rome.

[5] Seneca, *Oedipus*, ll. 949–51.

[6] Seneca, *Phoenissae*, ll. 27–33.

[7] *OLD* 4, 6.

back (*reposcit*); he calls upon it to give him back (*redde*) his death as if it were something which this place had unreasonably withheld from him; to restore (*restitue*) to him his lodging, *hospitium*. But *hospitium* is only a temporary dwelling, a place for a guest, *hospes*. The repeated *re-* forms mark Oedipus' desire to turn away from the present and to replace himself in a revised version of his own history. But such a return is beyond his capacity: tragedy invites but refuses it.

The spaces of Senecan drama provide places of retreat and self-definition, and ultimately of judgement and punishment, in Thomas Kyd's English Renaissance drama, *The Spanish Tragedie*.[8] While the action unfolds in the Renaissance Spanish and Portuguese courts, it is also acted out, unbeknown to the protagonists, on a stage which is precariously located between Renaissance and classical worlds. The play begins with an echo of Seneca's *Thyestes*, as Revenge and the ghost of Don Andrea recall how, after his death at the hands of the Portuguese prince Balthazar, the Spanish nobleman's spirit travelled through the underworld to the throne of Pluto for judgement. Andrea has left the underworld through the gates of horn, through which, according to Homer and Virgil, true dreams pass into the world of men, while false dreams come from the gates of ivory.[9] This places the play which then ensues as a true dream—but in whose mind? By contrast with the scenario in *Thyestes*, where the ghost of Tantalus is dragged reluctantly out of the underworld and compelled by the Fury to inspire his descendants to commit new horrors, Andrea is promised by Revenge that he will see his death avenged. They constitute almost a court of moral judgement, and at the end of the play the various wrongdoers are consigned to the classical underworld for punishment, replacing Sisyphus, Tantalus, and Ixion in their torments, as Revenge promises that 'heere, though death hath end their miserie, | Ile there begin their endles Tragedie'.[10] Their true tragedy begins only when the play ends, and one form of time and

[8] The play was probably written *c*.1587–8. Kyd is quoted from *The Works of Thomas Kyd*, edited by Frederick S. Boas (Oxford, 1901; corrected reprint 1955).

[9] Virgil, *Aeneid*, vi 893–6.

[10] *The Spanish Tragedie*, IV v 47–8.

space opens out into another. '*Qui iacet in terra non habet vnde cadat*', says the Portuguese Viceroy,[11] 'He who lies on the ground has nowhere further to fall', yet in this play characters can and do fall further, through the ground which they think is secure and into another form of space whose existence they hardly suspected.

And within these layered places of the drama, Hieronimo—increasingly distracted by his grief at the murder of his son, and his inability to obtain justice in the public world—is driven into further and further recesses of the mind, a solitude which is defined partly through Latin quotations. Holding a book, which conventionally signifies contemplation, prayer, or melancholy in Renaissance drama,[12] he says:

> *Vindicta mihi.*
> I, heauen will be reuenged of euery ill;
> Nor will they suffer murder vnrepaide.
> Then stay, *Hieronimo*, attend their will:
> For mortall men may not appoint their time.
> *Per scelus semper tutum est sceleribus iter.*
> Strike, and strike home, where wrong is offred thee;
> For euils vnto ils conductors be,
> And death's the worst of resolution.
> For he that thinks with patience to contend
> To quiet life, his life shall easily end.
> *Fata si miseros iuuant, habes salutem:*
> *Fata si vitam negant, habes sepulchrum.*[13]

What form of Latin speaks through Hieronimo and shapes his inner world? The opening '*Vindicta mihi*' seems to be a quotation from St Paul's admonition that 'Vengeance is mine', and the following two lines paraphrase the continuation of the verse, 'I will repay, saith the Lord'.[14] But this is not the Latin of the Vulgate, which reads *mihi vindictam ego retribuam dicit Dominus*: rather, the wording is closer

[11] *The Spanish Tragedie*, I iii 15.

[12] Alan C. Dessen and Leslie Thomson, *A Dictionary of Stage Directions in English Drama 1580–1642* (Cambridge, 1999), pp. 34–5.

[13] *The Spanish Tragedie*, III xiii 1–13.

[14] Romans xii 19.

to a phrase from the Senecan or pseudo-Senecan *Octavia*, *vindicta debetur mihi*.[15] Hieronimo's Christian resignation dissolves as his Latin pulls him away from St Paul to Seneca, a move which is prepared for as his singular Christian 'heauen' takes on the plural pronoun 'they' which is more apposite to the classical gods.[16] The book which he carries is evidently not a Bible but a copy of Seneca's plays, for he reads out: '*Per scelus semper tutum est sceleribus iter*': 'the safe way for crimes is always through a crime', a quotation from Seneca's *Agamemnon*.[17] It is a reading of Seneca which impels Hieronimo's plot, as he is drawn into replicating the words of his Senecan prototype. Then he quotes further lines from Seneca, this time from *Troades*: '*Fata si miseros juvant, habes salutem*; | *Fata si vitam negant, habes sepulchrum*.'[18] The words are spoken by Andromache as she tries to conceal Astyanax in the tomb of his father Hector: 'If the Fates help the wretched, you have a refuge; if the Fates deny you life, you have a tomb.' Words from another world come into Hieronimo's mind, and shape his own will. His repeated turns to Latin detach him from the milieu which he shares with other characters, and soon he is immersed in his own geography, the imagined scene of a justice which his own social world cannot deliver:

> Downe by the dale that flowes with purple gore,
> Standeth a firie Tower; there sits a iudge
> Vpon a seat of steele and molten brasse,
> And twixt his teeth he holdes a fire-brand,
> That leades vnto the lake where hell doth stand.
> Away, *Hieronimo*; to him be gone:
> Heele doe thee iustice for Horatios death.[19]

[15] *Octavia* (attrib. Seneca), l. 849: *haec vindicta debetur mihi?* ('Is this the vengeance I am owed?'); Nero speaking.

[16] There is also an ambiguity in Hieronimo's 'I, heauen', where 'I' is an Elizabethan spelling of 'Ay', 'yes'; but aurally one is simultaneously presented with an alignment between Hieronimo and heaven: 'I, heauen'.

[17] Seneca, *Agamemnon*, l. 115, spoken by Clytemnestra.

[18] Seneca, *Troades*, ll. 510–12; the lineation is different in Seneca and Kyd.

[19] *The Spanish Tragedie*, III xii 7–13.

And he tells Lorenzo (Horatio's murderer),

> Away, Ile rip the bowels of the earth,
> *He diggeth with his dagger.*
> And Ferrie ouer to th' Elizian plaines,
> And bring my Sonne to shew his deadly wounds.[20]

Hieronimo moves more and more into spaces of the mind where he can shape figures of revenge.

The tragic protagonist cannot inhabit collective space in the same way that other characters do, and often he moves into his own milieu to which the others have no access. He is held in parenthesis. In the second scene of *Hamlet* (a play much indebted to *The Spanish Tragedie*) the prince is set apart from the rest of the court by being dressed in black, while the others are in costumes suitable for the wedding of Claudius and Gertrude which has just taken place. This is an immediate visual sign for the audience of Hamlet's self-separation from the court, and his first words establish that he belongs on a plane which is set at a tangent to their world:

> KING. But now my Cosin Hamlet, and my Sonne?
> HAM. A little more then kin, and lesse then kinde.[21]

Though there is no such indication in the original Quarto or Folio texts, editors often mark Hamlet's line as an aside; but whether or not the King and the courtiers hear Hamlet's reply, it is a linguistic move, at once defensive and aggressive, which marks out a space opposed to Claudius and his court, a space in which Claudius' usage of 'Sonne' can be rebutted through a riddling play on 'kinde', juggling the concepts of kinship, kindliness, and nature. Hamlet's asides, or half-asides, continue to be ways in which he delineates for himself an inset space within the discourse of Elsinore, bending its language through savage word-play so that it becomes his own fortification.

From these liminal asides, barbed sentences which patrol the boundary between self and non-self, fashioning a kingdom for the dispossessed heir, Hamlet moves into other spaces which lie within

[20] *The Spanish Tragedie*, III xii 71–3.

[21] Shakespeare, *Hamlet*, I ii 64–5.

his own imagination, the worlds of the soliloquies which sit oddly with the text around them. Though some of these speeches respond to external stimuli (the Player's emotion, Fortinbras' resolution), others do not ('To be, or not to be' starts *ex nihilo*), and they characteristically traverse a terrain which is that of Hamlet's own uncertainty and self-dissatisfaction; they promise action, but action rarely issues directly from them. 'To be, or not to be' begins with what seems to be a debate about whether to commit suicide, but moves into the world of dreams and a syntax of rhetorical questions, at once describing and exemplifying a mental state in which

> enterprizes of great pith and moment,
> With this regard their Currants turn away,
> And loose the name of action.[22]

In the space of the mind, action is turned away, or turned 'awry' as the Second Quarto text has it.

There are other worlds into which Hamlet is drawn, for the irruption of the Ghost into Elsinore effects a contamination of one world by another. As a dramatist may create a new plot by the splicing of one story into another, the compositional strategy called *contaminatio*,[23] the Ghost's narrative of the killing of King Hamlet provides a potent but unverifiable narrative which insinuates itself into the action in Elsinore, distorting relationships and making much of Hamlet's behaviour unintelligible to onlookers in the everyday world of the court. Though 'forbid | To tell the secrets of my Prison-House',[24] the Ghost creates another form of prison house within his son's imagination. Initially the Ghost appears to Hamlet in the company of Marcellus, Barnardo, and Horatio, but after the end of the first Act it appears once more only to Hamlet himself in the middle of a violent interview with Gertrude: the Ghost starts by haunting Elsinore but ends by haunting only Hamlet's mind, for the space shared by Hamlet and Gertrude in her bedchamber is not the same space as that shared by Hamlet and the Ghost when he

[22] *Hamlet*, III i 86–8. [23] *OED* s.v. contamination 1c. [24] *Hamlet*, I v 14.

interrupts their meeting, as the Ghost draws Hamlet away into another dimension which his mother cannot enter, and draws from him words which she cannot understand.[25] However we interpret this scene, the play has created a new kind of stage space, a stage within a stage, which seems to be partly a way of talking about an inner space,[26] a psychological structure; this encounter between father and son takes place in a world within a world, or rather, the father creates within the psyche of his son a space in which his own commands take priority. The protagonist becomes both fissured and multiplied.

In such dream-like spaces, trances, hallucinations, or whatever terms we reach for to tame and normalize these moments ('extasie' is Gertrude's word), the protagonists of tragedy dwell with greater intensity than in the communal spaces around them. When Leontes in *The Winter's Tale* says to Hermione 'Your Actions are my Dreames',[27] he is unwittingly speaking the truth, since his wife has not been unfaithful; tragedy is produced by his own imagination creating a scenario of her adultery which is the space within which he traps himself, and her. As his wife and his boyhood friend Polixenes retire to another part of the stage, Leontes communes with his jealousy:

> Affection? thy Intention stabs the Center.
> Thou do'st make possible things not so held,
> Communicat'st with Dreames (how can this be?)
> With what's unreall: thou coactive art,
> And fellow'st nothing. Then 'tis very credent,
> Thou may'st co-joyne with something, and thou do'st,

[25] The Folio and Second Quarto texts disagree as to whether Gertrude says that Hamlet is speaking to the 'incorporall ayre' (Q2) or 'corporall ayre' (F) (III iv 114). Logically the air is incorporeal, but the image of corporeal air, even if it is a compositorial error, is an inspired one.

[26] For diverse representations of interiority in Renaissance drama see Katharine Eisaman Maus, *Inwardness and Theater in the English Renaissance* (Chicago, 1995), and Alistair Fowler, 'Shakespeare's Renaissance Realism', *Proceedings of the British Academy*, 90 (1996), 29–64.

[27] Shakespeare, *The Winter's Tale*, III ii 82.

(And that beyond Commission) and I find it,
(And that to the infection of my Braines,
And hardning of my Browes.)[28]

Leontes' tortured syntax is hard to follow, but it is clear enough that he is thinking about the way in which sexual passion ('Affection': the word was much stronger in seventeenth-century usage than it is now) makes possible things which would normally be thought impossible. He seems to be constituting Affection as a personified presence which can be spoken to within the enclosed world which is created by his own speech. The 'Center' which Affection stabs could be the centre of the universe (either literally, or metaphorically in the sense of the central values of the human world) or Leontes' own heart: this is a doubled geography. He then goes on to say that Affection communicates with dreams, that it is 'coactive' with 'what's unreall',[29] and may 'co-joyne with something'. These three 'co-' forms fall strangely on the ear,[30] and make Affection a conspirator in a drama with various unreal partners (as, indeed, is Leontes himself). This weird and illusory scenario of the insubstantial couplings of an allegorical figure is as insubstantial as the other narratives of illicit relations which he devises. The repeated parentheses mark out spaces within spaces, grammatical and imaginative withdrawals to further recesses of his mind.[31]

[28] *The Winter's Tale*, I ii 138–46. For a discussion of the problems of this passage see *The Winter's Tale*, edited by J. H. P. Pafford, The Arden Shakespeare (London, 1963), pp. 165–7. *The Winter's Tale* is usually thought of as a romance rather than a tragedy, but the first three Acts are undoubtedly tragic, and the romance motifs of regeneration and forgiveness only become prominent later in the play.

[29] The punctuation and syntax of the First Folio ('Communicat'st with Dreames . . . | With what's unreall: thou coactive art, | And fellow'st nothing') are often emended by editors to create the sense 'Communicat'st with Dreames; With what's unreall thou coactive art'.

[30] *OED s.v.* co-join cites only two examples, including this one; *OED s.v.* co-active 2 cites this example as its first instance of the sense 'acting in concert'.

[31] The lavish use of parentheses in the Folio text of *The Winter's Tale* is usually held to be a characteristic of the scrivener Ralph Crane, who probably prepared the fair copy from which the Folio text was set, but even if they are attributable to Crane's personal style they nevertheless respond to striking grammatical features of the speech.

These imagined enclosures are densely textured spaces which provide a different ontological grounding for the character, and become a locus of fear and longing in which strange narratives are generated.[32] Tragedy often works with particular forms of *analepsis* and *prolepsis*:[33] it is not simply that the narrative reaches backwards or forwards; rather, the past is liable to erupt, or the future to overwrite the present, within the imagination of the protagonist. To the protagonists these self-generated, mythic scenarios are often more cogent and persuasive, more powerful in initiating action, than what is taking place around them on the visible stage. Such is Phèdre's recollection of the *coup de foudre* in the temple when she first saw Hippolyte, a memory which has such force that it is hardly a memory of a past event but rather an experience which transcends time, or joins the present to the past in a private continuum. The moment of her meeting with Hippolyte is what defines her, and this is where she dwells.[34] Such too is the inset story of Othello's handkerchief, a fable inlaid into the marquetry of Othello's speeches. Othello's handkerchief, purloined by Iago, is seen by him as a token of Desdemona's betrayal, and this throws him back into a narrative of its origins (unverifiable to anyone else on stage) which is also a way of laying claim to his own origins, his own place outside the mundane worlds of Venice and Cyprus:

That Handkerchiefe
Did an Ægyptian to my Mother give:
. . . .
There's Magicke in the web of it:
A *Sybill* that had numbred in the world
The Sun to course, two hundred compasses,
In her Prophetticke furie sow'd the Worke:
The Wormes were hallowed, that did breede the Silke,

[32] Cp. Roland Barthes' discussion of 'Les trois éspaces extérieurs: mort, fuite, événement' in *Sur Racine* (1963) (*Œuvres complètes*, 5 vols. (Paris, 2002), ii 61–3).

[33] For the importance of *analepsis* and *prolepsis* to novelistic narrative see Gérard Genette, *Figures III* (Paris, 1972). One can usefully extrapolate Genette's procedures to an analysis of the drama.

[34] See pp. 192–3 below.

> And it was dyde in Mummey, which the Skilfull
> Conserv'd of Maidens hearts.[35]

In such a narrative delineating an off-stage space and time inaccessible to the other characters is located Othello's or Phèdre's sense of who they are, what defines them and gives them purpose, or what slackens their grasp on the present. Such narrated spaces have their own autonomous time scheme (Othello's handkerchief was sown by a two-hundred-year-old sibyl) and cannot be slotted neatly into the time and space of the rest of the drama.

Such spaces are often opened up by *unheimlich* things, by objects out of place which reconfigure the dramatic space around them and open out vistas of imagined worlds, new connections. At the same time, tragedy makes certain things remote by impeding our route to them, by blocking or suspending access. Such things are no longer merely instrumental objects, nor can they easily be made symbolic: they cannot be construed as an element of metaphor, since they do not exist on the same plane as any other object; nor can they be metonymic, for there is no readily conceivable whole of which they can be thought to be a part. Othello's handkerchief becomes important precisely because it is lost and inaccessible, and with that loss—as he thinks—comes the loss of his own standing in Venetian society, his marriage to one of its noble women, his new-found groundedness in the relationship with Desdemona. The handkerchief out of its proper place not only opens up Othello's past, and the exotic spaces of sibyls and Egyptian mummies, but creates for the unwitting Desdemona a new and dangerous space, a scenario (of which she is wholly unaware) which constitutes her as an adulteress, and transposes her into a new time scheme of illicit rendezvous with Cassio in secret spaces. The tapestries which Clytemnestra spreads out before her returning husband in the *Agamemnon* are also things out of place which create a new space. These are the treasures of the house, valuable fabrics which represent the labour of generations as well as

[35] Shakespeare, *Othello*, III iv 57–77.

realizable assets: riches and rich histories. To take them out of the house and spread them on the ground is to initiate an unaccustomed action, to invite an unexpected scenario. To walk on them with a traveller's unwashed feet is to ruin them; more, it is to commit *hubris*, to accept as a human that tribute which should properly be paid only to the gods. As Agamemnon walks on them, his path from the chariot to the door of his house is a path into a new dimension: he is drawn into the terrible narrative of revenge which Clytemnestra has plotted out for him, and is translated into being a player on a different stage. These things out of place are more than objects, and more than symbols; they are gateways into a space of stored-up resentment and retribution.

And then there is Alonzo's finger. In Act Three of *The Changeling*,[36] the servant Deflores has killed Alonzo de Piracquo at the behest of Beatrice, who wishes to be rid of an unwelcome suitor. As a token that the deed has been properly done, Deflores presents her with the ring that she had been obliged to give Alonzo—but the ring is still attached to his severed finger. Beatrice tries to discharge her obligation to Deflores by offering him the ring, and then three thousand florins, and then double the sum. But Deflores will not be bought off: what he wants is Beatrice herself. Not understanding what he seeks, she muses, 'I'me in a labyrinth'; indeed, she is being drawn into a wholly new and intricate space, a new set of unwelcome connections. 'Justice invites your blood to understand me', he says, using 'blood' in the sense of 'sexual appetite'.[37] To protect herself from this demand she in turn appeals to her 'honor', to her 'modesty', and to her superior social status, her 'blood' in the sense of 'noble birth':[38] 'Think but upon the distance that Creation | Set 'twixt thy blood and mine, and keep thee there'. But Deflores effaces such distance by showing her how she has forfeited any claim to use such terms as honour and modesty, and turns her face back to confront the primary

[36] Thomas Middleton and William Rowley, *The Changeling* (London, 1653), sigs. E4^{r}–F2^{r}.

[37] *OED* 6. [38] *OED* 12.

physical meaning of blood:[39] 'A woman dipt in blood, and talk of modesty', he exclaims. Deflores continues:

> Push, flye not to your birth, but settle you
> In what the act has made you, y'are no more now,
> You must forget your parentage to me,
> Y'are the deeds creature, by that name
> You lost your first condition.

The spatial verbs in 'flye' and 'settle' map for Beatrice a new space in which she must now trace her lineage not back to her father but back to the murder of Alonzo; the 'deed' is now her creator, she its creature—its offspring, but also its servant, dependant, instrument, or puppet.[40] The deed has initiated a new set of relationships and names, and has inaugurated a new time scheme in which everything is now dated from the murder. Alonzo's finger is an *unheimlich* thing, an object out of place; more than a synecdoche for murder, it is the physical token of a reconfigured world for Beatrice.

The time and space of the protagonist are also transformed by the eruption of ghosts from a world elsewhere. 'I see that all of us who live are nothing but ghosts, or a fleeting shadow', says Sophocles' Odysseus,[41] but the insubstantiality of man, his precarious standing in his home spaces, is revealed particularly when ghostly figures from another world make demands upon him. They come from another dimension (though exactly what this dimension is may not be clear), and bring with them a form of the past which disturbs the equanimity of the present. They are indeterminate, only partially legible versions of the human, and they challenge the autonomy of the protagonist. They are the traces of past narratives, both because they recall the play's own proto-narrative and because they are literary and theatrical in their manifestations: the Ghost in *Hamlet* speaks a heightened and slightly archaic language which sets him apart from the rest of the text and connects him to the idiom used in Elizabethan translations of

[39] *OED* 1. [40] *OED* 4, 5.

[41] Sophocles, *Ajax*, ll. 125–6: ὁρῶ γὰρ ἡμᾶς οὐδὲν ὄντας ἄλλο πλὴν | εἴδωλ' ὅσοιπερ ζῶμεν ἢ κούφην σκιάν.

Seneca. In turn, his words will haunt, will inhabit, Hamlet's own speech. The Ghost of King Hamlet is of uncertain status: as Hamlet summons the courage to address the Ghost directly, he lists the possibilities:

> Be thou a Spirit of health, or Goblin damn'd,
> Bring with thee ayres from Heaven, or blasts from Hell,
> Be thy events wicked or charitable . . . [42]

The Ghost himself says that he is

> thy Fathers Spirit,
> Doom'd for a certaine terme to walke the night;
> And for the day confin'd to fast in Fiers,
> Till the foule crimes done in my dayes of Nature
> Are burnt and purg'd away?[43]

This 'honest Ghost', as Hamlet calls him,[44] does not fit the theological categories of the day: Catholic theology taught that the spirits of the dead resided for a term in Purgatory, but this one seems to walk at night and return to purgatorial fires by day; Protestant teaching insisted that the spirits of the dead went straight to heaven or hell.[45] For a Protestant, a ghost could only be a devil who has assumed the form of a human being in order to work evil; as Hamlet himself admits:

> The Spirit that I have seene
> May be the Divell, and the Divel hath power
> T' assume a pleasing shape, yea and perhaps
> Out of my Weaknesse, and my Melancholly,
> As he is very potent with such Spirits,
> Abuses me to damne me.[46]

Is this spirit the devil? Can a devilish spirit act on Hamlet's spirits, on the vapours which produce melancholy?[47] Is it an external visitation or the external manifestation of an inner state of mind? The double

[42] *Hamlet*, I iv 40–2. [43] *Hamlet*, I v 9–13. [44] *Hamlet*, I v 144.

[45] *Hamlet*, edited by Harold Jenkins, The Arden Shakespeare (London, 1982), p. 454.

[46] *Hamlet*, II ii 594–9. [47] Jenkins, p. 273.

use of 'Spirit' troubles the distinction between self and non-self, between external forces and internal motions.

Hamlet not only takes on the task which the Ghost has set him of avenging his father's murder, he also takes on the appearance of a ghost, to Ophelia's eyes, when he approaches her 'with a looke so pitious in purport, | As if he had been loosed out of hell, | To speake of horrors'.[48] (But no ghost can be loosed from hell in either Catholic or Protestant theology: he is therefore placed in a non-category.) We cannot simply locate the Ghost; in Gertrude's bedroom the Ghost appears as Hamlet becomes increasingly overwrought. Psychologically it is easy to read this intervention as Hamlet's recollection of his father's injunction, now made over-vividly manifest, and the morality-play tradition of the protagonist accosted by his good and bad angels, revived in Marlowe's *Dr Faustus*, might lead us to imagine that this is an external dramatic manifestation of Hamlet's internal psychomachia; but we cannot tell. Dramatists use multiple theatrical languages to map and re-map the same psychological state or moral dilemma. Aeschylus' Furies are an external manifestation of Orestes' guilty memory, visible to him alone at the end of the *Choephori*, but they are also autonomous presences who interact with other characters in the *Eumenides*. Revenge in *The Spanish Tragedie* may be a supernatural force standing outside the plane of human affairs which foresees and perhaps determines the actions of the play's characters; or it may be an allegorical image expressing the power which the desire for revenge has to determine human lives. Because Kyd's dramatic language is legible either through reference to Seneca or through reference to the late-medieval morality play, we cannot quite place the ontological status of Revenge, and therefore do not know whether the characters do have the power to shape their own ends. Tragedy opens out a terrain in which we cannot be sure whether the external is autonomous or a metaphor for the internal; whether the boundaries of the self are permeable; or quite how the time and space experienced by the protagonist may or could connect with the quotidian time and

[48] *Hamlet*, II i 82–4.

space around him, with the milieu of the other characters and, often, of the audience. He loses one *Heimat*, but the strange form of *Heimat* which replaces it is scarcely habitable.

Nor does the protagonist's language quite mesh with the language of those around him.[49] Speech is difficult, and silence often a preferable retreat. Speech may break off into uncomfortable silence in the rhetorical figure of *aposiopesis* which, by failing to complete a sentence, draws the protagonist back into the silence which is their preferred mode, and guards them there.[50] *Hamlet* presents many interrupted narratives, and ends on a half-line.[51] Tragedy is also, not only locally but structurally, a form of *anacoluthon*, a sentence which fails to follow the expected grammatical sequence, in which a word fails to find its expected companion to complete the sense.[52] In tragedy the expected grammar—the sequence of cause and effect, the distinction between subject and object, the link between agent and verb—is persistently thwarted. Sometimes tragic figures thwart connections by the way in which they use language not as a means to communicate with others but as a means of isolating themselves into a world which they can control. Leontes and Othello both build narratives of their wives' adultery, and in so doing destroy the relationship between language and the external world, as every principal signifier points to the same signified, which is always adultery. In *The Winter's Tale*, while Leontes watches his wife Hermione and

[49] On some characteristics of tragic language see M. S. Silk, 'Tragic Language: The Greek Tragedians and Shakespeare', in *Tragedy and the Tragic: Greek Theatre and Beyond*, edited by M. S. Silk (Oxford, 1996), pp. 458–96. Silk suggests that 'in concrete linguistic terms, tragedy tends to foreground *must* and *too* and the *name*' (p. 465).

[50] Silvia Montiglio suggests that in Greek tragedy silence is a veil which prevents a character being truly known by others (*Silence in the Land of Logos* (Princeton, 2000), pp. 177–9). She also argues that silence often surrounds the perpetrator of polluting crimes, and that characters may hold silence responsible for precipitating a tragic development in the plot. (*Phèdre* exemplifies both the latter points.)

[51] 'Go, bid the Souldiers shoote' (V ii 408). Michael Neill makes the point in *Issues of Death: Mortality and Identity in English Renaissance Tragedy* (Oxford, 1997), p. 220.

[52] See Jacques Derrida's extended discussion of *anacolouthon* in *Le Parjure, peut-être («brusques sautes de syntaxe»)* (Paris, 2005).

his friend Polixenes conversing, he sees that his young son Mamillius needs to have his nose wiped, and says:

> Come Captaine,
> We must be neat; not neat, but cleanly, Captaine:
> And yet the Steere, the Heyfer, and the Calfe,
> Are all call'd Neat. Still Virginalling
> Upon his Palme? How now (you wanton Calfe)
> Art thou my Calfe?[53]

Leontes wants his son to be 'neat', clean, but no sooner has he spoken the word than he remembers that 'neat' as a noun means 'horned cattle', and horns signify cuckolds. Glancing at Hermione, Leontes sees her taking Polixenes' hand, 'Virginalling' on it: her fingers move like the fingers of one playing the virginals, but erotically, not virginally. The inset phrase '(you wanton Calfe)' is probably addressed to Mamillius, with 'wanton' here meaning 'frisky, lively, playful', but it may also be addressed *sotto voce* to Hermione, with 'wanton' meaning 'lascivious'.[54] So 'Calfe' may be a term of endearment to Mamillius, or of insult to Hermione; 'Art thou my Calfe?' may mean 'Are you a playful boy?' or 'If we call you a calf that makes me a horned creature', or (with the emphasis on *my*) 'Are you really my son or someone else's?' Leontes' grimly playful speech becomes over-determined, and words have either too many meanings (generating multiple interpretations, but each to do with adultery) or too few meanings (each new notion simply connoting 'adultery'). Leontes destroys the referential capacity of language as each signifier signifies his wife's transgression. No argument from his trusted adviser Camillo or from Hermione herself can pierce this carapace; even the words of the oracle of Apollo are dismissed as lies.[55] No sooner has Leontes denounced the oracle, than a messenger announces the death of Mamillius; Leontes sees this as the god's judgement on

[53] *The Winter's Tale*, I ii 122–7. [54] *OED* 1c, 2, 3.

[55] Whereas in the source story, Robert Greene's *Pandosto*, the equivalent figure to Leontes admits the truth of the oracle's words (*Narrative and Dramatic Sources of Shakespeare*, edited by Geoffrey Bullough, 8 vols. (London, 1957–75), viii 171).

him, and he repents. But only death, death seen as a sign of divine wrath, can undo the linguistic structure which Leontes has built around him.

In *Richard II*,[56] the King begins the play as the pinnacle of the feudal system and the upholder of its semiotic code, but as the drama develops he destroys the capacity of language to function as the bond between ruler and subject; rather, it becomes his own plaything, and as such it creates emblems, narratives, and rituals which appeal only to him, and lack persuasive force. The dispute between Thomas Mowbray and Henry Bullingbrooke is to be settled by a trial by combat over which Richard will preside; but before the matter can be submitted to God's judgement in this way, the combat is stopped by a word from the King; other words pronounce sentence of banishment on both men; further words remit part of Bullingbrooke's term. Richard has intervened in a social ritual which had assumed that the hand of God would reveal the truth, and has substituted the power of his own voice. Language is no longer submitted to God, and thereby underpinned by a *signifié transcendantal*; nor, as the play unfolds, is it a socially accepted convention which carries political efficacy. Here Richard may speak words which are performative: he pronounces banishment, and the man is banished. But later his words will become only performances. By seizing Henry Bullingbrooke's lands on his father's death, Richard has left him Duke of Lancaster in name only, 'Barely in title, not in revennew' (II i 226); and Henry himself complains that Richard's henchmen have

> From mine owne Windowes torne my Household Coat,
> Raz'd out my Impresse, leaving me no signe,
> Save mens opinions, and my living blood,
> To shew the World I am a Gentleman.[57]

[56] *Richard II* is normally treated as one of Shakespeare's history plays, but the Quarto calls it a tragedy (*The Tragedie of King Richard the second* (London, 1597)), and it is clearly shaped as such, lending itself to analysis in terms of an Aristotelian fall of Richard, or a Hegelian conflict between Richard and Bullingbrooke (or between the forms of political conduct and ideology which they represent).

[57] Shakespeare, *Richard II*, III i 24–7.

Henry wants to re-establish signs, to insist on the use of signifiers and to make sure that signifiers and signifieds properly connect. Meanwhile, as events move against him, Richard takes refuge in a rhetoric which is increasingly divorced from military and political reality. He charges the earth to fight his enemies by marshalling spiders, toads, stinging nettles, and adders, even to turn her stones into soldiers.[58] Armed only with hyperbole, Richard invests too much power in imagery, and presses the metaphor of the King as the sun to extravagant lengths in imagining that the mere appearance of him as sun-king will scatter the night of treason.[59] As his soldiers desert him, he cries, 'Is not the Kings Name fortie thousand Names? | Arme, arme my Name');[60] but there is no more power in names.[61]

When he is deposed, this master of emblems tries to take control of the procedure of resignation. His opponents hope that he will simply resign the crown to Henry, but Richard insists on a ritual. There is no form of ceremony for uncrowning a king, so Richard invents one; but since ceremony is no longer functional in this society, this is a ritual in which, as he says, Richard is both priest and clerk. No one will speak the words which he has prescribed for the people, and which would corroborate his own utterance:

> God save the King: will no man say, Amen?
> Am I both Priest, and Clarke? well then, Amen.[62]

And he enacts a ceremony of resignation in which it seems that more is happening than the resignation of an office:

> BULL. Are you contented to resigne the Crowne?
> RICH. I, no; no, I: for I must nothing bee:
> Therefore no, no, for I resigne to thee.
> Now, marke me how I will undoe my selfe.

[58] *Richard II*, III ii 12–26.

[59] *Richard II*, III ii 36–62.

[60] *Richard II*, III ii 85–6.

[61] Cp. Silk: 'the *name*: the striving individual is a special someone with an identity, which must, by his or her striving, be lived up to, in a sense created, certainly *realized*' (p. 465). Richard's tragedy is, in part, his inability to realize his name, or to make that name realized by his subjects.

[62] *Richard II*, IV i 173–4.

I give this heavie Weight from off my Head,
And this unwieldie Scepter from my Hand ...[63]

'I' in early-modern spelling is both the first person pronoun and 'aye', meaning 'yes'. To agree to resign the crown will, thinks Richard, undo his own self: he is unable to separate self from office. He has no name, 'No, not that Name was given me at the Font'.[64] Having used language to rule, then to invent imaginary spaces peopled with imaginary subjects to do his bidding, he now uses it to speak his own dissolution. This is the tragedy of an individual, but also the tragedy of medieval English society and its linguistic system: ritual is no longer a social act but an individual one; a word such as 'king' has become a sign with a contested application; metaphor and simile have proved dangerously facile; the signs which make the social world cohere have been razed out.

In tragedy the conceptual building blocks of society are questioned, and the most elemental terms through which we construct and construe our world are made fragile. Tragedy is a failure of translation, as certain key terms cannot any longer be carried across the boundaries which tragedy fashions between its protagonist and the other characters. In the *Oresteia* the concept of justice is turned round and round as various characters appropriate it for their own purposes, while in *Antigone* the vocabularies of the law and of family ties are similarly in play between Antigone and Creon.[65] *King Lear* queries the nature of 'nature':[66] *Othello* undoes the honesty of 'honest'.[67] *Titus Andronicus* is likewise focused upon the concept of *pietas*.[68] *Pietas* draws, or should draw, the various elements of Roman society

[63] *Richard II*, IV i 200–5.

[64] *Richard II*, IV i 256. Cp. Silk again: 'The name ... seems to embody all the endeavour that isolates them from society, so that any belated compromise with the social order can induce, ironically enough, a distancing from the name as well' (p. 470).

[65] See Simon Goldhill, *Reading Greek Tragedy* (Cambridge, 1986).

[66] See p. 166 n. 21 below.

[67] See William Empson, *The Structure of Complex Words* (London, 1951; third edition, 1977), pp. 218–49.

[68] Act I of *Titus Andronicus* was probably written by George Peele: see Brian Vickers, *Shakespeare, Co-Author* (Oxford, 2002), pp. 148–243.

into a coherent whole. It denotes an attitude of dutiful respect towards those to whom one is bound by ties of reciprocal obligation, and applies to the reverence of man for the gods, the conduct of children towards parents, and the duties which the individual owes to the state.[69] But in *Titus* the concept disintegrates along with the society which it once cemented.

At the outset of *Titus Andronicus*, Titus is 'Sur-named *Pious*, | For many good and great deserts to Rome'.[70] He inherits the term which Virgil had assigned to Aeneas, where it designated his interlinked concern for his city of Troy, the gods of the city, and his father and child. It functions in the play as an indication that Titus embodies the classic values of Rome. He brings home the bodies of his sons who have died fighting for Rome against the 'barbarous Gothes',[71] and inters them with due solemnity in the family tomb. He is at home here in Roman spaces. The ritual which he performs links family and city. Titus' son Lucius asks his father to sacrifice the principal prisoner from the Goths *ad manes fratrum*; and when Titus agrees to sacrifice Alarbus, son of Queen Tamora, she begs Titus for mercy, invoking the Roman concept of *pietas*: 'O! If to fight for King and Common-weale, | Were piety in thine, it is in these'.[72] But Titus replies that his surviving sons require a sacrifice 'T'appease their groaning shadowes that are gone': the ghosts of the dead demand the death of the living. Indeed, he claims that 'Religiously they aske a sacrifice', to which Tamora replies, 'O cruell irreligious piety'.[73] This rhetorical clash of opposites, the blatant oxymoron, points to the crumbling of the idea which had helped to provide Rome with its

[69] *OLD* 1–4. In English the word, 'piety', when it is taken over from Latin, first refers to the bonds between parents and children (*OED* 3) before then coming to designate religious feeling and duty (*OED* 2). The adjective 'pious' is recorded in the *OED* as Shakespeare's coinage (in the years 1602–3) in the sense of showing religious devotion. See also pp. 113–14 below.

[70] Shakespeare, *Titus Andronicus*, I i 23–4; 'pious' is spelt in the Latin way, '*Pius*', in the First Quarto (1594), but '*Pious*' in the First Folio (1623), which suggests that the adjective had become naturalized in English during the intervening thirty years.

[71] *Titus Andronicus*, I i 28.

[72] *Titus Andronicus*, I i 117–18.

[73] *Titus Andronicus*, I i 127–33.

conceptual stability. Her son Chiron compares Rome to barbarous Scythia,[74] but his brother Demetrius introduces a more telling rhetorical development when he wishes that

> The selfe same Gods that arm'd the Queene of Troy
> With opportunitie of sharpe revenge
> Upon the Thracian Tyrant in his Tent,
> May favour *Tamora*, the Queene of Gothes,
> (When Gothes were Gothes, and *Tamora* was Queene)
> To quit the bloody wrongs upon her foes.[75]

This is a significant moment in the decomposition of the forms of Romanness in the play, as the Gothic prince invokes the foundation myth of Rome, and wishes that his mother may be aided by the same gods who armed Hecuba, sometime Queen of Troy. Previously, 'Gothes were Gothes', but now we see the beginning of the process by which Tamora becomes incorporated into the body of Rome, for soon the Emperor makes her his wife, and she says: 'I am incorparate in Rome'.[76] As those who represent Rome and its historic values turn to barbarous practices such as human sacrifice, the Gothic queen is brought into the heart of the city and its culture. Soon she is swearing by the gods of Rome, and calling Rome 'our City'.[77] Meanwhile, Titus kills his son Mutius for opposing him, and refuses him burial in the family monument. His brother Marcus calls this 'impiety', and pleads: 'Thou art a Romaine, be not barbarous'.[78] Titus is turned from being the epitome of Rome (its defender, the one whose voice determines who will be emperor) to being the outsider. Tamora, the barbarian queen, becomes empress. The city becomes, in Titus' words, 'a wildernes of Tigers'.[79] At the end of the play, Titus' son Lucius restores

[74] *Titus Andronicus*, I i 134.

[75] *Titus Andronicus*, I i 139–44.

[76] *Titus Andronicus*, I i 467. This is glossed as 'formally admitted, by legal procedure' in *Titus Andronicus*, edited by Jonathan Bate, Arden Shakespeare, third series (London, 1995), but the meaning 'united in one body' (*OED* 1), which draws on the Latin root *corpus* ('body'), seems more appropriate and evocative.

[77] *Titus Andronicus*, I i 439–41; IV iv 77; 'our City' is the First Folio reading, but the First Quarto has 'your': there is a textual uncertainty here as to whether Tamora really belongs in Rome.

[78] *Titus Andronicus*, I i 360; I i 383.

[79] *Titus Andronicus*, III i 54.

order to Rome, but at the head of an army of Goths. The almost antithetical terms which had defined life *more Romano*, 'piety' and 'barbarous', are in danger of exchanging their applications.

All this is a way of saying that tragedy undoes the self. It prises apart the coherence of the language which we use for consolidating the individual. This argument runs counter to Hegel's insistence on the solidity and unity of the tragic individual: such characters, he says, 'have risen to become, as it were, works of sculpture, whether they be living representatives of the substantive spheres of life or individuals great and firm in other ways on the strength of their free self-reliance'; for 'truly *tragic* action necessarily presupposes either a live conception of *individual* freedom and independence or at least an individual's determination and willingness to accept freely and on his own account the responsibility for his own act and its consequences'.[80] But the tragic individual is neither so firm and independent, nor, indeed, so individual, so undivided. The tragic 'I' may be multiple, and may be discontinuous. And though the protagonists may accept responsibility for their actions, tragedy often demurs. Running through tragedy is the problem of agency and of freewill, as tragedy asks, 'Who is it that acts?' and 'Who is it that speaks?' Though these are philosophical problems, tragedy devises its own language in which to speak these deep perplexities. Tragedy asks 'Who acts?' when Oedipus, driven on, he says, by Apollo, drives the pins of Jocasta's brooches into his own eyes; and in this case 'Who acts?' is a question partly about the influence of the gods but also about the accumulated burden of a man's history as it weighs upon the moment of decision, and the fear, the anticipated shame (the weight of adopted social imperatives) which lead Oedipus to recoil from seeing his parents in the

[80] G. W. Hegel, *Aesthetics: Lectures on Fine Art*, translated by T. M. Knox, 2 vols. (Oxford, 1975), ii 1177–8, 1195, 1205; see also i 576–85 on the independence of the individual character. Hegel's writings on tragedy are conveniently anthologized in *Hegel on Tragedy*, edited by Anne and Henry Paolucci (New York, 1962), and discussed by A. C. Bradley in his *Oxford Lectures on Poetry* (London, 1909), pp. 69–95.

underworld. Tragedy asks 'Who acts?' when Othello is led by Iago to kill his wife because he suspects her of adultery. But it is Othello who constructs the false story, Iago who only hints. And yet, are Othello and Iago two separate characters? Is there not a sense in which Iago, like Mephistopheles, is an external manifestation of an inner drive, or an inner insecurity, which theatre makes visible to us by splitting it off from the protagonist and reconstituting it as an apparently independent actor? Freud asks this question about Macbeth and Lady Macbeth, when, citing an idea of Ludwig Jekels, he writes: 'Shakespeare often splits a character up into two personages, which, taken separately, are not completely understandable and do not become so until they are brought together once more into a unity.'[81] Faustus and Mephistopheles, Othello and Iago, Hamlet and the Ghost, Macbeth and the witches—these are all instances of a protagonist who meets a visibly autonomous being who nevertheless articulates his own innermost thoughts: this is a form of psychomachia which is given its own language, one whose subtlety, and whose terror, we would risk taming by translating it into the pre-cast terminology of philosophy or psychology.

So the boundaries of the self are blurred, and neither we nor the protagonist can truly say what is self and what is not-self. The individual is haunted by the burden of inheritance, and in this respect cannot be autonomous: Hamlet is in part possessed by his father; Antigone is repeatedly seen as her father's child, not simply as herself. Tragedy asks, 'Who acts?', and again, 'Who speaks?' Characters begin to sound like other characters: Lady Macbeth speaks the words of the witches; *King Lear* is a play of multiple forms of ventriloquism which replace authentic individualized speech.[82] The self is multiplied into external manifestations, but is also fissured, with anguished internal

[81] 'Some Character-Types met with in Psycho-analytic Work', *Standard Edition*, xiv 323–4; 'Einige Charaktertypen aus der psychoanalytischen Arbeit', *Gesammelte Werke*, x 379: 'Er meint, daß Shakespeare häufig einen Charakter in zwei Personen zerlegt, von denen dann jede unvollkommen begreiflich erscheint, solange man sie nicht mit der anderen wiederum zur Einheit zusammensetzt'.

[82] See pp. 127 n.19 and 166–7 below.

dialogues from Hamlet, Lear, or Leontes, as self speaks to self. And the self is discontinuous. Richard II struggles to maintain a continuity with the 'I' he used to be when 'I' and 'King' were synonymous. When Lear thinks of homeless beggars and cries 'O I have tane | Too little care of this', is this 'I' continuous with the proud royal 'we' of the opening scene? Or with the humbled and confused 'I' who tells Cordelia, 'I am bound | Upon a wheele of fire', words spoken from the depths of an imagined purgatory?[83] Those who claim that Lear learns through his suffering fail to see that despite a nominal continuity in the role there is hardly any continuous and integral Lear who could learn anything, as he—as some form of 'he'—moves into the storm and madness. After watching Cressida's defection to Diomed, Troylus asks bitterly 'Was *Cressed* here?', and 'She was not sure', and again, 'Rather thinke this not *Cressid*':

> This she? no, this is *Diomids Cressida*:
> If beautie have a soule, this is not she:
> If soules guide vowes; if vowes are sanctimonie;
> If sanctimonie be the gods delight:
> If there be rule in unitie it selfe,
> This is not she:
>
> . . . .
> This is, and is not *Cressid*.[84]

Troylus knows what he has seen, but recoils from acknowledging the continuity of this Cressida who has given herself to Diomed with the woman whom he loves. The passage of rhetorical *gradatio* which builds up clauses beginning with 'if' is an attempt to invoke a moral and religious order which would prohibit this from being Cressida, for the whole fabric of the intelligible universe should argue against it. The argument culminates in Troylus saying, 'If there be rule in unitie it selfe'; but in tragedy there is no rule in unity: unity is fractured, and

[83] Shakespeare, *King Lear*, III iv 32–3; IV vii 46–7.

[84] Shakespeare, *Troilus and Cressida*, V ii 131–53. The genre of the play is indeterminate: the 1609 Quarto calls it a 'Historie', while the Folio calls it 'The Tragedie of Troylus and Cressida'. That it has tragic elements, if not a clearly tragic form, is not in doubt, however.

the woman whom he has been watching is not, any longer, one. 'This is, and is not *Cressid*.'

For in tragedy there are ways in which the self dies and decomposes long before the actual physical death of the body, which, however horrific or pitiful, is often but an afterword to the deep work of the drama: it is not death which makes tragedy tragic, but the path which leads to it. And to this we shall return at the end of the book.

2

AESCHYLUS

Oresteia

Agamemnon, the first play of the trilogy, presents the return of the king to Argos after the fall of Troy. For the Greeks the *nostos* or return home was a familiar literary motif, exemplified by the return of Odysseus to Ithaca at the end of the Trojan war.[1] But to what home does Agamemnon return? For him, the *heimlich* turns into the *unheimlich*, the homely and the place of safety into the strange and the place of ultimate danger, as he crosses the threshold. As Clytemnestra remarks ironically, ἐς δῶμ᾽ ἄελπτον ὡς ἂν ἡγῆται Δίκη, 'Justice may lead him to the home he never hoped to see!'[2] At a literal level, home is Argos—the city ruled by Agamemnon and his father Atreus before him—and his house, the *oikos*. In Greek the word *oikos* refers both to the house as a physical structure, a dwelling place, and to the household goods which furnish it and constitute the family's wealth, and also to the family which lives there, especially if it is the ruling family.[3] More than a

In this chapter the Greek text is quoted from Denys Page's Oxford Classical Texts edition, *Aeschyli Septem Quae Supersunt Tragoedias* (Oxford, 1972), though without following his use of the lunate sigma and adscript iota, while the translations (unless otherwise stated) are from *Aeschylus: Oresteia*, translated by Hugh Lloyd-Jones (London, 1982). I have also drawn on *Aeschylus: Agamemnon, Libation-Bearers, Eumenides, Fragments*, edited by Herbert Weir Smyth, Loeb Classical Library (Cambridge, Mass., 1926, reprinted 1999); *Choephori*, edited by A. F. Garvie (Oxford, 1986); *Eumenides*, edited by Alan H. Sommerstein (Cambridge, 1989); and *Aeschylus: Oresteia*, translated by Christopher Collard (Oxford, 2002).

[1] For the *nostos* see Garvie, pp. ix, xiv.

[2] Aeschylus, *Agamemnon*, l. 911.

[3] *LSJ*, Chantraine, *s.v.* See also Émile Benveniste, *Le Vocabulaire des institutions indo-européennes*, 2 vols. (Paris, 1969), i 293–319.

building, the *oikos* is the means of life, even the way of life. Contained within the idea of the *oikos* is an implicit narrative, for the present is defined by the past history of the family. The physical house is present throughout, as the play opens with the speech of the watchman on its roof, who begins, elliptically, to touch on the past of the *oikos*, and it is represented by the building which forms the back wall of the stage (the *skēnē*) of the Athenian theatre.[4] The masonry physically limits our view, while at the same time enticing us to read what it conceals. The space which we imagine behind the theatrical *skēnē* stands for the interior of the house of Atreus, but it is a complex topography. It is the inhabitable space where the descendants of Atreus live, and where Agamemnon expects to be received with adulation and to enjoy its material comforts after the rigours of war. But it is also a conceptual space which encompasses the history of the family. Such a space is constituted by the stretch of past time, and time in this case is mythic, for the murder of Thyestes' children by Atreus is contained within the space of the house as a memory. It is also an element in a narrative which is as yet unfinished. Because the mythic past is neither narrated nor explained, but remains suspended in this loaded space—a space heavy like humid air full of incipient rain—it forms the material of the uncanny. The *oikos* is *unheimlich*.

A special kind of fear attaches to this past because we know that it haunts the time and space which we can actually see, and yet we cannot know in advance the form in which the past will erupt into view. It is contained, temporarily yet atemporally, in a space which we as an audience never see with our eyes, for the *skēnē* never opens out to reveal an actual interior; instead, across its threshold emerge the dead bodies of Agamemnon and Cassandra who had entered that space alive and are now returned transformed. The Chorus calls war χρυσαμοιβὸς, the 'gold-changer of bodies' which transmutes men into ashes which are brought home in urns,[5] but the intangible off-stage

[4] For the theatrical spaces in which the Greek tragedies were performed see David Wiles, *Tragedy in Athens: Performance Space and Theatrical Meaning* (Cambridge, 1997).

[5] *Agamemnon*, ll. 437–44.

space also transforms the living into the dead. It is a space which the prophetess Cassandra can read, for she alone sees beyond the back wall of the stage into the storied space which contains the past, present, and future of the house of Atreus. So she foresees her own death; or rather, she sees in the present the death which is already stored up for her in this space beyond the *skēnē*; and her description of these events—which for her all seem to inhabit the same space and time—is expressed in a language which no one around her on stage can understand. She is the only one whose speech engages fully with this densely-stored off-stage space; others speak about it only obliquely.

Oblique speech typifies this play. Speech is oblique because characters speak less than they know, and reveal less than they purpose. Speech is dangerous, because when speaking about the gods it may trespass on territory into which humans should not venture. And throughout the *Agamemnon* there are forms of estrangement between the speaker and his words, or between the image and its supposed referent. The boldly metaphorical language of Aeschylus often estranges us from the world, whereas one might have expected metaphor to domesticate the unfamiliar by translating that which seems strange into some recognizable terms of our own choosing. It is particularly in the area of man's relations with the gods that the language seems to occlude rather than to clarify, or to offer multiple and not always compatible readings. Such audacity of imagination combined with reticence about the precise application of words comes partly from the Greek fear of speaking the wrong word: so the Herald is reluctant to say anything ill-omened which might mar the celebratory home-coming with an account of the army's sufferings, and the Chorus is cautious about naming Zeus in case the title by which it honours him may be displeasing to him.[6] But caution and indirection are also politic. The Watchman says less about the affairs of the house than he knows, yet even so his words are caught up in an irony beyond him. The light which he greets does indeed

[6] *Agamemnon*, ll. 636–45, 160–2.

signal the fall of Troy and the return of his lord, but that return will bring grief rather than joy; this light, a chain of beacons stretching from Troy to Argos, is itself uncanny, the product of human artifice proclaiming an unprecedented human control over time and space which the Chorus does not quite understand or trust. It particularly distrusts it as a device arranged by Clytemnestra, and light will not be purged of its contamination by Clytemnestra until the torchlit procession which honours the Eumenides at the end of the trilogy.

The Watchman's opening speech draws us into a disturbed time and space. He guards the house against danger, but the danger which will ravage the house of Atreus will not come from outside, and cannot be seen by any lookout. He is kept awake by fear which stands by his side (*παραστατεῖ*[7]) as if it were a personified presence, not simply a fear which he feels within him but his own emotion which now stands outside him and oppresses him. He says that the house is no longer managed in the best way, as it was in the past, but this past of his is a selective memory, and appears not to stretch back to incorporate the fratricidal rule of Atreus. Indeed, the watchman's words consciously suppress both past and present: 'for I of my choice | speak to those who know, but for those who do not I forget'.[8] The house itself could say many things if it found a voice, he muses, but it waits to be voiced by others. In particular, it waits to be voiced by the stranger, Cassandra.

Agamemnon is returning to an *oikos* which he has himself violated through the sacrifice of Iphigenia. This sacrifice forms the unseen backdrop to the play, and lives on in a series of oblique allusions, and a difficult, disturbed narrative by the Chorus. It is a while before the Chorus finds the words with which to address this subject. In the first ode it is gestured towards tangentially with a reference to vultures grieving for their offspring.[9] Formally, the battle-cry of the outraged Greeks is being compared here to the scream of the outraged birds; but as the metaphor develops it fits less neatly with its ostensible subject, and begins to generate unsettling kinds of unlikeness. The

[7] *Agamemnon*, l. 14.

[8] *Agamemnon*, ll. 38–9.

[9] *Agamemnon*, l. 50.

chicks which have been stolen from their nest are not much like Helen abducted from the bed of Menelaus; and the word which is used for the vultures' chicks is *παίδων*, which is applied in Greek only to human offspring.[10] So this exceptional usage directs our attention to the destruction of human children, and the simile threatens to re-apply itself to a new subject, to find a new victim, Iphigenia. The sons of Atreus are sent by an Erinys or Fury to avenge the theft of Helen.[11] But we know that the Erinyes are specifically charged with avenging not abduction and adultery but murder, especially the deaths of those killed by their own kin, which again does not fit the scenario of Paris and Helen. So the loose simile unwinds and curls again around the figure of Agamemnon, who has killed his own daughter and will at some point be pursued for vengeance. Formally, Agamemnon is presented here as the agent of the Erinyes, but implicitly the simile points to a time when the avenger will be the victim.

The bird imagery returns later in the ode, when the Chorus sings about the eagles which attack and feed upon a pregnant hare.[12] The eagles seem to represent the Atreidae, and the hare, teeming with young, the city of Troy and its people. Artemis is apparently enraged by what is destined to happen as it is encoded in this metaphor. Her wrath against Agamemnon and the Greeks therefore seems to be proleptic: the future is brought into the present, the guilt is anticipated and punished in advance. In other, earlier, versions of the story, Artemis is said to have been offended when Agamemnon killed a deer and boasted that not even she was a better hunter than he.[13] In such

[10] As Lloyd-Jones points out (p. 18). The usage is unusual enough in the surviving corpus for *LSJ* to cite this instance as its sole example of the use of the word for animals.

[11] *Agamemnon*, l. 60.

[12] *Agamemnon*, ll. 115–38. Lloyd-Jones (p. 18) notes that the Greeks did not distinguish sharply between vultures and eagles, so the second passage is linked to the first. For a discussion of the image and its possible interpretations see John J. Peradotto, 'The Omen of the Eagles and the *Ethos* of Agamemnon', in *Aeschylus*, edited by Michael Lloyd, Oxford Readings in Classical Studies (Oxford, 2007), pp. 211–44; originally published in *Phoenix* 23 (1969), 237–63.

[13] Timothy Gantz, *Early Greek Myth: A Guide to Literary and Artistic Sources* (Baltimore, 1993), pp. 582–5.

accounts the demand that Agamemnon sacrifice his daughter is an easily legible example of *nemesis* following *hubris*, but as Aeschylus presents it the moral logic of the demand is veiled because of the temporal uncertainty: it appears that Agamemnon is being challenged over something which he is destined to do in the fairly distant future. And so the protagonist of tragedy is held in a non-space without the usual relations of cause and effect, without his guilt being specifically for something which has actually been committed. This tragic displacement is compounded here by the typically Greek anxiety that guilt is complex and fluid: guilt does not pertain solely to the agent as a result of his actions, but it spreads as a pollution over the family and associates of the guilty one, so that in the telling of the stories it often seems that the descendants of Atreus in Argos or of Labdacus in Thebes exist in a different spatial and temporal world from other people, a dimension in which the crime of their ancestor is eternally present, its consequences always liable to break out, and its name always inescapably their name.

Past, present, and future are held in unsettling relation when the Chorus quotes the prophet Calchas as praying that Artemis may not bring about 'another sacrifice' (*θυσίαν ἑτέραν*[14]), thus alluding both to the sacrifice of Iphigenia which is to come, and the sacrifice by Atreus of the children of Thyestes which is past—but not safely past. For, says Calchas,

μίμνει γὰρ φοβερὰ παλίνορτος
οἰκονόμος δολία, μνάμων Μῆνις τεκνόποινος.[15]

there abides, terrible, ever again arising,
a keeper of the house guileful, unforgetting, Wrath, child-avenging.

Wrath here (*Μῆνις*) seems to be personified, a force which abides in a disturbingly continuous form of the present tense, and emphatically linked to its verbs by alliteration (*μίμνει . . . μνάμων Μῆνις*); it is recurrently rising up, standing outside of any individual (the avenger is not specifically Aegisthus avenging his brothers nor Clytemnestra

[14] *Agamemnon*, l. 150. [15] *Agamemnon*, ll. 154–5.

avenging her daughter, though it may suggest both); and it is, in a jarring paradox, a 'guileful' (Lloyd-Jones) or 'treacherous' (Collard) guardian of the house (*οἰκονόμος δολία*). Against whom is the house being guarded in this way? The word *οἰκονόμος* may be construed either as abstract ('household management', 'economy') or as concrete ('manager', 'steward'), and as it includes the word *νομός* ('law'), one wonders what kind of law it is that Wrath maintains in this house. It seems that the house of Atreus is guarded not only by the fearful watchman but by *Μῆνις*, by Wrath itself, which like the watchman's fear stands outside the characters. But since classical Greek did not have the modern typographical distinction between upper- and lower-case letters, one cannot specify that an abstract noun is a personification by using a capital letter, and the words were anyway originally intended to be spoken rather than read: so the status of abstractions in the original Greek script remains uncertain, and we cannot readily place and tame such abstract nouns into the relative comfort of allegory. Much of the work to define *Μῆνις* and other abstract nouns is done by the verbs, strangely human verbs. We do not, therefore, quite know where to place this mention of wrath or Wrath—is it inside or outside an individual, a rationalized abstraction or an avenging deity? Does this keeper guard or destroy the house? Does Wrath the *οἰκονόμος* ruin the economy of the house by having Agamemnon walk on its tapestries? And is this the same *μῆνις* which is said later to have accomplished a fateful marriage to Troy (l. 701)? Where in the human world does *Μῆνις* fit? In us, or beyond us?

In a formulation which is typical of Greek thought, Agamemnon at Aulis puts on the yoke of necessity,[16] so that the action is seen simultaneously as willed and imposed. Often Greek characters are represented as being taken over by some force larger than themselves which is nevertheless part of them: anger, desire, pride, infatuation.[17] In the Chorus's distanced account of what happened we see Agamemnon as the individual fully aware of his dilemma, saying

[16] *Agamemnon*, l. 218.

[17] E. R. Dodds, *The Greeks and the Irrational* (Berkeley, 1951), pp. 1–27.

that to disobey is 'grievous' (*βαρεῖα*: literally, 'heavy', for it will weigh upon him as a yoke would[18]), yet it is also grievous to sacrifice his daughter, 'the pride of my house',[19] which will pollute the father's hands.[20] The image of 'his spirit's wind veering to an impious blast' (*φρενὸς πνέων δυσσεβῆ τροπαίαν*)[21] connects his inner state with the shifting of the winds which he wants to bring about. In such images we are presented with a mode of individuality whose boundaries are indeterminate: we are told that Zeus has thrown a net over Troy, and that Agamemnon has uprooted Troy with the mattock of Zeus;[22] so is Agamemnon acting as Zeus' instrument or as his agent? Agamemnon is also said to cast the yoke around the neck of Troy,[23] which is the same image which had been used for Agamemnon himself, for his compulsion, or self-compulsion, at Aulis.[24] Is he victim or victor; or does tragedy dismantle the stability of such an antithesis?

These linguistic paradoxes, repetitions of key images, and temporal dislocations are ways of showing how the individual both is and is not autonomous. 'Autonomous' is the necessary term here, for *αὐτόνομος* means 'living by one's own laws', and Agamemnon seems to be colliding with laws that he can only partly recognize. The Chorus likes to think that it can enunciate the laws of Zeus: 'Zeus, who put men on the way to wisdom | by making it a valid law | that by suffering they shall learn', it says.[25] And again, 'it abides, while Zeus abides upon his throne | that he who does shall suffer, for it is the law'.[26] The verb here is *μίμνει*, the same verb used for Wrath earlier; both Wrath and the law of Zeus 'abide' in a dimension beyond the flux of human life. But here the terminology of 'law' in the translation

[18] The Loeb translation 'hard' is insufficient.

[19] Though present in the Loeb, Lloyd-Jones, and Collard translations, 'my' is not actually in the Greek: *δόμων ἄγαλμα*, so 'pride of [the] house'.

[20] *Agamemnon*, ll. 206–10.

[21] *Agamemnon*, l. 219.

[22] *Agamemnon*, ll. 358, 525.

[23] *Agamemnon*, l. 528.

[24] The words *λέπαδνον* (l. 217) and *ζευκτήριον* (l. 529) both refer to yokes; the former is the leather strap which fastens the yoke around the head of the animal, and the latter the wooden yoke itself.

[25] *Agamemnon*, ll. 176–8.

[26] *Agamemnon*, ll. 1563–4.

may mislead us. In the first quotation there is no Greek noun equivalent to 'a … law': instead, the Greek has an adverb *κυρίως*, 'rightly'. In the second, the word translated as 'the law' is *θέσμιον*, a neuter adjective without a definite article, so 'a lawful thing'. To slide an adverb into an indefinite noun (to make 'lawfully' into 'a law'), and an indefinite noun into a definite one (to make 'a lawful thing' into 'the law') is to reify as a divine principle what the Greek leaves as an *ad hoc* description.

But even when translated less assertively, the apparent elegance of these balanced formulations is at odds with the jagged complexity of the characters' attempts to understand the actual collisions of men and gods. For the apparent logic of cause and effect, action and consequence, is complicated by the temporal uncertainties in the Chorus's descriptions of events. It is unclear where, temporally, the events are located which are being described. The Chorus says:

βαρεῖα δ' ἀστῶν φάτις σὺν κότῳ,
δημοκράντου δ' ἀρᾶς τίνει χρέος·
μένει δ' ἀκοῦσαί τί μου
μέριμνα νυκτηρεφές·
τῶν πολυκτόνων γὰρ οὐκ
ἄσκοποι θεοί, κελαι-
ναὶ δ' Ἐρινύες χρόνῳ
τυχηρὸν ὄντ' ἄνευ δίκας[27]

Grievous is the talk of the citizens when they are angry;
the curse the people has pronounced ordains that a penalty must be paid.
My anxious thought waits to hear
a thing shrouded in darkness.
For the killers of many do not go
unwatched by the gods; and the black
Erinyes in time consign to darkness
him who is fortunate without justice.

The Chorus waits—and so much of the *Agamemnon* is concerned with waiting, waiting for the present tense of the drama to catch up with the events which have been adumbrated, and which therefore are

[27] *Agamemnon*, ll. 456–64.

already waiting to occur; the Chorus waits to hear something which it thinks will happen, but which is even now shrouded in darkness, as if it lurks already in some other unattainable dimension. But 'shrouded in darkness', as Lloyd-Jones has it, though it seems an appropriately sombre image, is a misleadingly comfortable cliché.[28] The word νυκτηρεφές is more literally 'covered by night',[29] and the verb from which the second element comes, ἐρέφω, is to cover or roof over, or to cover with a crown, or to wreathe with garlands. The image is therefore more troubling than 'shrouded', and implies that this thing for which the Chorus is waiting is roofed over like a (dark) house, or covered with a (dark) garland like a returning hero. This weird thing which waits in darkness is momentarily an anti-*oikos*, an anti-Agamemnon. The comment is oblique and generalized, but it is hard to avoid the impression that what the Chorus fears is some retribution on the Atreidae for their fortune—or their fortune without justice—in capturing Troy. We are not told which people have pronounced a curse, nor on whom, nor for what reason. Agency is suspended just at the moment when we might hope for moral clarity about who has acted, what they have done, and who is to punish them. There seem to be too many explanations offered in advance for the downfall of Agamemnon, without that fall ever being specifically alluded to: is it the result of his offending Artemis, or killing his daughter, or destroying the temples of the gods at Troy, or killing many, or being fortunate without justice, or being cursed by the people, or being the victim of child-avenging Wrath? Though the outlines of Agamemnon's story are clear, there are uncomfortably multiple ways of understanding its cause, and hence its moral status—whether his death is a punishment, or a new crime, or indeed both. The thing which the play roofs over or garlands in darkness is the moral status of Agamemnon's death, the problem of how we read it within a moralized narrative (which would have to be abstracted from the text) of guilt and retribution, where the standing of each

[28] The Loeb translation has 'shrouded in gloom' and Collard 'veiled over by night'.

[29] *LSJ*.

action is placed *sous rature* by its being both willed and unwilled, a human action impelled by a superhuman force; and by its being not an act in isolation but both a repetition of an earlier act and a prefiguration of another still to come. How can we think the morality of a single act which is neither exactly single nor exactly acted?

Unsettled and unsettling also is the language associated with Helen, as the Chorus plays on the supposed link between her name and the root *hel-* associated with killing, because the proper name Helen, Ἑλέναν, appears to be linked to ἑλέναs, 'ship-destroying', ἕλανδρος, 'man-destroying', and ἑλέπτολις, 'city-destroying'.[30] Someone unseen (τις ὅντιν' οὐχ ὁρῶμεν[31]) guided the naming of Helen, thinks the Chorus, so that her nature and the consequent destiny of the ships, the men, and the cities which she destroys are all already enfolded in her fatal naming. Can a name determine what happens to men? Can it, if conferred not by man as an element in human language, but by some unseen (and here unnamable) power? The narrative seems to be already encapsulated in this 'real' naming (ἐτητύμως, 'real, true'; ὀρθώνυμον, 'rightly named'[32]). The Chorus also sees as appropriate the double meaning of κῆδος, saying that Helen 'was for Ilium a *kedos* true to its name', for the word moves out from its root sense of 'care' to mean both 'marriage alliance' and 'mourning'.[33] At the end of this ode the Chorus's concern to perceive a pattern, especially one spoken by the gods, turns to a consideration of whether the acme of human prosperity generates misery, or whether it is the evil action which begets more evil. Though these commonplace reflections on the fall of houses into misfortune appear to generalize from the preceding lines on the fall of Troy, they immediately preface the entry of Agamemnon; and so, in a way which is typical of this play, the apparently judicious exposition of eternal laws hangs suspended between two points of application: one, we know, past, and one, we intuit, in the near future.

30 *Agamemnon*, ll. 688–9.

31 *Agamemnon*, l. 683.

32 *Agamemnon*, ll. 682, 700.

33 *Agamemnon*, l. 699. Its root is κήδω, 'to wound, to trouble' (Chantraine).

When Agamemnon arrives, he pauses—or is made by Clytemnestra to pause—before the threshold of the house.[34] It is Clytemnestra who commands the threshold, commands the access to the house, and thereby commands the meaning of the house. Agamemnon says that by spreading tapestries in front of him she greets him as if he were a barbarian, and remarks that the tapestries should be reserved for the use of the gods. Whether seen as barbarian or god, Agamemnon is displaced from his proper position as a Greek king, his proper position being a proto-Aristotelian mid-point between the two extremes. The tapestries are part of the wealth of the household, so that by marring them with his tread he is continuing the damage to the *oikos* which he began with the killing of Iphigenia, the 'pride of the house' as he called her.[35] But there is an unhappy doubling in the word which is translated 'pride'. For ἄγαλμα means not only 'glory, delight, honour', but also, and ominously, a 'pleasing gift for the gods', as it is used for objects which are offered in sacrifice, and also for any rich item which is reserved for the use of a king or a god, such as gold, weapons, vessels—or tapestries.[36] The multiple meanings of ἄγαλμα stretch out into the play, connecting the sacrifice of Iphigenia with that other form of household wealth which Agamemnon is about to trample.[37]

Cassandra too is made to pause before the threshold. Her speech, though made in Greek, is in another sense cast in a language which the Chorus cannot understand, as it presents a riddling vision of past, present, and future, going back to the killing by Pelops of his own children, the killing by Atreus of his nephews, and then forward to Clytemnestra's preparations for the murder of Agamemnon and of Cassandra herself. Her vocabulary at this point[38] falls strangely on the ear of Chorus and audience. Does μισόθεον, applied to the house,

[34] For the staging of this scene, see Oliver Taplin, *The Stagecraft of Aeschylus* (Oxford, 1977), esp. pp. 308–16 for the significance of the tapestries.

[35] *Agamemnon*, l. 208.

[36] *LSJ*, Chantraine *s.v.* ἀγάλλομαι.

[37] In the production at the National Theatre in 1999 it was a bold but crude piece of directorial imagination to have the pathways of fabrics which led Agamemnon into the house made from Iphigenia's blood-stained dresses.

[38] *Agamemnon*, ll. 1090–2.

mean that the house hates the gods, or that the house is hated by the gods;[39] is the house transgressor or victim? Or does Aeschylus fuse the two possibilities? Had anyone previously heard her strange compound word ἀνδροσφαγεῖον ('slaughterhouse of men')? Or πεδορραντήριον ('ground sprinkled with blood')?[40] She destabilizes the very idea of the house in these weird coinages. She sees the statue of Apollo guarding the threshold and puns bitterly on the name of the god who possesses her: ὤπολλον . . . ἀπόλλων ('O Apollo . . . destroyer'), seeing something inevitable in the similarity of names.[41] To what house has he brought her, she asks? The word for house which Cassandra uses here is στέγην, whose root means 'shelter' but also 'cover, conceal, hide',[42] and Cassandra, who finds no shelter here, is about to uncover in her prophetic speech the secrets which the house of Atreus hides. She sees the house occupied by the Erinyes. She sees the children of Thyestes sitting by the door, ghostly occupants of the house. She sees the gates of the house of Atreus as the gates of Hades.[43] And so the visible spaces of the house are turned into the entrances to this uncanny off-stage space where the past and future crimes of the family are stored. It is indeed an entrance to the underworld. Time is speeded up as she describes what Clytemnestra will do to Agamemnon, and the verbs slip from the future into the present tense as she describes the killing, or sacrifice, of Agamemnon.[44]

Many of the events narrated or staged in this play are presented as forms of sacrifice.[45] The formal sacrifices of Thyestes' children by Atreus and of Iphigenia by Agamemnon seem to be laid as a template over the deaths of other characters, as if they are compelled to

[39] Lloyd-Jones understands the former, Loeb the latter; Collard has 'godless', which loses the idea of hatred altogether.

[40] The Loeb text; Page prints πέδον ῥαντήριον. In both cases this is *LSJ*'s only example of the word, and both readings result from an emendation of the MSS. It is revealing that this speech of horrified vision is textually uncertain, for the scribes appear to have had difficulty understanding Cassandra's tortured speech.

[41] *Agamemnon*, ll. 1080–1.

[42] *LSJ*, Chantraine.

[43] *Agamemnon*, ll. 1185ff.; 1215ff.; 1291.

[44] *Agamemnon*, ll. 1107ff.

[45] See Pierre Vidal-Naquet, 'Chasse et sacrifice dans l'«Orestie» d'Eschyle', in Jean-Pierre Vernant and Pierre Vidal-Naquet, *Mythe et tragédie en Grèce ancienne*, 2 vols. (Paris, 1972–86; reprinted 2001), i 133–58, and Wiles, pp. 58–9.

replicate those deaths in some form of requital. We are presented with the difficulty of matching one event against another, as no event ever quite seems stable and completed, and this also generates a difficulty in assigning events to moral categories. The fall of Troy is metaphorically presented as a sacrifice which no sacrifice made by Paris can avert,[46] while Clytemnestra attempts to normalize and make moral the murder of Agamemnon by describing it as a votive offering made to Hades or to 'the Zeus beneath the earth'.[47] She changes the rationale, however, in saying later that she has sacrificed him to Justice, Ruin, and the Erinyes.[48] But who acts, who performs this sacrifice? The Chorus had spoken of the *daimon* falling upon the house and ruling through the hands of women,[49] so according to this view Clytemnestra is the agent or the instrument of the *daimon* of the family. By *daimon* here we might understand some supernatural power,[50] though Lloyd-Jones interprets it as 'the personified curse upon the family';[51] but to call it a personification neuters the terror and returns us in the word 'curse' to another abstract noun which no one seems to have pronounced.

The concept of *daimon* is actually more terrible. The Chorus returns to the subject:

ἦ μέγαν οἴκοις τοῖσδε
δαίμονα καὶ βαρύμηνιν αἰνεῖς,[52]

Mighty for this house is the spirit you tell of, heavy his wrath.

The idea of the destructive *daimon* which is heavy in its wrath (βαρύμηνιν, another instance of μῆνις) is seized upon by Clytemnestra to evade full responsibility for her act, denying that the deed was hers and asking the Chorus to imagine, in a counter-factual narrative, that she is not Agamemnon's wife.[53] She claims that it is the *daimon* of the house which has sacrificed the grown man in requital for the death of

46 *Agamemnon*, ll. 65, 69–71.
47 *Agamemnon*, ll. 1386–7.
48 *Agamemnon*, l. 1435.
49 *Agamemnon*, ll. 1468, 1470.
50 See also pp. 79–81 below.
51 Lloyd-Jones, p. 96. Collard (pp. xxxiii–xxxiv) lists occurrences of what he calls the personification of the curse.
52 *Agamemnon*, ll. 1481–2.
53 *Agamemnon*, ll. 1475–80, 1497–9.

the children of Thyestes,[54] so according to Clytemnestra it is a supernatural force beyond her control which has done this. But the text here is difficult to interpret. She speaks of the 'ancient savage avenger of Atreus', *φανταζόμενος δὲ γυναικὶ νεκροῦ*, 'manifesting himself to this dead man's wife' as Lloyd-Jones translates it.[55] But *φανταζόμενος*, meaning 'making oneself visible to', has also been interpreted to mean 'taking on the form of'.[56] So does the *daimon* show itself to Clytemnestra and prompt her to act, or does it take on the physical form of Clytemnestra and act through her body without her will? We enter here an area where semantic uncertainty stretches into and undermines our understanding of the claim which Clytemnestra is making about the degree of her responsibility for the killing.

Later Clytemnestra says that she is 'willing to swear a covenant with the demon [*δαίμονι*] | of the Pleisthenids so that I bear all this, | hard though it is to endure',[57] an ostensibly self-sacrificial gesture which is a staged response to the Chorus's despairing question, 'Who shall cast out the brood of curses from the house?', *τίς ἂν γονὰν ἀραῖον ἐκβάλοι δόμων;*.[58] The phrase translated as 'a brood of curses' is *γονὰν ἀραῖον*, where *γονὰν* means 'generation, family, offspring', and *ἀραῖον* 'cursing, cursed, bringing mischief', with both active and passive senses possible: a cursed brood, or a cursing brood. So what is to be expelled from the house, a family which is cursed (the family of Atreus) or a group of beings, such as the Erinyes, which brings disaster to the house? The lexical uncertainty provides two alternative images of the inhabitants of this house. And Cassandra had seen the house doubly occupied when she said that 'this house is never left by a choir | that sings in unison, yet with no pleasant sound... | ... a band of revellers | not easily sent away, composed of the Erinyes bred with the family [*συγγόνων Ἐρινύων*]'.[59] Though the

[54] *Agamemnon*, ll. 1500–4. [55] *Agamemnon*, l. 1500.

[56] Thus Loeb, Collard. This example provides *LSJ*'s only example of this sense.

[57] *Agamemnon*, ll. 1569–71. [58] *Agamemnon*, l. 1565.

[59] *Agamemnon*, ll. 1186–90. For interpretations of curses and the Erinyes see N. J. Sewell-Rutter, *Guilt by Descent: Moral Inheritance and Decision Making in Greek Tragedy* (Oxford, 2007).

Erinyes will have a more visibly active role later in the trilogy, it seems that they already inhabit the house—perhaps, then, in some way inhabiting the human agents who carry out its killings.

Responsibility for these crimes is mapped in complex ways, though often for reasons of self-interest. After the murder of Agamemnon, Clytemnestra claims that 'If we could have had enough of these troubles, we should be content, | grievously struck as we have been by the spirit's hoof';[60] here δαίμονος χηλῇ is a vigorously physical image, suggesting the kicking of a vicious animal, but at this point in the play all the principals are invoking the concept of a *daimon* for their own purposes. Clytemnestra does too in a gesture of exculpation, attributing the action to the *daimon* and casting herself as its victim. Aegisthus warns the Chorus not to make 'trial of their fortune [δαίμονος]' (i.e. 'don't push your luck'), while the Chorus responds by hoping that a δαίμων may lead Orestes back to Argos as an avenger.[61] Though the repeated references suggest some form of supernatural agency oppressing the house of Atreus, each usage of *daimon* reflects the speaker's own viewpoint and rhetorical purpose: the resulting theological framework around the action is oppressive but imprecise.

Multiple explanations for the killing, multiple descriptions of it, present its moral status in varying ways, and in so doing attempt to re-align the responsibility of the killer towards the action. The one event is offered as a repetition and vengeance for the earlier ones, but in the *Oresteia* characters are caught up in a chain of events which are differently emplotted according to the characters' perceptions: murder can be redescribed as sacrifice, a wife can imagine that she is no wife. The repeated imagery of nets similarly invites us to perceive one event as a repetition of, or as a version of, another. Zeus casts a net over Troy (δίκτυον, a hunting or fishing net[62]), Agamemnon's body is said by rumour to have as many wounds as a net has holes (δίκτυον[63]), and Cassandra sees 'some net [δίκτυον] of Hades. | But it is the net [ἄρκυς] that shares his bed, that shares the guilt | of

[60] *Agamemnon*, ll. 1659–60. [61] *Agamemnon*, ll. 1663, 1667.
[62] *Agamemnon*, l. 358. [63] *Agamemnon*, l. 868.

murder',[64] so eliding Clytemnestra as autonomous actor into the image of the instrument of Agamemnon's death, while still preserving her guilt. Agamemnon is killed with the help of a hunting net (ἀρκύστατ'[65]). Nets are woven, and these images suggest a link to the woven tapestries on which Agamemnon treads, and the woven net or robe[66] in which he is ensnared. Finally, Aegisthus says that Agamemnon lies 'in the woven robes of the Erinyes',[67] as if it is they, not he and Clytemnestra, who have accomplished all this. It seems as if no act is autonomous, no agent wholly free to act; every act is a version of a previous act, every agent compelled or influenced by some power, barely nameable, beyond themselves. Or perhaps this power is both within and beyond them.[68]

The *Agamemnon* is a liminal tragedy. Man is placed uncannily on the threshold of his home, which turns into the place of his death as he passes through the doorway. The unseen space into which he moves, driven by pride and folly, is a conceptual space in which the rich substance of the house, signified externally by its defiled tapestries, turns out to be composed of deaths from the past. But in this play the past is never past; rather it is repeated in new versions, with images such as the net implying that there is a pattern to events which is larger than anything seen or willed by the participants. And yet responsibility for the design of such a pattern is withheld from view. The pattern-seeking Chorus, standing at the threshold of the house, which is the threshold of death, recognizes the strangeness of its own utterance:

> τίπτε μοι τόδ' ἐμπέδως
> δεῖμα προστατήριον
> καρδίας τερασκόπου ποτᾶται;
> μαντιπολεῖ δ' ἀκέλευστος ἄμισθος ἀοιδά[69]

[64] *Agamemnon*, ll. 1115–17. [65] *Agamemnon*, l. 1375.
[66] *Agamemnon*, l. 1382. [67] *Agamemnon*, l. 1581.
[68] For a discussion of the representations of the individual will in Greek tragedy, particularly in the *Oresteia*, see Jean-Pierre Vernant, 'Ebauches de la volonté dans la tragédie grecque', in Vernant and Vidal-Naquet, i 41–74.
[69] *Agamemnon*, ll. 975–9.

Why, ever constant, does this
terror, set before my divining heart,
hover,
and prophecy speaks in a song unbidden, unpaid for?

Fear is 'standing before' (προστατήριον) the heart, as the Chorus stands before the door. But fear also hovers (ποτᾶται), and like the fear which stood alongside the Watchman, or the wrath which was abiding in the house, fear is both inside and outside of the body. The heart is 'sign-seeing' (τερασκόπου), but there are no secure signs to read. The Chorus's song comes unbidden (ἀκέλευστος), without anyone willing it. The autonomy of the characters is lost, or at least lost from our understanding. Tragic man is partly compelled, partly a free agent; but Aeschylus presents that double recognition in language which leaves it just beyond our grasp.

The second play of the trilogy, *Choephori* or 'Libation Bearers', repeats and reverses some of the principal actions of the *Agamemnon*:[70] both Agamemnon and Orestes return home to be greeted by Clytemnestra; Clytemnestra is led over the threshold of the house to be killed by Orestes as she had killed Agamemnon; Orestes stands over the bodies of Clytemnestra and Aegisthus as she had stood over the bodies of Agamemnon and Cassandra. As we read the events of the *Choephori* we come to see that no principal act is isolated, and no principal actor autonomous. Each may be understood as a repetition of an earlier element in the story of the house of Atreus. Who is it who acts? Who carries out the actions which are attributed to Orestes? Orestes is partly his father's representative; he is also seen as the agent of the chthonic powers; he will be pursued by the Erinyes if he does not avenge his father; he kills his mother on the instructions of Apollo (who says that he is speaking for Zeus); and he appears in Clytemnestra's dream as a serpent biting her breast, suggesting that in some dimension the killing has already been carried out.[71] When Orestes

[70] Garvie, pp. xxxv–xxxvi.

[71] The Erinyes are portrayed as snakes, or as having snake-like hair (Garvie, pp. xvii, xxxvi–xxxvii), which provides an association between Orestes and the Erinyes.

says that Clytemnestra's dream portends that 'I turn into a snake | and slay her', the verb κτείνω is in the present tense: 'I kill her', 'I am killing her'; there is a form of time in which Orestes is even now (or, is always) killing Clytemnestra. The Chorus asks Electra to pray that 'some god or mortal' (δαίμον' ἢ βροτῶν τινα[72]) may come to punish Clytemnestra and Aegisthus, and she duly calls upon 'the deities below the earth [τοὺς γῆς ἔνερθε δαίμονας] to hear my prayers';[73] so Orestes, if not himself a *daimon*, is nevertheless envisaged as the instrument of such a *daimon*. 'Orestes', therefore, names a complex collection of agents and influences. The *Choephori* takes place around the tomb of Agamemnon, which now commands the entrance to the house; it is a disturbing presence, making the dead king a participant in the action in ways which we cannot quite determine. The underworld is very close here to the world of Argos, for those beneath the earth cry out and demand vengeance upon their killers.[74] Agamemnon's mind has not been subdued by the funeral fire, says the Chorus, 'but late in time he shows his anger'.[75] Orestes invokes the rulers of the underworld, and exclaims 'Look on us, powerful curses of the dead!'[76] These curses, Ἀραί, seem personified through the apostrophe here, and made capable of sight. Zeus sends up from below 'late-avenging ruin', 'ruin' here being ἄταν.[77] *Atē* can be construed as ruin, disaster, or as a form of delusion or blindness sent by the gods, or, personified as Atē, the goddess of ruin. We do not know quite what form this intervention from Zeus will take—if indeed it happens, for this is simply part of the Chorus's prayer. Human and

Garvie notes that 'Orestes . . . has taken upon himself the character which belonged to his mother . . . and will act as she did . . . and . . . the power of the dead Agamemnon has entered into his son' (p. 193).

[72] *Choephori*, l. 119. [73] *Choephori*, l. 125.

[74] *Choephori*, ll. 40–1. 'Those below the earth make angry complaint' (τοὺς γᾶς νέρθεν περιθύμως), but it is not clear whether this refers to the chthonic powers or to Agamemnon himself. Garvie (p. xxxiii) notes that Agamemnon is envisaged as being both close by in his tomb, and far away (almost unreachable) in Hades. In the production cited in note 37 the grave was open, and a video screen projected the view up from inside the grave—Agamemnon's view, in effect.

[75] *Choephori*, ll. 324–6. [76] *Choephori*, ll. 405–6. [77] *Choephori*, l. 383.

divine, living and dead, interact to bring about the killing of Clytemnestra.

Things, too, take on forms of agency through Aeschylean metaphor. Blood demands further blood, through a verb which denotes the action of an importunate suppliant (προσαιτεῖν: demand in addition, beg persistently).[78] And 'because of blood drained by the fostering earth | the vengeful gore stands clotted, and will not dissolve away'.[79] The blood is drained or drunk up (ἐκποθένθ') by the earth, and yet it is also coagulated (πέπηγεν) and will not drain away (οὐ διαρρύδαν); the blood itself takes vengeance (τίτας). Thus the blood is both drained away and not drained away; because of past bloodshed, the shed blood is still present. Acts are not confined to the past; and it is not only human agents who act.

And when human agents do act, they are not necessarily conceptualized as integral and autonomous beings. The Chorus says that 'The child of older bloody murders | is being brought into the house': τέκνον δ' ἐπεισφέρει δόμοις | αἱμάτων παλαιτέρων.[80] So who or what is this child? It seems to be both Orestes and the act of killing, as if the two were now fused.[81] Orestes is the killing; and this is the kind of child which inhabits the house of Atreus. Who kills Clytemnestra? As Orestes confronts his mother, she repeatedly evokes the maternal bond between them, placing him as her child, but he tries to reposition himself as his father's child, not hers, and insists, with emphatic pronouns, σύ τοι σεαυτήν, οὐκ ἐγώ, κατακτενεῖς, '*You* will kill yourself, not *I*',[82] thus making her the agent of her own death. And again: πατρὸς γὰρ αἶσα τόνδε σουρίζει μόρον, 'It is my father's destiny

[78] *Choephori*, ll. 400–2. [79] *Choephori*, ll. 66–7.

[80] *Choephori*, ll. 648–9; Collard's translation. Lloyd-Jones has: 'But the child is brought into the house | of ancient murders'.

[81] *Pace* Lloyd-Jones, who says categorically that 'the child' 'refers not to Orestes but to the new murder that will soon take place' (p. 46); Collard more flexibly says that the child 'is both figurative and also literally Orestes, after the acts involving his ancestors Atreus and Agamemnon': in Collard's reading, the image would transform Atreus and Agamemnon into 'bloodshed' (αἱμάτων in the plural meaning 'streams of blood' or 'bloodshed'), another translation of the human into the non-human, whereby individuals are conceptualized solely as the bloodshed which they produce.

[82] *Choephori*, l. 923; my translation.

which determines this death of yours'.[83] And again, when she says that Fate (*Μοῖρα*) had some responsibility for Agamemnon's death, Orestes replies: *καὶ τόνδε τοίνυν Μοῖρ' ἐπόρσυνεν μόρον*, 'Well, Fate has dealt you this death too'.[84] In each of these rejoinders to Clytemnestra, Orestes is constituting the agent of this killing as someone or something other than himself—as Fate, Agamemnon's death, Clytemnestra herself. And in the eyes of the Chorus, Orestes' hand was guided by Justice, breathing (*πνέους'*) wrath against her and his enemies, touching his hand as he raised it to strike.[85] Justice is a physical, though invisible, agent.

Yet in the *Eumenides* Orestes is not severed from the murder of Clytemnestra even after he has performed the prescribed ritual acts of purification. The Priestess describes Orestes sitting in the temple of Apollo, 'his hands and newly drawn sword . . . dripping with blood':[86] time seems suspended here, the moment of the killing turned into an ever-present continuum in which the sword has just been drawn (*νεοσπαδὲς ξίφος*) and the hands are, as we watch, still dripping (*στάζοντα χεῖρας*). Is there any escape from the prison of such suspended time, such ever-present blood?

In the *Eumenides* there is a dramatic movement away from the house of Atreus and its embodied bloodshed, which had haunted the first two plays of the trilogy; we move first to the temple of Apollo, and then to the altar of Athene. The movement is from the hearth of all woes, *πάνοιζυς ἑστία*,[87] to the hearth of the god Apollo, *πρὸς ἑστίαι θεοῦ Φοίβου*,[88] for purification, and thence to the hearth of Athene for judgement, *ἑστίας ἐμῆς πέλας*.[89] The same word *ἑστία*, which means both the human domestic hearth and the altar of a god, is used by Aeschylus to mark the necessary progress of the story from

[83] *Choephori*, l. 927; Collard's translation.

[84] *Choephori*, l. 911; Collard's translation.

[85] *Choephori*, ll. 958–51. Lloyd-Jones has 'guided his hand', but Collard translates 'lent her hand's touch'. Whether Aeschylus is referring to the hand of Orestes (as Garvie also thinks, p. 309) or the hand of Justice, the physicality of Justice's intervention is clear from the verb *ἔθιγε* (touched).

[86] Aeschylus, *Eumenides*, l. 42.

[87] *Choephori*, l. 49.

[88] *Eumenides*, ll. 281–2.

[89] *Eumenides*, l. 440.

the blood-stained hearth of Argos to the purificatory altars of the Olympian gods.[90] Although the drama does not return to Argos, and does not explicitly purge the house, it does allow Orestes to return to his father's house to take possession of his inheritance. The Erinyes protest, 'Shall he who has spilt his mother's kindred blood upon the ground | then live in Argos in his father's house?'[91] But Orestes himself thanks Athene for his acquittal by saying:

> *ὦ Παλλάς, ὦ σώσασα τοὺς ἐμοὺς δόμους,*
> *γαίας πατρῴας ἐστερημένον σύ τοι*
> *κατῴκισάς με. καί τις Ἑλλήνων ἐρεῖ*
> *"Ἀργεῖος ἀνὴρ αὖθις, ἔν τε χρήμασιν*
> *οἰκεῖ πατρῴοις."*[92]

> O Pallas, you who have preserved my house,
> I was deprived of my native land, and it is you
> who have brought me home! And the Greeks shall say,
> 'The man is once more an Argive, and lives
> among the possessions of his father.'

The speech resonates with the repeated loaded words 'house' (*δόμους ... κατῴκισάς ... οἰκεῖ*) and 'paternal' (*πατρῴας ... πατρῴοις*). He is once more a true inhabitant of Argos (*Ἀργεῖος*), even though we do not see him cross the threshold. For Aeschylus is preparing a different form of *nostos*, a different form of return.

The reconfiguration of dwelling takes place instead on a communal scale. At the end of the *Choephori* the Erinyes moved into the space of Orestes' mind, where he alone could see them. At the opening of the *Eumenides* they have taken over the sacred space of Apollo's temple, occupying the realm of light and reason and healing with their dark chthonic retribution; two principles and two modes of justice contend

[90] For the significance of the concept of *ἑστία* see Jean-Pierre Vernant, 'Hestia-Hermès: Sur l'expression religieuse de l'espace et du mouvement chez les Grecs', in his *Mythe et pensée chez les Grecs: Études de psychologie historique* (Paris, 1965; second edition 1985, reprinted 1996), pp. 155–201, esp. pp. 165–9 for its importance in the *Oresteia*.

[91] *Eumenides*, ll. 653–4. Sommerstein's gloss on *δῶματ' οἰκήσει* is: 'not just "dwell in the house of" but "enter into the inheritance of"' (p. 205).

[92] *Eumenides*, ll. 754–8.

for supremacy in the same space, this space being at once the character 'Orestes' and the moral discourse of Athens. Then at the climax of the trilogy the Erinyes sanctify the civic space of Athens itself. After the acquittal of Orestes, they are persuaded to take up residence in Athens, where they will bless the inhabitants and promote the fertility of the place. Whereas before they 'have chosen the ruin | of households; when violence | nurtured in the home strikes a dear one down', now no house will thrive without their blessing.[93] The Erinyes had been pursuing the perpetrators of slaughter, Ἄρης, which is often personified as Ares the god of war.[94] Men had become habituated to such barbaric slaughter (or is it Ares, the divinity?); and it had been domesticated (τιθασὸς) as one would tame a wild animal, and had grown to be part of the home. This is one of many images in the *Oresteia* which encapsulate the perverted domesticity of the Atreidae, and recalls the fable of the lion nurtured as a household pet which eventually revealed its innate savagery,[95] and the snake which suckled the breast of Clytemnestra.[96] The image of Ἄρης τιθασὸς places within the domestic space a concept of slaughter which is at once divine—the god Ares—and animalistic—needing to be tamed. Thus is the appalling *locus* of the human defined. The concluding speeches of the *Eumenides* seek to recuperate the spaces of human dwelling by transforming the avenging divinities into guardians and nurturing powers; and the trilogy ends with a torchlit procession which escorts to their new residence these childless children of night, Νυκτὸς παῖδες ἄπαιδες:[97] they are both 'children who are no children' because they are ancient, and 'children who are childless' because crime will no longer breed retribution.[98] No longer will the house nurture bloodshed as its perpetual offspring. Time and space have been transfigured.[99]

93 *Eumenides*, ll. 354–6, 895.

94 Ares guards the city of Athens: *Eumenides*, l. 918.

95 *Agamemnon*, ll. 717–36; Sommerstein, p. 143.

96 *Choephori*, ll. 526–33.

97 *Eumenides*, l. 1034.

98 Sommerstein's translations and gloss, p. 283.

99 But the ending is not without unresolved elements: see (e.g.) Vernand and Vidal-Naquet, i 25–7, n. 3.

3

SOPHOCLES

Electra

Sophocles' *Electra* is shadowed by the past of the house of Atreus, a past which survives and is reshaped in the minds of its principals; in particular, in a departure from the emphasis in the *Oresteia*, the tragic milieu is the mind of Electra. At the beginning of the play the old slave's speech establishes the setting as more than the geographical Argos: 'home' is a complex fabric of biography and myth,[1] for he recalls that it was here that he received the boy Orestes from the arms of his sister and carried him to safety; but this is also the place of Io and of Apollo; it is at once rich in gold (πολυχρύσους) and rich in disasters (πολύφθορόν).[2] The Chorus even traces the woes of the house back to the original killing by Pelops of his own son.[3] Though memory plays its part, more than memory is at work here, for the very way that the characters exist in time is determined by the death of Agamemnon, which remains present throughout in its own dimension, and is restaged at the end of the play when Orestes kills Aegisthus on the same spot where Aegisthus had killed Agamemnon.[4]

In this chapter the Greek text and English translations are taken from *Sophocles*, edited and translated by Hugh Lloyd-Jones, Loeb Classical Library, 2 vols. (Cambridge, Mass., 1994), unless otherwise stated. I have also drawn on *Sophocles: The Plays and Fragments*, edited by Sir Richard Jebb, *Part VI: The Electra* (Cambridge, 1894, reprinted 1924) and on *Electra*, edited by J. H. Kells (Cambridge, 1973).

[1] Jebb's notes on this passage trace the mixture of geographical precision and mythic layering.

[2] Sophocles, *Electra*, ll. 9–10.

[3] *Electra*, l. 502.

[4] *Electra*, ll. 1494–6.

Agamemnon's death is not confined to being an event in a sequence, but is rather the invisible premise which underlies all the actions which we watch. The central character, Electra, lives in a version of the past, not only never forgetting the murder of her father, but having her whole life and way of thinking, from moment to moment, compelled by it: she seems to be one in whom mourning has never mellowed into commemoration. By contrast, her mother Clytemnestra tries to keep that past dormant, sending her other daughter, Chrysothemis, to make offerings on her behalf at the tomb of Agamemnon, thus hoping to ward off the consequences of his killing, to deter his angry irruption into her comfortable present.[5] The Chorus is cautious in its recollections, saying of the murder that 'Cunning was the teacher, passion was the killer; horribly they brought into being a shape horrible [δεινὰν δεινῶς], whether it was a god or a mortal who was the doer'.[6] The phrasing almost takes agency away from the individuals Clytemnestra and Aegisthus by making 'cunning' (δόλος) devise the murder and 'passion' (specifically, sexual desire: ἔρως) execute it. Are these attributes of the two characters, or abstract nouns into which the characters have been transformed, or autonomous superhuman forces? (Justice was his killer, according to Clytemnestra's self-exculpatory claim.[7]) And the Chorus is carefully non-committal about whether this was the work of men or of the gods. The verb translated as 'brought into being' is προφυτεύσαντες, which means 'giving birth to', thus making the killing of Agamemnon a gross kind of child—and one which will grow in time.

Electra seems to have no future, or at least no future among the living. She laments that she has lost much of her life—more precisely, that a great part of her life has abandoned her without hope,[8] as if her life were something or someone outside her which has forsaken and deserted her (ἀπολέλοιπεν). In an expressive verb she 'melts away' (κατατάκομαι,[9]

[5] For the conduct of relations between the living and the dead in the Greek world see Sarah Iles Johnston, *Restless Dead: Encounters between the Living and the Dead in Ancient Greece* (Berkeley, 1999).

[6] *Electra*, ll. 197–200.

[7] *Electra*, l. 538.

[8] *Electra*, ll. 185–6.

[9] *Electra*, l. 187.

a passive form, so in effect 'I am melted away') without offspring and without husband, and so without a stake in the future, contributing nothing to the continuation of the house of Atreus in which she is made to serve as if she were a slave, an *ἔποικος*.[10] An *ἔποικος* is a stranger or alien, one who dwells temporarily in a place which is not their own home. Through these lexical and grammatical nuances, Sophocles shows how Electra is no longer in possession of her home or herself. She exists, undeveloping, in a kind of stalled time in which the murder of Agamemnon is kept perpetually present through her laments. She has, she tells Chrysothemis, decided on her course of action long ago,[11] so the present is subordinate to the past. The Chorus warns her against excessive anger, but she says that there will be no measure or proportion to her sorrow.[12] She is, one might say, unbalanced by her grief, for she herself says that she no longer has the strength to bear alone the weight of sorrow which is *ἀντίρροπον*,[13] 'counterpoising', the image suggesting that the sorrow outweighs her own body and so tips her over.

Electra's time and place are with the dead. Her opening speech begins with an invocation to 'holy light' (*ὦ φάος ἁγνὸν*[14]), but this light is called upon only in order to witness that she has spent her days singing dirges and beating her breast, while her nights are filled with sleepless lamentations. Night and day alike are but stretches of mourning. And when she speaks of the sorrows of her sleepless nights, she uses a word, *παννυχίδων*, which usually refers to night-time rituals, to joyous torch-lit festivals or even revelling.[15] The irony is clear—hers is no shared festival, but a solitary lamentation; and this is one of several examples of distorted or perverted ritual, instances when the proper means of communicating between men and gods, between living and dead, have been disrupted. She is aware of the

[10] *Electra*, l. 189. [11] *Electra*, l. 1049.

[12] *Electra*, ll. 179–80, 236. The Loeb translation renders *μέτρον* as 'limit', which is possible, but the word also means 'due measure or proportion' (*LSJ, s.v.*). The Chorus says that she has acquired *excessive* troubles (l. 217).

[13] *Electra*, l. 120. [14] *Electra*, l. 86.

[15] *Electra*, l. 92; Jebb, *ad loc.*; *LSJ, s.v.*

shining constellations—in fact, of the wonderfully 'quivering' rays of starlight, as Jebb translates ῥιπάς[16]—but she looks on them like the grieving nightingale: twice she compares herself with Procne, who killed her own son Itys in order to avenge the rape of her sister by her husband;[17] and she also compares herself with Niobe, weeping for the loss of all her children.[18] While the comparison with these two mothers marks out Electra's loss by imagining her now impossible future as a mother, the principal point of the comparison is that the grief of Procne and Niobe is perpetual: Procne, turned into a nightingale, never ceases to cry 'Itun, Itun', while Niobe never ceases to weep. Niobe, in Electra's eyes, is even 'divine' (θεόν) because of her complete absorption in mourning. The devotion of Procne and Niobe to mourning is an obsession beyond the human, and they have been translated into non-human forms, Procne into a bird, Niobe into stone. Electra seems to be precariously placed on such a boundary of the human.

She seems to exist tangentially to the time and space shared by other characters. 'Time is a god which brings relief', says the Chorus,[19] but it is hard to see how. The Chorus says that Electra will never raise Agamemnon from Hades with her weeping,[20] but in a sense this is what she does. In her opening speech she invokes the powers of the underworld and asks them to send Orestes as avenger.[21] When she hears that Orestes is dead, she appeals to Chrysothemis to join her in killing Aegisthus, and urges her: 'work with your father, labour with your brother',[22] so trying to draw her sister into a temporal and spatial dimension in which the dead work with them as their helpers. Orestes, by not coming, has destroyed, she says, 'the hopes I had and the hopes I had not': τὰς οὔσας τέ μου | καὶ τὰς ἀπούσας ἐλπίδας.[23] The phrasing strikingly enacts Electra's simultaneous possession and lack of possession even of those very hopes which define her existence.[24]

[16] *Electra*, l. 106. [17] *Electra*, ll. 107, 147–8. [18] *Electra*, ll. 150–2.
[19] *Electra*, l. 179. [20] *Electra*, ll. 137–9. [21] *Electra*, ll. 110–17.
[22] *Electra*, ll. 986–7. [23] *Electra*, ll. 305–6.
[24] Jebb's gloss, 'simply, "all possible" hopes', smoothes away the expressive strangeness of the wording.

Into this static time comes Orestes, who is conscious of the right time, *καιρός*, the time in which one has to act.[25] In the play's first speech the slave tells Orestes that this is no time to hesitate, but the moment to take action:

ἵν' οὐκέτ' ὀκνεῖν καιρός, ἀλλ' ἔργων ἀκμή.[26]

And at the end of his first speech, Orestes echoes the old man's words: it is time, *καιρὸς γάρ*.[27] At several points the characters urge each other to act rather than to spend their time on speech,[28] and Orestes asks Electra to tell him what course of action will suit the present time.[29] But this decisive intervention of the avenger into the present is itself a form of repetition. The play dramatizes various kinds of return, of *nostos*, the insistence on the difficulty of return perhaps alluding to the fatal *nostos* of Agamemnon memorably presented in Aeschylus' play. True return is impossible, for both the person and the place have changed, have been displaced. Orestes does return, but not simply: he is both multiplied and fragmented. First the old slave arrives at the house alone, carrying Orestes' death with him in his false story of the chariot race. Then Orestes himself returns, but not as himself; he appears as a stranger from Phocis with the urn in which, he says, are the ashes of Orestes. He carries the sign of his own death, but like other signs in this play it is misleading.[30] Then there is a third return of Orestes, *in propria persona*, when he reveals his identity to Electra. During this third and final return, Orestes requires Electra to give up the urn which supposedly contains his ashes—to give up the false sign, to give up her mourning—and in exchange he gives her himself. But there are other revenants which haunt this stage: Agamemnon returns in Clytemnestra's dream,[31] where she imagines him coming into the

[25] In Greek usage *χρόνος* is time in general, while *καιρός* is the right time for action, the critical moment.

[26] *Electra*, l. 22. [27] *Electra*, l. 75.

[28] *Electra*, ll. 1326–38, 1363–73, 1483–4. [29] *Electra*, l. 1292.

[30] Ironically, Chrysothemis is persuaded that she is wrong in interpreting the offerings laid on the tomb of Agamemnon as signs that Orestes has returned, though she is, of course, correct.

[31] *Electra*, ll. 417–23.

light (ἐς φῶς), taking back his staff from Aegisthus and planting it on the hearth (ἐφέστιον), thereby reclaiming his home. The hearth (ἑστία) is for the Greeks the sacred central space of the house, the word sometimes being used for an altar, and signifying the place where the gods which protect the household are reverenced.[32] Electra, in her joy at her brother's return, says that she would not be surprised if Agamemnon himself were to return alive.[33] And Aegisthus returns from the country, only to be killed. Orestes forces him to go inside the house in order to kill him on the spot where Aegisthus himself had killed Agamemnon,[34] thus linking up the past and the present on the same ground. In order for time to be released, the past has to be restaged: another killing and the same, *alter et idem*, on the same spot, with almost the same participants but with their roles reversed, with Orestes standing for his father and so reclaiming his inheritance: agent now, not victim.

Here we have both tragic and non-tragic forms of displacement, some destructive, some recuperative: Orestes allows temporary displacements of himself (into the person of a stranger from Phocis, into ashes in the urn, into his father when killing Aegisthus) in order to return to his home and to reclaim that identity which is grounded in his membership of the house of Atreus. As Electra says, he was dead by a stratagem, and has returned safely home by a stratagem.[35] But Electra herself suffers more tragic displacements, unable to inhabit the time and space of the other characters, treated as a slave indoors in her father's house and rebuked when she ventures outside, for Clytemnestra regards Electra as bringing shame on the family by moving around 'without restraint' out of doors.[36] Electra says that she will never again enter the house, but will stay at the gates and waste away,[37] while Clytemnestra and Aegisthus apparently plan to shut her up in some dungeon outside their territory, in an echo of the fate of Antigone. She is unable to maintain any kind of self which is

[32] Chantraine, *LSJ*, *s.v.* See p. 61 n. 90 above.
[33] *Electra*, l. 1316.
[34] *Electra*, ll. 1493–5.
[35] *Electra*, ll. 1228–9.
[36] *Electra*, l. 516.
[37] *Electra*, ll. 817–19.

not either made or unmade by reference to Agamemnon or to Orestes.

In this play hypothetical narratives take up much of the drama's time, transposing characters into might-have-been times and spaces which cannot be woven into the actual fabric of the everyday world. In the desolate speech in which she laments the death of Orestes,[38] holding the urn which she thinks contains his ashes, Electra wishes that she had died before rescuing her brother and sending him away, because if that had happened he would at least have died at home in Argos and shared his father's tomb. A *heimlich* death. As it is, his death has destroyed her: *τέθνηκ' ἐγὼ σοί*.[39] The phrasing is unusual:[40] literally, 'I-have-died, I, to you'. Greek verbs need no pronouns, so the extra 'I' is emphatic in its juxtaposition with the other pronoun, the sister with the brother. The dative (*σοί*: 'to or for you') is normally used in Greek to identify the indirect object, to indicate an instrument or cause ('he died of a disease'), or to express a relationship of possession, likeness, or unlikeness. So there are various ways of paraphrasing *τέθνηκ' ἐγὼ σοί*: 'I am dead in relation to you', 'I am dead through you', 'I am dead because of you, i.e. because of your death'.[41] The relationship between the 'dead' Electra and the dead brother cannot quite be established: we hear the psychological scandal through the strained grammar. She then implores the dead Orestes to take her with him to the underworld: 'receive me into this mansion of yours, receive me who am nothing into nothingness, so that in future I may live with you below'.[42] The word which is here translated 'mansion' is *στέγος*, which means both house and burial urn: she is exchanging the house of Atreus for a dwelling in Hades, which is a version of the urn of Orestes. This is the only place where she can join him. When she says 'nothing into nothingness', the Greek is *τὴν μηδὲν ἐς τὸ μηδέν*: literally, 'the nothing [in]to the

[38] *Electra*, ll. 1126–70. [39] *Electra*, l. 1152.

[40] Indeed, it has been emended by editors, as Jebb records in his collation, p. 157.

[41] Lloyd-Jones in the Loeb edition translates this as 'you have killed me', which is too loose.

[42] *Electra*, ll. 1165–7.

nothing', associating herself with what she had said of Orestes, that he is now nothing, *νῦν μὲν γὰρ οὐδεν*,[43] and emptying herself further with a poignant movement from the feminine *τὴν μηδὲν* into the neuter *τὸ μηδέν*, giving up her gender as she loses all trace of identity. It is also an echo of her earlier lament that her father was now 'earth and nothing', *γᾶ τε καὶ οὐδὲν*,[44] so that all three Atreidae are now turned into nothing.

Throughout the play the characters struggle to establish relations with the dead. Clytemnestra has instituted a monthly festival to celebrate the death of Agamemnon, but despite this gesture of triumphalism she is afraid: she had apparently cut off the extremities of her husband as a way of preventing him from walking as a ghost,[45] and smeared his head with his own blood in an attempt to make him responsible for his own death. After Agamemnon appears in her dream, she sends Chrysothemis to place offerings on his tomb, only for Electra to intercept her and replace these tokens with her own. Such ritual gestures cannot rid Clytemnestra of her guilt. Electra laments that she has been unable to care ritually for the dead body of Orestes. The play is full of deformed, perverted, or misplaced rituals, notably Electra's misplaced lament for the not-dead Orestes. Her continued mourning links her not only to the actual death of Agamemnon but also to the gods of the underworld: Clytemnestra's irate words to Electra—'may the gods below never release you from your lamentations!'[46]—recognize that she is unusually bound to the gods below, and while Clytemnestra regards this as a curse, for Electra it is simply a continuation of her state. Electra wishes to speak on behalf of the dead man.[47] She honours the dead, but wonders whether they can feel any pleasure.[48] Are they in full possession of their faculties, or mere shadows, both physically and mentally?[49] What reaches the dead from the world of the living? Can a voice travel below the earth and tell Agamemnon of his dishonour?[50] Electra

43 *Electra*, l. 1129.
44 *Electra*, l. 245.
45 *Electra*, l. 444.
46 *Electra*, ll. 291–2.
47 *Electra*, ll. 554–5.
48 *Electra*, ll. 355–6.
49 *Electra*, ll. 833–41.
50 *Electra*, l. 1066.

laments that it was not Ares the god of war who made Agamemnon his guest (ἐξένισεν) in a barbarian land.[51] Having spoken about lamenting at the doors of her father's house, she turns to invoke the house of Hades and its occupants.[52] The one house stands adjacent to the other. She prays that Agamemnon will come from the underworld to avenge his murder, while the Chorus says that Agamemnon will not forget, and neither will the axe which killed him; and the brazen-clawed Erinys will come too.[53] The victim and the murder weapon are both endued with memory.

In their different ways, Clytemnestra's and Electra's rituals are awkward and unavailing attempts to pacify the dead, the former trying to free the present from the past, the latter trying to make the past a shaping force in the present. When Orestes arrives he carefully makes offerings at his father's tomb, and greets the household gods before he crosses the threshold to avenge his father's death. As Clytemnestra is killed—in the very act of adorning the supposed urn of Orestes for burial—we are told by the Chorus that the dead live again as the blood flows. It seems as if the dead themselves are performing the killing. 'Look, they are here', exclaims the Chorus, referring apparently to the dead, at which point Orestes and Pylades enter from the house, having carried out the murder of Clytemnestra.[54] There is a need to repeat the past, to perform it repeatedly in a ritual way, with the living taking on the roles of the dead. Reversal is important, as the second performance reverses the significance of the first. Re-enactment is the means by which Orestes gains control.

But despite his success, this remains Electra's tragedy. As in *Oedipus at Colonus*, the Aristotelian reversal from high estate to low has already happened, and the reversal which does take place on stage is from misery into some transformation of that condition. But this play is tragic because of its sustained imaginative attention to Electra's suffering, especially to the way in which the history of

[51] *Electra*, ll. 95–6.
[52] *Electra*, ll. 110.
[53] *Electra*, ll. 482–91.
[54] *Electra*, ll. 1416–23.

her family forces her into a realm of time and space which is hers alone, however much she may appear to interact with the other characters. It achieves this partly through her own speeches expressing her condition, but more especially through two painful scenes in which Electra is displaced further into her grief and ensconced more deeply within her own parenthetical space of perpetual and reiterated mourning: the old man's false account of the chariot race in which Orestes was supposedly killed; and the arrival of the urn, carried by Orestes' servants, which is said to contain his ashes. Each of these episodes takes us into the territory of the *unheimlich*, where the protagonists do not know the strange from the familiar, or rather, accept as familiar that which is strange, accept as true that which is false, as absent that which is present. At the threshold of the living and the dead, the dead and the living change places. The old slave's narrative of Orestes' death works on Electra's emotions and on ours because it is long enough to create its own drama, to fashion its own temporal and spatial world into which we too are led. We witness the pain of the long detour through the false and the estranged in order to reconnect man with time and with place, and in order to reconfigure the home. This is the estranged territory of tragedy, and here in *Electra* we have a tragedy within a tragedy. The story of the urn and the story of the chariot race recapitulate Electra's suffering, stage again for us, in her response to these two fictions, her pain at the death of Agamemnon, and her pain at living in her own mental world. False forms of the past recapitulate and complete Electra's embedding in the past only to prepare the way for her release. The play concludes with the Chorus saying, 'Seed of Atreus, after many sufferings you have at last emerged in freedom, made complete by this day's enterprise!'[55] The ending, though brief, is clear: unlike the ending of the *Choephori*, where the Furies are already beginning to torment Orestes, this ending gives no hint of trouble to come, and the play ends on the emphatic word

[55] *Electra*, ll. 1508–10.

'completed': τελεωθέν.[56] But the damaged Electra does not herself give voice to this new freedom: alone on stage with the Chorus, she remains enclosed in silence.[57]

[56] As Jebb notes. Ritter (reported by Jebb, p. 203) deleted the final lines as he believed this ending to be spurious.

[57] For the importance of silence in Greek tragedy see Silvia Montiglio, *Silence in the Land of Logos* (Princeton, 2000), who discusses Electra on pp. 207–9.

4

SOPHOCLES

Oedipus the King
& Oedipus at Colonus

Who is Oedipus? Where does he belong? In *Oedipus the King* the *heimlich* and the *unheimlich* undo each other before his own eyes. The play opens with Oedipus as king of Thebes, thinking that his home—that is, his place of origin—is Corinth, and his parents King Polybus and Queen Merope. He has made Thebes his adopted, second, home by freeing it from persecution by the Sphinx, using his reason to defeat a monster and to solve a riddle, showing that the strange creature which goes on four legs, on two legs, and on three, is no monster other than man himself. Thebes is now assailed again, by a plague which can only be removed if the killer of his predecessor King Laius is discovered and expelled. Step by step it is revealed to Oedipus that he himself is the one indicated by the oracle, and hence the source of the city's pollution; that his origin is not in Corinth but here in Thebes—indeed in the very household over which he now presides, for Laius was his own father, and his wife Jocasta his own mother. The words 'father', 'mother', 'son', which establish our

In this chapter the Greek text and English translations are taken from *Sophocles*, edited and translated by Hugh Lloyd-Jones, Loeb Classical Library, 2 vols.(Cambridge, Mass., 1994), unless otherwise stated. I have also drawn on *Sophocles: The Plays and Fragments*, edited by Sir Richard Jebb, *Part I: The Oedipus Tyrannus*, third edition (Cambridge, 1914), *Part II: The Oedipus Coloneus*, third edition (Cambridge, 1928); *Oedipus Rex*, edited by R. D. Dawe (Cambridge, 1982); and Jean Bollack, *L'Oedipe roi de Sophocle: Le texte et ses interprétations*, 4 vols. (Lille, 1990).

elementary connections to and separations within the world, become unspeakable as they become interchangeable definitions: both husband and son, both father and brother. Each individual has too many names.

In ways which are too well known to require analysis here,[1] Sophocles presents us with reversals for which the word 'irony' seems inadequate. Aristotle observed that the most satisfying tragic plot—exemplified, in fact, by *Oedipus the King*—not only included both recognition (ἀναγνώρισις) and reversal (περιπέτεια) but made them coincide.[2] Recognitions and reversals abound: the king becomes an exile, the hunter turns out to be his own quarry, the stranger from Corinth is revealed to be the native-born son; the blind prophet Tiresias sees the true state of affairs, while the sighted and insightful Oedipus is metaphorically blind, and when the truth is revealed to him he literally blinds himself to avoid the continual pain of seeing. Tragic irony, we might call this, but the word falls short. For the Roman rhetoricians such as Cicero and Quintilian, *ironia*[3] was an artifice, a forensic or philosophical tactic in which one said the opposite of what one meant, or feigned an ignorance in order to promote a line of argument. *Ironia* is a form of mastery. But as we trace the word back to its Greek roots, it takes on a darker hue: εἰρωνεία is dissimulation, dissembling, often with pejorative connotations; and an εἴρων is one who says less than he thinks. There are two words which stand as opposites to εἴρων: the opposite to the ironist who says what he does not mean is the ἀληθευτικός who tells the truth, while the opposite to the ironist who tells less than he knows or thinks is the ἀλαζὼν, the braggart who says more than he does. Fittingly, not ironically, the etymological origin of εἰρωνεία is unknown, with scholars attempting to derive it from verbs meaning

[1] Illuminating analyses of the play include Jean-Pierre Vernant, 'Ambiguïté et renversement: Sur la structure énigmatique d' «Œdipe-Roi»', in Jean-Pierre Vernant and Pierre Vidal-Naquet, *Mythe et tragédie en Grèce ancienne*, 2 vols. (Paris, 1972–86; reprinted 2001), i 99–131; Bernard Knox, *Oedipus at Thebes: Sophocles' Tragic Hero and His Time* (New Haven, 1957; revised edition 1998).

[2] Aristotle, *Poetics*, 1452a30. [3] *OLD, s.v.*

'to say' or 'to question'.[4] Irony is an untraceable swerve away from speech and questioning. It is an irony that Oedipus himself is no ironist who says less than he believes (he cannot, in fact, restrain himself from telling Creon and Tiresias what he thinks of them), but he actually is, all unknowingly, more than he says. Tiresias initially says less than he knows, reluctant to cause pain, and so, in the end, does Jocasta, unable to share the truth with Oedipus face to face. The oracle, too, says much less than the full truth. The play moves around the danger of speech, feeling how far speech is from being fully truthful. Irony here is not a mark of rhetorical mastery, but a fearful uncovering of Oedipus' own lack of mastery, the turning of the riddle-solver into his own paradox. But to make Oedipus himself an irony, to structure the play around ironic reversals, is perhaps a protective gesture which would attempt to save human definitions and distinctions—to keep faith in the value of fundamental concepts: blindness and sight, prophetic perception and rational skill; and to keep faith with the necessary work of metaphor. But by metaphor we are at once comprehended and displaced.[5]

Who is Oedipus? He is regarded by all as singular, standing above the crowd; he is addressed by the priest as 'the first of men' and 'mightiest'; he is the man who answered the riddle of the Sphinx because of extra strength given to him by a god.[6] Oedipus regards himself as specially gifted and privileged when he accuses Creon of envying not only his 'riches and kingship' but his 'skill surpassing skill', *τέχνη τέχνης | ὑπερφέρουσα*.[7] The word *τέχνη* is at root the idea of building or making,[8] but a strange form of deconstruction takes place in the unitary figure of Oedipus, the skilful maker: he is multiplied, and he is fragmented. Multiplied: he pursues the killer of Laius as if this were a separate person from himself; and the killer is even

[4] Chantraine, *s.v.*

[5] 'nous sommes . . . compris et déplacés par métaphore' (Jacques Derrida, 'Le retrait de la métaphore' in his *Psyché: Inventions de l'autre*, second edition (Paris, 1998), p. 63).

[6] Sophocles, *Oedipus the King*, ll. 33–40.

[7] *Oedipus the King*, ll. 380–1.

[8] Chantraine, *s.v.*

imagined plurally as a group of robbers, which allows him to dissociate himself, albeit temporarily, from being implicated in this narrative, because 'one is not the same as many'.[9] (But it is, in the case of Oedipus.) He is given a double when the Chorus maps out a narrative which imagines the killer of Laius fleeing through wild places,[10] but here a reference to the wounded foot of the limping fugitive fleetingly connects him to Oedipus, the 'swollen-foot'. Oedipus is multiplied because he has too many birthplaces—Thebes and Corinth, but also Mount Cithaeron, which the Chorus prematurely praises as the 'nurse and mother' of Oedipus[11]—and too many parents: Laius and Jocasta, then Mount Cithaeron itself and the two shepherds, then Polybus and Merope. Too many people stand in for his original parents. Jubilant, temporarily, Oedipus himself says: 'I, who hold myself son of Fortune that gives good, will not be dishonoured. She is the mother from whom I spring; and the months, my kinsmen, have marked me sometimes lowly, sometimes great.'[12] He claims to derive from, and to belong to, a realm separated from the world of ordinary human kinship, in which he is the child of Fortune (παῖδα τῆς Τύχης) and kinsman to the months (οἱ δὲ συγγενεῖς | μῆνές). But Fortune does not always give the good to its children. Earlier, after Oedipus has boasted of his skill (τέχνη) in interpreting riddles, Tiresias had said that 'it is that very happening [τύχη] that has been your ruin': αὕτη γε μέντοι σ' ἡ τύχη διώλεσεν.[13] One can understand τύχη in several ways: as an agent or cause beyond human control, as a person's fortune or fate, as the action of a god, as the action of a human, as the result of such an action.[14] What is it, then, which has been the ruin of Oedipus: some cause beyond him, or his own action? The explanation lies just out of reach in the complex semantic field of τύχη. The assonance of τέχνη (*technē*) and τύχη

[9] *Oedipus the King*, l. 845. [10] *Oedipus the King*, ll. 463–82.

[11] *Oedipus the King*, ll. 1090–1.

[12] *Oedipus the King*, ll. 1080–3; Jebb's translation, as the Loeb misleadingly calls Oedipus 'child of the event that brought good fortune': there is no Greek word for 'event' here, and to make him the child of an event rather than of Fortune is misleading.

[13] *Oedipus the King*, l. 442. [14] *LSJ*, *s.v.*

(*tuchē*) draws the two terms together, and disturbs them, the one speaking of man's mastery over his environment, the other of man's helplessness in the face of powers which are set over him. Oedipus is also given birth, as Tiresias says, by the tragic moment, the tragic present which we witness in the play: 'This day shall give you birth and shall destroy you' (ἥδ' ἡμέρα φύσει σε καὶ διαφθερεῖ).[15] This day is yet one more of Oedipus' metaphorical parents, but it will give him birth definitively, as it will reveal his true names, the whole network of intolerable names. And for Oedipus himself to have become a parent will be shown to be an appalling excess.

Multiplied, but also fragmented: the will of Oedipus becomes a concept which is at once necessary and untenable, as Sophocles invites us to see his actions as being in some way the work of the gods.[16] But in what way? It is this double and irresolvable representation of the will, in which the action both is and is not the work of the protagonist, that tragedy offers, opening out through image, through paradox, and through the juxtaposition of incompatible readings the necessary incompleteness of our understanding. When Oedipus has learned that he is the murderer of Laius—but before the revelation of his parentage—he exclaims:

> ἆρ' οὐκ ἀπ' ὠμοῦ ταῦτα δαίμονός τις ἂν
> κρίνων ἐπ' ἀνδρὶ τῷδ' ἂν ὀρθοίη λόγον;[17]
>
> Would one not be right who judged that this came upon me by the action of a cruel deity?

[15] *Oedipus the King*, l. 438; my translation. Jebb's 'this day shall show thy birth' weakens the bold idea that the day will metaphorically give birth to Oedipus, not simply reveal the facts about his birth. Lloyd-Jones's 'this day shall be your parent and your destroyer' unnecessarily changes the verbs into nouns.

[16] For discussions of the Greek conceptual equivalents to what we might now call 'the will', and Greek ways of understanding the relations between human action and divine intervention, see E. R. Dodds, *The Greeks and the Irrational* (Berkeley, 1951); Jean-Pierre Vernant, 'Ebauches de la volonté dans la tragédie grecque', in Vernant and Vidal-Naquet, i 41–74; Christopher Gill, *Personality in Greek Epic, Tragedy, and Philosophy: The Self in Dialogue* (Oxford, 1996); and, with specific reference to Oedipus and the question of his freedom or fate, Knox, esp. ch. 1; and R. P. Winnington-Ingram, *Sophocles: An Interpretation* (Cambridge, 1980), ch. 7, 'Fate in Sophocles'.

[17] *Oedipus the King*, ll. 828–9.

Even in this moment of agony the protest is cautiously worded as a rhetorical question, with the responsibility for accusing some (unnamed) god being placed first on the man who is imagined as saying these things, and then on those who agree that such a saying would be right; so Oedipus distances himself from this attribution of blame even as he utters it, anxious not to offend further by inopportune speech. The word translated 'deity' here is δαίμονός, and δαίμων has a range of meanings which mark out an area of uncertainty as Oedipus confronts the limits of his own will: it can mean an individual god or goddess, and is sometimes used to avoid naming a god in circumstances where such speech would be unpropitious; it can mean the good or evil genius of a person or family; or divine power; or, specifically, the power controlling an individual's destiny, and hence one's lot or fortune.[18] So the field of meaning stretches from an autonomous supernatural power to the lot of the individual. Etymologically the word derives from the verb δαίομαι which means 'to assign, to allocate'—in this sense, to allocate destinies.[19] Plato toyed with the idea that δαίμονες were so called because they were δαήμονες, wise,[20] but the usage in tragedy is by no means so comforting. The adjective attached to δαίμων at this point in the play is ὠμός, 'savage': it is a word used to designate that which is outside of human culture,[21] so this superhuman power is implicitly sub-human in its conduct.

So Oedipus wonders whether what he has discovered himself to have done may have been the action of some divine power. But the Loeb translation 'by the action of a cruel deity' interpolates the word

[18] For δαίμων see *LSJ*, *s.v.*; Dodds, pp. 39–43; Felix Budelmann, *The Language of Sophocles: Communality, Communication and Involvement* (Cambridge, 2000), pp. 143–54; and cp. the discussion of *Agamemnon*, pp. 53–5 above. Walter Burkert says that '*Daimon* is occult power, a force that drives man forward where no agent can be named' (*Greek Religion: Archaic and Classical*, translated by John Raffan (Oxford, 1985), p. 180).

[19] *LSJ*, Chantraine, *s.v.*

[20] Plato, *Cratylus*, 397e–398c. Socrates would refer to his δαίμων, which was the warning voice he would hear whenever he was on the point of making a mistake (Plato, *Apology*, 31d, 40, 41d).

[21] See the discussion of the word in the context of *Antigone*, p. 96 below.

'action', for there is no such idea in the Greek, which speaks of 'these things from a savage god': *ἀπ' ὠμοῦ ταῦτα δαίμονός*. So the text leaves suspended the question of exactly how this unnamed divine power brought about Oedipus' killing of Laius.[22] Was it by physical intervention, or by taking over the will of Oedipus, or by verbal suggestion? Later, some unnamed god (*δαίμων* again[23]) is said to have shown him the way to the dead Jocasta, though the messenger says that the horrors which he will narrate were 'willed and not unwilled' (*ἑκόντα κοὐκ ἄκοντα*[24]), so attributing the actions to the will of Oedipus himself. As in the case of Aeschylus' Agamemnon, we find here the characteristic Greek habit of imagining that exceptional actions are produced by the individual's will being taken over, as if from outside, and this taking over can be construed as a passion or a god, can be conceptualized as a movement within the human being or as a superhuman force outside him; or perhaps the former is explained as being caused by the latter: passions come upon a man from outside him. After the Chorus has learnt that Oedipus has blinded himself, it exclaims: *τίς σ', ὦ πλῆμον, | προσέβη μανία;* 'What madness has come upon you, unhappy one?', but immediately adds, *τίς ὁ πηδήσας | μείζονα δαίμων τῶν μηκίστων | πρὸς σῇ δυσδαίμονι μοίρᾳ*, 'Who is the god that with a leap longer than the longest has sprung upon your miserable fate?'[25] Is Oedipus overcome by madness (*μανία*) or a god (*δαίμων*)? Are the two compatible or incompatible models for the same event? What is the relation between the god and the fate: is Oedipus' fate the result of the god's actions, or did the fate pre-exist Oedipus and find expression through the god? The two are linked by Sophocles' description of Oedipus' fate as *δυσδαίμονι*, which might be translated literally

[22] And it is not clear what 'these things' (*ταῦτα*), and therefore the scope of divine intervention, refers to: the killing of Laius, the revelation that Oedipus is the killer, or the whole scenario of Oedipus' life which is now unfolding.

[23] *Oedipus the King*, l. 1258.

[24] *Oedipus the King*, l. 1230.

[25] *Oedipus the King*, ll. 1299–1302. Jebb has a useful note on this image: 'The idea of a malignant god leaping *from above* on his victim is frequent in Greek tragedy', but here we should 'conceive the *δυσδαίμων μοῖρα*, the ill-fated life, as an attacked region, *far into* which the malign god springs' (p. 170).

as 'hard-fated',[26] and clearly suggests a connection with δαίμων.[27] But exactly what connection remains unclear. Oedipus cries out, ποῖ γᾶς φέρομαι τλάμων; 'To which place am I being carried in my sorrow?',[28] as if he is being carried along into an unknown region by forces beyond his control. He hears his voice carried in the air apart from him,[29] for now as a blind man he seems to be experiencing his voice as if it were something separate from his ruined body. Fragmented, his voice seems distinct from him, his body displaced into barely conceivable territory.

The Chorus asks Oedipus:

> ὦ δεινὰ δράσας, πῶς ἔτλης τοιαῦτα σάς
> ὄψεις μαρᾶναι; τίς σ᾽ ἐπῆρε δαιμόνων;[30]

> Doer of dreadful deeds, how did you bring yourself so to quench your sight? Which of the gods [δαίμονων] set you on?

And he replies, perhaps gesturing towards the statue of Apollo which guards the threshold of the house,[31] as it did in the *Agamemnon*:

> Ἀπόλλων τάδ᾽ ἦν, Ἀπόλλων, φίλοι,
> ὁ κακὰ κακὰ τελῶν ἐμὰ τάδ᾽ ἐμὰ πάθεα.
> ἔπαισε δ᾽ αὐτόχειρ νιν οὔ-
> τις, ἀλλ᾽ ἐγὼ τλάμων.[32]

> It was Apollo, Apollo, my friends, who accomplished these cruel, cruel sufferings of mine! And no other hand struck my eyes, but my own miserable hand!

The Chorus asks both, 'How did *you* do it', and 'Which *god* made you do it?' The word translated 'dreadful' here is δεινὰ, and δεινός has a semantic field which it is important to map. It means 'fearful, terrible' but also 'strange, wonderful', and 'strong, powerful', and 'clever, skilful'.[33] It might even be translated 'uncanny'.[34] The word, which

[26] It is translated in the Loeb edition as 'miserable', which loses the connection with δαίμων.

[27] See Dawe, p. 230; Bollack, iv 897.

[28] *Oedipus the King*, l. 1309; my translation, as the Loeb version fails to translate γᾶς.

[29] *Oedipus the King*, l. 1310.

[30] *Oedipus the King*, ll. 1327–8.

[31] As Dawe suggests, p. 231.

[32] *Oedipus the King*, ll. 1329–33.

[33] *LSJ*, Chantraine, *s.v.*

[34] See Heidegger on *Antigone*, p. 105 below.

etymologically is grounded in the sense of 'fear',[35] unites reactions of horror with reactions of admiration and wonder, as if any action of a human being which was exceptional and aroused admiration might also, from another viewpoint, be dangerous in attracting the envy of the gods: it might be a form of *hubris*. To be clever, to have τέχνη τέχνης ὑπερφέρουσα, is wonderful but also fearful. And as for the actions of the gods, the word for 'god' which is used here is once again the wide-ranging δαίμων. The verb in 'which of the gods set you on' is ἐπῆρε ('rouse, induce, persuade'), of which the fundamental meaning is, ironically, 'lift, raise'. But the exact form of such rousing, inducing, or persuading is beyond both our conceptual and our dramatic reach, for the moment of decision which led to Oedipus' self-blinding is displaced into the inaccessible offstage space.

Oedipus replies to the Chorus's question with a similar recognition that it was both he and another: 'It was Apollo, Apollo, my friends, who accomplished these cruel, cruel sufferings of mine! And no other hand struck my eyes, but my own miserable hand!' How far does the intervention of the god extend? Scholars have debated whether the role assigned to Apollo here applies to the whole sorry story of Oedipus, or more specifically to his self-blinding.[36] There is also a tension—unexplained because this is tragic poetry, and an utterance of extreme anguish—between the two verbs τελῶν ('accomplish', 'complete'), used of Apollo, and ἔπαισε ('strike'), used of Oedipus, particularly since the former is a present participle ('Apollo is accomplishing') and the latter an aorist (indicating a completed action on the part of Oedipus).[37] How does the single past act of Oedipus relate to the apparently continued (and perhaps still continuing) accomplishing of Apollo's purpose? Time and tense evade rational, and therefore moral, analysis. There is also an emphatic personal pronoun here—ἐγώ, 'I'—which is all the more prominent because Greek grammar does not require personal pronouns with verbs. But just

[35] Chantraine, *s.v.* δείδω.

[36] Bollack, iv 916–18. Budelmann argues that τάδ' must refer specifically to Oedipus' self-mutilation (p. 172).

[37] For disputed interpretations of τελῶν see Bollack, iv 917.

what constitutes the prominent 'I' who is the agent in this case? In such extreme states, the individual both is and is not himself. Some role may be attributed to the gods, but exactly what this role is, tragedy leaves suspended. Narration cannot avoid assigning moral responsibility, even implicitly through the shaping of the narrative, but because Sophocles has suppressed much of the story of Oedipus and his family, or transferred it into a fragmentarily recalled past, the moral logic of the story remains occluded. In certain versions of the myth which were known to Sophocles and his audience, Laius is punished for his rape of a boy called Chrysippus: the boy's father curses him, wishing either that Laius may have no son of his own, or that if he does have a son, that child will kill him.[38] But with this prelude to Oedipus' story removed from the play, the moral question of why Oedipus is fated to do what he does remains inscrutable.

If recognition and reversal unfold the horror of *Oedipus the King*, in *Oedipus at Colonus* they are instead a means through which Oedipus is drawn with grace towards his ending. The meaning of the *heimlich* is reconfigured again, and the symbolic status of Oedipus himself undergoes a reversal in the course of the play, as he is brought into a new relation with the gods. At the end of his life, Oedipus the wanderer (πλανήτην Οἰδίπουν[39]) comes to a place which he does not recognize. It is Colonus, on the outskirts of Athens.[40] Here he seeks rest, either on ground which is not holy (βεβήλοις, 'permitted to be trodden', from βηλός, a threshold[41]) or on ground which is ἄλσεσιν θεῶν, a grove sacred to the gods.[42] Normally this is an important

[38] Lowell Edmunds, *Oedipus: The Ancient Legend and its Later Analogues* (Baltimore, 1985), pp. 7–8.

[39] Sophocles, *Oedipus at Colonus*, l. 3.

[40] For the importance of place in *Oedipus at Colonus* see Winnington-Ingram, pp. 339–40, and Lowell Edmunds, *Theatrical Space and Historical Place in Sophocles' 'Oedipus at Colonus'* (Lanham, Md., 1996).

[41] Greek also has a cognate verb βεβηλόω, to profane or pollute.

[42] *Oedipus at Colonus*, l. 10. Jebb (p. 12) notes that although the grove of the Eumenides at Colonus was ἀστιβὲς (l. 126), not to be entered, many sacred groves were open to visitors.

antithesis, marking out two distinct kinds of territory, defining the limits of what is permissible to man, but here it is a boundary which Oedipus will cross. He has come to the threshold which separates the human world from that of the gods, for at Colonus there is a brazen threshold (ὀδός[43]) which marks the entrance into the underworld.

His daughter Antigone, who is accompanying him, realizes that the place is sacred, for the bay trees, olives, and vines mark it out as a sanctuary—as does the song of the nightingales, an aural rather than a visual sign which she selects as one which her blind father can appreciate.[44] Oedipus wonders whether this place is ἐξοικήσιμος,[45] which might mean either 'inhabited' or 'habitable': in part he is asking whether anyone lives here who might give them information and help, but because its root is in οἶκος ('house') the word implies that Oedipus is seeking a final dwelling which will replace the abandoned homes of Corinth and Thebes. The man who arrives from Colonus orders him to move, as the ground which he occupies cannot be trodden without pollution; it is, he says, not to be touched and not to be inhabited (ἄθικτος οὐδ' οἰκητός[46]). The gods to whom this space is sacred are called by different titles in different places, but here, says the man, they are known as the 'all-seeing Eumenides'. Oedipus may be blind, but these goddesses are 'all-seeing' (πάνθ' ὁρώσας[47]); and when he says that he will confer a blessing on King Theseus, and the local man asks sceptically what good a blind man can do, Oedipus replies that all the words he utters will have sight (πάνθ' ὁρῶντα[48]). The virtual repetition of the phrase, applied first to the Eumenides and then to Oedipus, draws the two together, giving Oedipus a more-than-human sight, and placing him rightly on their ground. This is not *hubris*: Oedipus' words will be all-seeing because he is now doing the gods' bidding, and it is significant that insight is ascribed to the words themselves, not to the speaker.[49] Once again there is a disjunction affecting Oedipus, separating him within

[43] *Oedipus at Colonus*, l. 57.
[44] As Jebb observes.
[45] *Oedipus at Colonus*, l. 27.
[46] *Oedipus at Colonus*, l. 39.
[47] *Oedipus at Colonus*, l. 42.
[48] *Oedipus at Colonus*, l. 74.
[49] As Jebb notes, p. 74.

himself as well as from the world around him, but now it is a disjunction which betokens grace rather than horror. This uncanny characteristic to his words (later he is said to 'see in sound'[50]) is one amongst several such signs which now cluster around the figure of Oedipus as he is moved from being the polluting outcast to being the honoured guest who brings blessing.

The play attends carefully to what it means for this stranger to be a guest. He is an exile, *ἀπόπολις*[51] (literally 'one who is at a distance from the city'), and 'cityless' (*ἄπολιν*[52]), and the play has many occurrences of *οἶκος*, *πόλις* and their derivatives. He has moved out of the inhabited spaces of house and city into the sacred space of the Eumenides, which is uninhabitable for ordinary mortals but the right place now for Oedipus, the strange-bodied, the shadow, the not-quite-ghost. Tentatively, as if the gift may not be offered this time, he speaks of his elementary need to receive what he expects to be 'scanty gifts'[53] from the local people, and he knows that as *ξένοι*, strangers, he and his daughter Antigone need to learn of the local inhabitants how to proceed. He addresses the man who arrives from Colonus as 'stranger' (*ὦ ξεῖν*'[54]), and the man replies with the same formula:[55] it is a commonplace Greek greeting. But the word becomes weighted.[56] In *Oedipus the King* it had been one of the words which marked the connection of Oedipus not only with Thebes but with the killing of Laius: Oedipus says that he is a stranger (*ξένος*) to the story and a stranger (*ξένος*) to the deed,[57] though he has now become a citizen; Tiresias says that although the killer of Laius was thought to be a stranger (*ξένος*), he will be shown to be a native Theban but will be forced to go away into a strange land (*ξένην*);[58] if the stranger

[50] At l. 138 Oedipus says *φωνῇ ὁρῶ*, which Lloyd-Jones translates as 'I see with my voice', but there is no 'my' in the Greek, and it seems preferable to translate it as 'I see in sound', as he is referring to his being able to hear the approaching citizens.

[51] *Oedipus at Colonus*, l. 207.

[52] *Oedipus at Colonus*, l. 1357.

[53] *Oedipus at Colonus*, l. 4.

[54] *Oedipus at Colonus*, ll. 33, 49.

[55] *Oedipus at Colonus*, ll. 62, 75.

[56] See Fridericus Ellendt, *Lexicon Sophocleum* (Berlin, 1872), *s.v.*; Edmunds, *Theatrical Space*, pp. 130–4.

[57] *Oedipus the King*, ll. 219–20.

[58] *Oedipus the King*, ll. 452, 455.

(ξένῳ[59]) whom Oedipus killed turns out to have been Laius (and therefore no stranger but his own father), then no one, neither citizen nor stranger (ξένων[60]), may give him shelter.

In *Oedipus at Colonus* Oedipus' status as ξένος is gradually translated from 'stranger' to 'guest'. Oedipus asks the man not to refuse him the knowledge which he asks for, and 'refuse' here is ἀτιμάσῃς from the root τιμή, honour: 'do not dishonour me', he says in effect, 'give me the honour which is due to a ξένος.'[61] For a ξένος is more than a stranger, he is one who is entitled to the graces of hospitality: in being received kindly, the stranger becomes a guest. 'Stranger, treat me as a guest.' In Greek ξένος is used for both aspects of the relationship between host and guest,[62] so in this dialogue 'stranger' is potentially 'guest', and potentially 'host'. It is a relationship with reciprocal duties, and one which envisages that at some point in the future the roles of the participants in the ξένος-bond may be reversed. The relationship is important because it establishes a familiarity in the territory of the strange, so that the traveller need not feel threatened or lost in a foreign land, but can rely upon strangers to show him the hospitality necessary for survival. The ξένος-bond makes the *unheimlich* into the *heimlich*. In the *Iliad* the Greek warrior Glaucus and the Trojan Diomedes meet in battle, but discover that Glaucus' grandfather Bellerophon was once the guest of Diomedes' grandfather Oeneus, so that the two are bound in a friendship which overrides their enmity: as Diomedes says, he is a 'dear guest-friend' to Glaucus, ξεῖνος φίλος.[63] Not for nothing is Zeus called ξένιος, protector of the bond between guest and host. At the end of the play Oedipus the guest becomes the inhabitant, as he leaves his body in the ground of Colonus rather than of Thebes. This movement answers an implicit, Heideggerian question: What is it to dwell rather than to wander? To be an inhabitant rather than a guest? More

[59] *Oedipus the King*, l. 813. [60] *Oedipus the King*, l. 817.

[61] *Oedipus at Colonus*, ll. 49–50.

[62] Émile Benveniste, *Le Vocabulaire des institutions indo-européennes*, 2 vols. (Paris, 1969), i 87–101.

[63] Homer, *Iliad*, vi 224.

particularly, how could this *unheimlich* Oedipus become a dweller rather than a wanderer? Here he wanders into the sacred space, and only later recognizes that this apparently aimless wandering has brought him to the final goal foretold by the god. Addressing the Eumenides, Oedipus says that Apollo had promised him rest or an ending (παῦλαν) in a place where he would find the seat of the Eumenides and ξενόστατιν, a lodging for guests. His dwelling (οἰκήσαντα) here would be an advantage to those who receive him kindly.[64]

When the Chorus arrives, it first asks where the man is who has violated the sanctuary: ποῦ ναίει?[65] Where is he dwelling? The verb is awkward, for ναίω normally means 'I dwell, abide, inhabit', so here it seems as if it ought logically to have a weaker meaning and be a verb, as Jebb puts it, of mere situation not habitation.[66] But the stronger meaning is resonant as an ironic absence: he cannot *dwell* here. This must be someone who is a 'wanderer not a dweller [ἔγχωρος] in the land', says the Chorus, using of Oedipus the same word πλανάτας, wanderer, that Oedipus himself had used.[67] Theseus offers to make Oedipus a dweller in their city, ἔμπολιν.[68] Yet Oedipus is never quite a dweller in this or any city: Creon asks him to return to the city and house of his fathers, ἄστυ καὶ δόμους . . . πατρῴους,[69] but Oedipus knows that Creon would never receive him into Thebes but intends merely to place him near its borders, ὡς πάραυλον οἰκίσῃς ('settle me as one living near').[70] Oedipus would not be a citizen, or even one who dwells in a city, but one who dwells on the borders. But this liminal status which is offered as part-bribe, part-punishment by Creon is rejected by Oedipus, who instead accepts a different form of *limen*, the burial place offered by Theseus on the borders not of Thebes but of Athens—which is also the point where earth and underworld meet.

64 *Oedipus at Colonus*, ll. 84–93.
65 *Oedipus at Colonus*, l. 117.
66 Jebb, p. 31. The verb is poetic: the normal prose equivalent is οἰκέω (Chantraine).
67 *Oedipus at Colonus*, ll. 123–4; cp. l. 3.
68 *Oedipus at Colonus*, l. 637, though this is a modern emendation of the MSS reading ἔμαλιν. Jebb notes (p. 108) that ἔμπολιν does not occur outside this play (though *LSJ* actually has one other example), so it may have struck its first hearers as unusual and emphatic. It is used again of Polynices at l. 1156.
69 *Oedipus at Colonus*, ll. 757–8.
70 *Oedipus at Colonus*, l. 785.

Oedipus himself is certain that this place is his destined end. He prays that the Eumenides will receive a suppliant graciously, and when he is asked what he means, Oedipus replies: ξυμφορᾶς ξύνθημ' ἐμῆς, 'It is the sign of my destiny!'[71] The two words beginning with the ξυν- prefix are striking: ξυν- or συν- means 'with, together', and these two words suggest that Oedipus' life, and the signs which represent it, are coming together: ξυμφορά literally means a 'bringing together', and so 'event, circumstance', while ξύνθημα means 'that which is put together', and so 'an agreed token or sign'. Things are coming together for Oedipus; and the material world around him now bears sure signs of the presence of the gods who are directing him. Oedipus prays to the Eumenides, saying that Apollo had predicted this end for him when he predicted all the evil[72]—which is a part of the prophecy that Sophocles had suppressed from *Oedipus the King*. It was, says Oedipus, a trustworthy omen (πιστὸν πτερὸν) which led him to the sanctuary of the Eumenides. Recuperating the deeply troubled linguistics of *Oedipus the King*, signs are now reliable, even though Oedipus himself is only an image or phantom (εἴδωλον[73]) of the former man.

Oedipus at Colonus also rehearses the question of the guilt of Oedipus, as he tells the Chorus not to drive him away simply for fear of his name, for it cannot, he says, be his person or his actions that they fear, because his 'actions consisted in suffering rather than in doing': ἐπεὶ τά γ' ἔργα με | πεπονθότ' ἴσθι μᾶλλον ἢ δεδρακότα.[74] He was not evil in his nature (φύσιν[75]), but his acts were done under provocation and in ignorance. But the Chorus persists in asking about what happened, and Oedipus begs them, 'For the sake of hospitality [πρὸς ξενίας], do not lay bare the shame I have suffered!'[76] In a

[71] *Oedipus at Colonus*, l. 47.
[72] *Oedipus at Colonus*, ll. 86–95.
[73] *Oedipus at Colonus*, l. 110.
[74] *Oedipus at Colonus*, ll. 263–7.
[75] *Oedipus at Colonus*, l. 270.
[76] *Oedipus at Colonus*, ll. 515–16; my translation, following Jebb; but editors disagree as to whether ἀναιδῶς should be construed as applying to Oedipus (the *shame* which he suffered) or to the Chorus (lay bare *shamelessly, ruthlessly*). Lloyd-Jones translates: 'do not ruthlessly lay bare my sufferings'.

passage which is unfortunately problematic textually, Oedipus exclaims:

> ἤνεγκ᾽ οὖν κακότατ᾽, ὦ ξένοι, ἤνεγκ᾽ ἀέκων μέν, θεὸς ἴστω.
> τούτων δ᾽ αὐθαίρετον οὐδέν.[77]

> I have borne terrible things, strangers, I have borne not by my own will, let the god be witness! And none of these things was my own choice!

The textual problem here besets the word ἀέκων or ἄκων, meaning 'against one's will', which is sometimes emended[78] on metrical grounds to its opposite, ἑκών. Is Oedipus saying that he bore (the verb ἤνεγκ᾽ is part of φέρω, to bear, carry, endure, suffer) these terrible things by his own will (ἑκών), or against his will (ἄκων)? The manuscript reading ἄκων effectively distances his will from the events which he has been instrumental in producing: this seems the stronger idea, and is consistent with his subsequent version of his story.[79] But whether one prefers ἑκών or ἄκων, one should not follow Lloyd-Jones's Loeb translation and render the opening clause as 'I endured evil', for 'evil' suggests a metaphysical power or abstract concept, whereas the Greek κακότατ᾽ is just a superlative adjective in the neuter plural, literally meaning 'very bad things' or 'the worst things'. It is important to avoid the metaphysical fallacy at this point, to avoid importing abstract nouns into a text which already has plenty of abstract nouns which may or may not be construed as metaphysical forces. Then the Chorus, probing the wound, says:

> Χο. ἔπαθες—
> Οι. ἔπαθον ἄλαστ᾽ ἔχειν.
> Χο. ἔρεξας—
> Οι. οὐκ ἔρεξα.[80]

[77] *Oedipus at Colonus*, ll. 521–3; Jebb's text, my translation. The verb translated 'be witness', ἴστω, is the imperative form of εἴδω: 'see, know'.

[78] For example by Lloyd-Jones in the Loeb edition. But Jebb's notes (p. 90) seem persuasive in favour of his reading ἀέκων.

[79] Antigone calls the events ἔργων ἀκόντων, 'unwilled actions' (*Oedipus at Colonus*, ll. 239–40); cp. ll. 964–6, 977.

[80] *Oedipus at Colonus*, ll. 538–9. Jebb's translation 'sinned' for ἔρεξας (simply 'did') is misleading as it imports quite extraneous concepts.

CHO. You suffered—
OED. I suffered woes unforgettable!
CHO. You did—
OED. I never did.

Oedipus firmly rejects the idea that he 'did' anything, and when the Chorus then asks how he can claim this, he says that after solving the riddle of the Sphinx he 'received a gift'.[81] That, receiving rather than doing, is how he remembers it, and how he delineates his share in the story. And his description of the killing of Laius again challenges the moral implications of the word which the Chorus chooses. 'You killed', it says, and he agrees, 'I killed', but then insists that 'according to the law I am clean!' (νόμῳ δὲ καθαρός), clean, or purged, καθαρός, because he acted in self-defence and in ignorance.[82]

Though the text draws back from specifying precisely the responsibility which might be assigned to Oedipus or to Apollo for the acts which Oedipus carried out or which he suffered, the relationship between Oedipus and the gods is transformed as the play draws towards its conclusion. Oedipus prays to the Eumenides, and Ismene is told the precise ritual which she has to perform. As he moves across the threshold towards the other world, he is 'led by the escorting Hermes and by the goddess below'[83] towards his final displacement. And the worlds of gods and mortals are linked when Theseus, having shielded his eyes as if the sight were something which he could not bear to look upon, reverently greets 'the earth and the sky, home of the gods, at the same moment'.[84]

[81] *Oedipus at Colonus*, l. 540.

[82] *Oedipus at Colonus*, ll. 547–8. Oedipus' self-exculpation that he acted in self-defence because 'they whom I slew would have taken my own life' (Jebb's translation) is unfortunately based on a corrupt and much-contested text. Lloyd-Jones's emendation produces this translation: 'I murdered and slaughtered as the victim of the power that sent me mad'. It is essential to note that the important idea that Oedipus was temporarily driven mad depends entirely upon a scholarly emendation, in this case Lloyd-Jones's introduction of ἄτα into the text.

[83] *Oedipus at Colonus*, l. 1548.

[84] *Oedipus at Colonus*, l. 1655. The translation 'at the same moment' rests on Lloyd-Jones's adoption of the emendation of χρόνῳ ('time') for λόγῳ ('word') in the MSS; the original reading would produce the translation 'in the same word' (or, as Jebb has it, 'in one prayer'), which seems preferable.

As the play had recuperated for Oedipus his status as *ξένος*, so too Sophocles returns to and transforms the notion of *δεινός*. Here the two English senses of the word 'fear' help to suggest the range of the Greek word: it inspires both reverence and terror. There are several points at which the word *δεινός*, so prominent in *Oedipus the King*, recurs here to describe the events of Oedipus' past. The Chorus exclaims that the old man before them is *δεινὸς* to see and *δεινὸς* to hear.[85] Oedipus himself says that his birth was *δεινά*.[86] The Eumenides are *δεινῶπες*,[87] 'terrible-eyed', an epithet which might also apply to Oedipus himself. But by the end of the play the response of the bystanders has changed to one of wonder, even though the sight which confronts Theseus at Oedipus' departure is also *δεινοῦ* and makes him cover his eyes.[88] For the significance of Oedipus is reversed, no longer a pollution but a blessing, a reversal which echoes the end of the *Oresteia* where the Erinyes are transformed from being the Furies into being the Kindly Ones. Now the words which the characters use are cognates of *θαῦμα*, a wonder or marvel: the Messenger who narrates Oedipus' death says that it was something to wonder at (*κἀποθαυμάσαι*[89]), and that his passing was 'by a miracle' (*θαυμαστός*[90]), even though he carefully, reverently qualifies this by adding 'if any among mortals', for it might be too much to claim that Oedipus was actually granted a miraculous passing. But finally Theseus confirms that the death of Oedipus is nothing which we should regret:

> *ἐν οἷς γὰρ*
> *χάρις ἡ χθονία νὺξ ἀπόκειται,*
> *πενθεῖν οὐ χρή· νέμεσις γάρ.*[91]

One should not mourn for those for whom the darkness below the earth is a treasure graciously bestowed; the gods would resent it!

[85] *Oedipus at Colonus*, l. 141.
[86] *Oedipus at Colonus*, l. 212.
[87] *Oedipus at Colonus*, l. 84.
[88] *Oedipus at Colonus*, l. 1651.
[89] *Oedipus at Colonus*, l. 1586.
[90] *Oedipus at Colonus*, l. 1665.
[91] *Oedipus at Colonus*, ll. 1751–3.

The darkness[92] below the earth is literally 'laid up in store', ἀπόκειται, implying that the place in which Oedipus now dwells is a treasury of grace provided by the powers of the underworld. But his tomb is not to be seen; it lies beyond our reach.

[92] Unfortunately 'darkness' is another reading which depends on an emendation: Lloyd-Jones (following Martin) prints *νὺξ ἀπόκειται* in place of the MSS reading followed by Jebb, *ξυναπόκειται* ('stored up as a common benefit'). Lloyd-Jones's 'treasure' is his reification of the verb *ἀπόκειται* 'to lay up in store'.

5

SOPHOCLES

Antigone

Where does Antigone stand? In this play there is no *heimlich* world for Antigone, as right from the beginning she is displaced, and the world around her rejects her—or she rejects it. She is placed in the territory of 'l'entre-deux-morts', as Lacan puts it,[1] held in the space between death and death. Her opening line addresses her sister Ismene as κοινὸν αὐτάδελφον, 'of common origin my own sister',[2] and this reminder of the sibling bond, so troubled and so troubling in this family, has the effect of establishing their uniqueness and their separation from others, for 'the origin which connects the sisters also isolates them', as Jebb observed.[3] Zeus, she says, is accomplishing (or perhaps 'completing, bringing to an end': τελεῖ[4]) the evils

In this chapter the Greek text and English translations are taken from *Sophocles*, edited and translated by Hugh Lloyd-Jones, Loeb Classical Library, 2 vols. (Cambridge, Mass., 1994), unless otherwise stated. I have also drawn on *Sophocles: The Plays and Fragments*, edited by Sir Richard Jebb, *Part III: The Antigone*, third edition (Cambridge, 1900), and Sophocles, *Antigone*, edited by Mark Griffith (Cambridge, 1999). A valuable account of this play which is congruent with the present discussion is Th. C. W. Oudemans and A. P. M. H. Lardinois, *Tragic Ambiguity: Anthropology, Philosophy and Sophocles' Antigone* (Leiden, 1987).

[1] *Le Séminaire de Jacques Lacan: Livre VII: L'Éthique de la Psychanalyse: 1959–1960*, edited by Jacques-Alain Miller (Paris, 1986), p. 315.

[2] Sophocles, *Antigone*, l. 1; my translation.

[3] Jebb, p. 8. Griffith notes that Sophocles uses many dual forms, 'describing natural but frustrated pairings' (p. 121).

[4] This is the same verb which Oedipus used of Apollo accomplishing his misfortunes (*Oedipus the King*, l. 1330); see above, p. 81.

which come from Oedipus.[5] A few lines later she speaks of the evils which come from their enemies, and there is an uncomfortable echo between the two phrases: *τῶν ἀπ' Οἰδίπου κακῶν* echoed by *τῶν ἐχθρῶν κακά*.[6] How do we decipher this link? The last line of her speech contrasts friends and enemies in a resolute piece of definition which sets up a dichotomy which will be much disputed: *πρὸς τοὺς φίλους στείχοντα τῶν ἐχθρῶν κακά*, 'the evils from our enemies as they come against our friends'.[7] The distinction between *φίλος*, friend, and *ἐχθρὸς*, enemy, polarizes Antigone's world, and it is an antithesis which effects an unbridgeable schism between her and the others. But it is also an antithesis whose application is challenged in the course of the play, notably by Creon, who assigns the labels 'friend' and 'enemy' in different ways.[8] It would be too simple to idealize Antigone as standing for the individual over against the state, the city, or the ruler; for what is the individual when separated (or, as here, when self-separated) from the city—a beast or a god?[9] The play will trace the contours and the consequences of such a separation, and the territory of the non-human (the territory which might be that of beast or god) receives in this play some strange and sometimes contradictory definitions. Nor is Antigone's appeal to the moral law which requires her to bury her brother simply in conflict with the civic law which requires her not to honour the city's enemy. For who makes such laws; who has the right to define them? Though both kinds of law are defensible principles, they are not simply antagonistic, in part because neither is pure here, for both are inflected by their proponent's self-interest.

The conflict is not between solid, unitary characters, or at least not between solid, unitary causes, as these causes tend to decompose under tragic pressure, to show themselves to be mixed in their motivation,

[5] *Antigone*, ll. 2–3. [6] *Antigone*, ll. 2, 10. [7] *Antigone*, l. 10.

[8] As Griffith notes, p. 123. Mary Whitlock Blundell discusses *philia* in *Antigone* in her *Helping Friends and Harming Enemies: A Study in Sophocles and Greek Ethics* (Cambridge, 1989), pp. 106–30.

[9] Aristotle says that he who cannot live in society must be either a beast or a god (*Politics*, 1253a 27–9).

ideals contaminated by egoism, self-will disguised as principle. This is not precisely a conflict between an individual and the state (or, to set aside the rather anachronistic concept of the state, between an individual and the city). Antigone is not claiming rights or duties as an individual but as the member of a community, in this case her family (most of whom now inhabit the underworld).[10] So it is a case of one form of community, or, we might say, one form of inhabited space, this family as defined by Antigone, set against another community, the city of Thebes, as defined, indeed as appropriated, by Creon. And two kinds of time meet in contention: Antigone's time, the eternity of the dead and the immemorial laws which she claims to know, and Creon's time, the political imperatives of the moment (albeit grounded, ostensibly, in principle and designed to secure the future of the city).

In determining to bury her brother Polynices, Antigone rejects Creon's law and maintains that it was not proclaimed *to her*[11] by Zeus or by Justice who lives with the gods below.[12] In the word which Antigone chooses for 'lives with', *ξύνοικος*, we hear the root *οἶκος*, 'house, dwelling', implying that she is invoking (perhaps even preparing for herself) some alternative space to the one which mortals inhabit, an alternative source of value to the home which is no longer her home. Antigone appeals, then, to the underworld, the world of Hades, which seems for her somehow closer, more compelling, than the world of the city. The space into which Antigone moves is a liminal space on the borders between two worlds: she carries out the burial of her brother on the plain outside the city, and she is punished by being immured alive in a cave; as she herself says, she is 'living neither among mortals nor as a shade among the shades, neither with the living nor with the dead'.[13] The word translated here as 'living' is

[10] Robert Parker says of Athenian burial customs: 'An ideal of collective burial existed, and was often realized in some measure. Funerary sculpture emphasized not the individual but the family, with particular stress on the idea of continuity between the generations' (*Polytheism and Society at Athens* (Oxford, 2005), p. 27).

[11] This important word, *μοι*, 'for me' or 'as far as I am concerned', is omitted from the Loeb translation.

[12] *Antigone*, ll. 450–1.

[13] *Antigone*, ll. 850–2.

μέτοικος. This is a resonant word, for it was the term applied to alien residents in a foreign city, especially in Athens, who did not enjoy rights of citizenship.[14] In Antigone's case it is part of a negative statement: she is not even an alien resident among either the living or the dead. She repeats the word a few lines later,[15] when she says that she goes to live with her parents in the underworld, so even here she will be a sojourner in another's house, still not a citizen. Creon too uses the word when he says that Antigone will be 'deprived of residence with us here above the ground',[16] implying that she has a resident's but not a citizen's rights in Thebes. A variant is used by Tiresias when he accuses Creon of lodging (κατοικίσας[17]) a living person in a tomb. Antigone has no place which is hers to dwell in by right.

Antigone justifies herself by telling Creon that his proclamation did not have the power to override 'the unwritten and unfailing ordinances of the gods' (ἄγραπτα κἀσφαλῆ θεῶν | νόμιμα).[18] But addressing Creon rather than replying to Antigone, the Chorus retorts:

> δηλοῖ τὸ γέννημ' ὠμὸν ἐξ ὠμοῦ πατρὸς
> τῆς παιδός·[19]

> The savage breeding of the daughter, from her savage father, is making itself plain.

The word which the Chorus uses here, translated 'savage', is ὠμὸν. As the Chorus's response to Antigone's invocation of divine rather than human laws, it places her outside the civilized space, but in the world of beasts rather than of gods, in a category in which the only other human being is her father Oedipus. The semantic field of ὠμὸς is worth pondering.[20] Its primary meaning (from the root represented by the

[14] *LSJ*, *s.v.* Lacan, while not discussing μέτοικος, has a suggestive paragraph on the emphatic placing of μέτα in Antigone's speeches in ll. 48, 70 and 73 which draws attention to the troubled idea of 'being with' in her idiolect (p. 308).

[15] *Antigone*, l. 868.

[16] *Antigone*, l. 890.

[17] *Antigone*, l. 1069.

[18] *Antigone*, ll. 454–5. Jebb and Griffith (*ad loc.*) helpfully cite Aristotle on the different kinds of law, written and unwritten, societal and natural.

[19] *Antigone*, ll. 471–2. Griffith's text and translation; Lloyd-Jones emends, and translates loosely.

[20] See *LSJ* and Chantraine, *s.v.*; Oudemans and Lardinois, p. 92.

Sanskrit *āmás*) is 'raw, uncooked'; then metaphorically 'savage, fierce, cruel, inhuman'; 'unripe' of fruits, and hence 'untimely, premature' when applied to human birth or death. The word places Antigone beyond the human community in a space occupied by the eaters of uncooked food, with the additional ominous implication that her death may be premature. She is untimely. But the Chorus's binary opposition between the civilized and the wild is unstable. The civilized city is being defended by Creon through the practice of leaving the body of Polynices unburied. To some extent this accords with Athenian law, which did not permit the burial of traitors within the territory of Attica.[21] Yet the burial of the dead was of profound importance to Greeks, and a prime responsibility of the family; and Creon is the man's uncle. Antigone and Creon argue over whether Polynices is to be thought of as kin or traitor;[22] he is, of course, both. But to leave the body of a man for dogs and birds to devour is to turn that man into carrion, to place him beyond the pale of the human. Eventually, the birds and dogs drop pieces of Polynices onto the city, on its altars and sacrificial fires, polluting it, and providing a graphic image of a civilization contaminated by the savagery with which it polices its civic survival.[23]

Creon's claim to be acting in defence of the city has plausible elements: the traitor and the enemy do not deserve to be honoured; to honour this enemy is to dishonour his brother Eteocles, the defender of the city; moreover, it is actually a duty (epitomized in the Greek ethical formula of helping friends and harming enemies[24]) to do harm to one's enemies; the rights of the individual have to give way to the safety of the city, which is the storm-tossed ship to which those individuals trust for their own survival. He will not, says Creon, make a friend of the enemy of his country.[25] Creon insists upon maintaining the distinction between friends and enemies: 'An enemy is never a friend, even when he is dead'.[26] But he is restricting

[21] Griffith, p. 127. [22] *Antigone*, ll. 502–25.

[23] *Antigone*, ll. 1016–18. On the significance of the birds see Oudemans and Lardinois, pp. 194–5.

[24] See Blundell. [25] *Antigone*, ll. 187–90. [26] *Antigone*, l. 522.

the meaning of φίλος,[27] which is for the Greeks not just 'friend' but also 'kinsman', and at root 'loved one'. Creon wants it to mean something more like 'ally' (for one chooses an ally) while distancing it from the bonds of kinship. For Antigone the φίλος is not chosen but given by birth: *οὔτοι συνέχθειν, ἀλλὰ συμφιλεῖν ἔφυν*: 'I was born not to join in hating, but to join in loving'.[28] The two verbs, *συνέχθειν* and *συμφιλεῖν*, are unique, found nowhere else in classical Greek,[29] so poignantly Antigone has to coin for herself the words with which she expresses the bonds which link her to another: this is her own lexis, not the vocabulary of any community. The repeated *συν-* or *συμ-* prefixes, signifying 'with', remind us that Antigone's case is the assertion not of her individuality but of her particular bonds, of her place within a special kind of community. Creon may seem to stand for community, but in his altercation with his son Haemon he begins to reveal his individual pride and defensiveness, and to assert ownership, rather than stewardship, of the city, while Haemon begins to speak for the citizens; and through their exchange there comes into focus the question of whether this Thebes is truly a city, a *πόλις* in the sense that the Athenians understood it, for as Haemon says, 'A city-state that belongs to one man is not truly a city-state'.[30]

What, then, is beyond the city? The space beyond the city (whose imagined contours act as a way of defining the city itself) is the plain where Polynices lies unburied. Here Antigone comes to perform the required rituals by covering the corpse with dust and pouring libations, bringing the rituals which should be part of man's civilized life, but are now proscribed within the city, out into the wild space beyond its limits. Who or what inhabits this terrain? This is the space where the mysterious storm suddenly erupts from nowhere, a storm which may perhaps be the work of the gods (*θείαν*).[31] Indeed, the timorous

[27] Griffith, *ad loc.*; Oudemans and Lardinois, pp. 163–4.

[28] *Antigone*, l. 523; my translation.

[29] Griffith, *LSJ*, *s.vv.*

[30] *Antigone*, l. 737; Griffith's neat translation (pp. 248–9), which expresses the point more sharply than the Loeb's 'Yes, there is no city that belongs to a single man!'

[31] *Antigone*, l. 421. Griffith (pp. 190–1) gives an account of the competing interpretations of this episode.

Chorus wonders whether the initial ritual burying of Polynices might be the work of some god (θεήλατον).[32] Then there is the cave, a richly ambiguous space,[33] which is both above and below ground, and which Antigone speaks of as 'the heaped-up mound of my strange tomb'.[34] It is a place of multiple significance:

> ὦ τύμβος, ὦ νυμφεῖον, ὦ κατασκαφὴς
> οἴκησις ἀείφρουρος, οἶ πορεύομαι
> πρὸς τοὺς ἐμαυτῆς,[35]

O tomb, O bridal chamber, O deep-dug home, to be guarded for ever, where I go to join those who are my own.

This dwelling (οἴκησις) is perhaps not 'guarded for ever' (ἀείφρουρος), as Lloyd-Jones has it: the point is not that Creon's guards will be stationed there for ever, but rather that this tomb is itself ever-watchful;[36] this could be normalized into the idea of 'everlasting', but the primary meaning of the word creates the stronger, more disturbing sense that the tomb itself will for ever be vigilant, watching the city of Thebes. This tomb is her bridal chamber where she will, as it happens, be joined by Haemon in death rather than in marriage, but Antigone does not know this; at this point she is thinking rather of joining her own people (τοὺς ἐμαυτῆς). It is her point of entry into the underworld, the other conceptual space which surrounds the city of Thebes. The city which repelled the invaders from its walls, and kept intact its seven gates, is finding that the uncanny fields of the conceptual spaces around it, which it cannot control, are powerful in their capacity to determine the life and death of its citizens.

Antigone, who inhabits, or is at least a μέτοικος in these strange spaces, is also placed strangely in time. That opening exclamation

32 *Antigone*, l. 278.

33 Oudemans and Lardinois, p. 181. For caves as sacred places and apt locations for myth see Richard Buxton, *Imaginary Greece: The Contexts of Mythology* (Cambridge, 1994), pp. 104–8, and John Boardman, *The Archaeology of Nostalgia: How the Greeks Re-created their Mythical Past* (London, 2002), pp. 104–6.

34 *Antigone*, ll. 848–9; 'strange' is ποταινίου, usually 'new', but also 'unexpected', 'unheard of'—and therefore *unheimlich*.

35 *Antigone*, ll. 891–2.

36 Thus *LSJ s.v.* ἀείφρουρος: 'ever-watching, i.e. everlasting'.

about Zeus accomplishing the evils which spring from Oedipus points to how her actions are being held in a temporal framework which stretches back to, and seems to make present again, the troubles of Oedipus. For Antigone seems to exist in a different temporal dimension from other characters. She does not live in the same time as Ismene, telling her that her life has long been dead, in order to help the dead (ἡ δ' ἐμὴ ψυχὴ πάλαι | τέθνηκεν).[37] And Creon says that she no longer exists (οὐ γὰρ ἔστ' ἔτι).[38] She appeals to 'the unwritten and unfailing ordinances of the gods',

> οὐ γάρ τι νῦν γε κἀχθές, ἀλλ' ἀεί ποτε
> ζῇ ταῦτα, κοὐδεὶς οἶδεν ἐξ ὅτου 'φάνη.[39]

> For these have life, not simply today and yesterday, but for ever, and no one knows how long ago they were revealed.

It is characteristic of Antigone, as Segal observes,[40] that she has a strong sense of ἀεί, 'always'; the tomb was always watchful (ἀείφρουρος), and she had previously told Ismene that the time for pleasing those below the earth is longer than that for pleasing those here, 'for in that place I shall lie for ever' (ἐκεῖ γὰρ αἰεὶ κείσομαι).[41] The verb κείσομαι means, in general, to lie down, but it is also used in epitaphs for a body which lies buried, and particularly of a body which lies unburied.[42] Will she be eternally unburied? Antigone envisages taking her place in the underworld alongside Polynices: φίλη μετ' αὐτοῦ κείσομαι, φίλου μέτα ('dear [to him] I shall lie with him, with the dear one').[43] Again the repetition of 'dear' (φίλη ... φίλου) and 'with' (μετ' ... μέτα) highlights Antigone's sense of belonging—but not to Creon's world.

In a play in which the characters exist, in some respects, in different temporal and spatial dimensions, we also find that they fail to share a common language at key points. The arguments of Antigone and of

[37] *Antigone*, ll. 559–60. [38] *Antigone*, l. 567. [39] *Antigone*, ll. 456–7.

[40] Charles Segal, *Tragedy and Civilization: An Interpretation of Sophocles* (Cambridge, Mass., 1981), p. 156.

[41] *Antigone*, l. 76; my translation, as the clause is oddly omitted from the Loeb translation.

[42] *LSJ*, senses 4, 5. [43] *Antigone*, l. 73; my translation.

Creon do not mesh, as the pair fail to address each other's principles, and deploy their key terms in selective ways.[44] Both use speech for self-assertion rather than persuasion. Creon frequently deploys generalizations and sententious, gnomic utterances,[45] as if the epigrammatic shape of the line were itself sufficient to give it truth, or at least authority. These dogmatic platitudes are infected by his egoism, however, and it becomes increasingly clear that they are not utterances made on behalf of the community. When Creon and Antigone clash, they do so fundamentally over two key concepts, for Creon appeals to law (νόμος) while Antigone appeals to nature (φύσις),[46] an opposition which animates, for example, their differing definitions of φίλος, he enlisting this alongside terms which relate to a system of control and obedience, she reminding him repeatedly of familial relations; he stresses choice, she appeals to the duties which she was born with.

The language of Antigone has a tiny linguistic feature which cumulatively shapes a desolate picture of the culture from which she is isolated. Greek uses the privative alpha prefix (ἀ-) to indicate a negative, and the play builds up a set of desolate ἀ- words through which Antigone laments what she is losing through her actions.[47] She goes to her death ἄκλαυτος, unwept by her friends; ἄγαμος, unmarried; then in a triplet ἄκλαυτος, ἄφιλος, ἀνυμέναιος, unwept, unfriended, unmarried; her fate is ἀδάκρυτον, unwept for; and she will die ἄλεκτρον, ἀνυμέναιον, unwedded, unmarried.[48] Even her appeal to the fundamental laws of the gods is an appeal to laws which are defined negatively, for they are 'the unwritten and unfailing ordinances of the gods'

[44] For this 'décalage' between the two characters' speeches see Paul Demont, '*Agôn* judiciare et *agôn* tragique: à propos de l'*Antigone* de Sophocle', in *Rhétoriques de la tragédie*, edited by Corinne Hoogaert (Paris, 2003), pp. 67–87 at p. 76. Segal (p. 183) offers a useful tabulation of the antitheses between Antigone and Creon. There is also a thoughtful discussion of the conflict between Antigone and Creon in Martha C. Nussbaum, *The Fragility of Goodness: Luck and Ethics in Greek Tragedy and Philosophy* (Cambridge, 1986), pp. 51–82.

[45] Griffith, pp. 36–7.

[46] Griffith, p. 210.

[47] Griffith notes (p. 200) how her speech of self-defence (ll. 450–70) is largely negative, denying the status of Creon's claims rather than expounding her own principles.

[48] *Antigone*, ll. 847, 867, 876–7, 881, 917.

(ἄγραπτα κἀσφαλῆ θεῶν | νόμιμα).[49] What she rejects in rejecting Creon's ordinance is a litany of shared pleasures. But Creon's denials are more serious. As Tiresias tells him, he has treated the body of Polynices without honour, ἀτίμως, by leaving it ἄμοιρον, ἀκτέριστον, ἀνόσιον: deprived (or unfortunate), without funeral rites, unholy.[50] There are two different kinds of denial here, as the alpha prefixes map the refusals of Antigone and Creon to acknowledge the force of claims which the community has embedded in the Greek language. In her speeches, Antigone's ἀ- words mark her abandonment of the shared human world, her sacrifice of the pleasures and consolations of communal living because of the dictates of the divine world, of Zeus and Justice under the earth, and their unwritten laws; Creon, however, has violated the morals of his own community, and offended the gods, through his egoistical definition of what the community requires.

These refusals create a form of autonomy, of self-law, for each character, albeit forms of autonomy which have different moral colorations, and different limitations. For, as in *Oedipus the King*, the problem of human agency and its limits, and, with that, the problem of moral responsibility and its limits, is brought to the fore through Sophocles' careful imprecisions. Antigone takes responsibility for her actions, but in denying that Zeus made the proclamation to her she aligns her cause with that of the gods; yet the Chorus in its comments seeks to deprive her of both autonomy and divine sanction: she inherits her savage nature from her father.[51] The house of Oedipus, it says, is now being triply destroyed: in a passage of violently mixed metaphor which has been debated and emended by scholars without any clear resolution, it is said of the house of Oedipus that 'the bloody dust of the gods below is harvesting it in turn',[52] as are 'folly in speech and the Erinys in the mind'.[53] It is unclear whether the reference to folly is to Antigone's behaviour, or Creon's, or both, but the Chorus

[49] *Antigone*, ll. 454–5. [50] *Antigone*, ll. 1069–71. [51] *Antigone*, ll. 471–2.

[52] Griffith's translation, keeping the MSS reading κόνις (dust); Lloyd-Jones in the Loeb edition prefers the emendation κοπίς (knife).

[53] *Antigone*, ll. 601–3.

strikingly joins divine agency and the work of the human mind.[54] It also speaks of the house being shaken by the gods, and compares a family overwhelmed by ruin to darkness running beneath the surface of the sea as the winds drive black sand up from the bottom of the ocean.[55] It believes that one generation cannot release another, *οὐδ' ἀπαλλάσσει γενεὰν γένος*,[56] and if this were true, then there could be no really autonomous action, and Antigone would indeed only be another manifestation of the savage nature of her family. But this is only the Chorus's (perhaps temporary) view. Through these difficult formulations we struggle to understand the nature and the limits of Antigone's autonomy. As for the psychology of Creon, the Chorus comments (without specifically applying this to him) that 'evil seems good to him whose mind the god is driving towards disaster':[57] in such a state of mind, evil and good are interchangeable terms. Creon admits his error, lamenting *ἐμῶν ἄνολβα βουλευμάτων* ('the wretchedness [or unblessedness] of my decrees [or decisions]'),[58] so clearly acknowledging that it was his own thinking which was at fault (the root *βουλ-* indicates thought); yet it was, he says at the end, not willingly (*οὐχ ἑκὼν*[59]) that he killed Haemon and Antigone, for 'a god bearing a great weight struck my head, and hurled me into ways of cruelty'.[60] It was both him and not him. The word which the Loeb edition translates as 'cruelty' is *ἀγρίαις*, 'wild, savage', with an etymological connection to *ἀγρός*, a field, so Creon, the defender of the city, has been behaving like one who lives out in the wild spaces beyond it.

At several such points *Antigone* touches on the boundaries which we draw between the wild and the civilized, and attends to the lines which man marks out between the human world and the non-human world. Both Antigone and Creon have in some respects crossed over from the

[54] As Griffith notes. [55] *Antigone*, ll. 584–92.

[56] *Antigone*, l. 596. [57] *Antigone*, ll. 622–4.

[58] *Antigone*, l. 1265; my translation; *ἄνολβα* is another word with a privative alpha prefix.

[59] *Antigone*, l. 1340.

[60] *Antigone*, ll. 1273–4. Griffith observes that the language suggests a chariot careering off course (p. 347).

human world, epitomized in the city, into some other territory, be it the cave or the plain, the underworld or the wild fields. A word which had been prominent in *Oedipus at Colonus* recurs here: δεινός. The root concept is 'fear', but the word branches out in Greek usage from 'fearful, terrible' to mean 'marvellous, strange', 'marvellously strong, powerful', 'clever, skilful'.[61] The range of meanings points to the range of Greek responses to the unusual natural phenomenon, the exceptional human achievement, the disturbed or disturbing state of mind. The word occurs most prominently in the celebrated chorus which begins:

πολλὰ τὰ δεινὰ κοὐδὲν ἀν-
θρώπου δεινότερον πέλει.[62]

'There are many things which are *deinos*, and none is more *deinos* than man.'[63] Some such things are just humanly terrifying: Creon's countenance is δεινὸν to a subject who tries to speak unwelcome truths to him, and his threats to the Guard are δείν'.[64] Creon thinks that to give way would be δεινόν, but in a debased sense, in that it would hurt his pride, make him lose face.[65] But some usages move the sense from consequences within the human sphere to consequences which bring in the gods, and in so doing mark out the limitations of human understanding. Antigone says that Creon viewed her action in burying Polynices as something which was δεινὰ, a heinous crime, and the punishment which she faces will be δεινὸν, terrifying;[66] but Creon's use of the term to describe her act of burial is tendentious, in effect demanding that she pay to his words the fear which should properly be paid to divine commands. Her punishment will indeed be appalling, but it would be more appalling to disregard the law of Zeus, and the consequences of the punishment will actually turn out to be terrible for Creon. The Guard, when he prepares to tell Creon that someone has buried the body, says that he is nervous when he has to speak of things which are δεινὰ;[67] and here he is thinking not of his

[61] Cp. p. 91 above; Chantraine, *LSJ*, *s.v.*
[62] *Antigone*, ll. 332–3.
[63] My translation.
[64] *Antigone*, ll. 690–408.
[65] *Antigone*, l. 1096.
[66] *Antigone*, ll. 915, 96.
[67] *Antigone*, l. 243.

master's wrath but of what may be the awesome intervention of the gods. Tiresias utters a prophecy which the Chorus thinks is δεινὰ, not just because it foretells disaster but because it is a speaking of the fearful will of the gods.[68] And the power of fate is δεινά; so much so, that neither god nor mortal can withstand it.[69] The notion of what is *deinos* is a way of marking out the precarious standing of the human within a world which is subject to divine rewriting. And this precarious, tragic, standing is what makes man himself *deinos*, a spectacle which stirs pity and fear. 'There are many things which are *deinos*, and none is more *deinos* than man'; or, as Heidegger puts it when he translates this chorus, there is nothing which is more '*unheimlich*', uncanny, than man.[70] *Antigone* attends to the terrible strangeness of man estranged from his society, located between savage and god; to the strange states of mind which drive him to do things which are fearful, marvellous, perhaps clever, but always *deinos*: standing on ground where reverence for that which makes us human places him tragically on the edge of the world.

[68] *Antigone*, l. 1091. [69] *Antigone*, l. 951.

[70] Martin Heidegger, *Höderlins Hymne »Der Ister«*, Gesamtausgabe 35 (Frankfurt am Main, 1984), p. 74; part of an extended discussion of this chorus.

6

SENECA
Thyestes

In reading Seneca's *Thyestes* the Aristotelian or Hegelian models of tragedy seem not to fit: there is no error, no trajectory which brings the protagonist from a height to a depth, nor is there any conflict between opposing principles. Aristotelian pity for undeserved misfortune and fear for a man like ourselves do not suffice as the appropriate terms for our response to the vengeance which Atreus wreaks upon his brother Thyestes by killing his children and making him eat them unawares: rather, horror, and a form of terror at the capacities of the human which are revealed to us. But the play is tragic in pushing human nature to the brink, and perhaps beyond: we are forced to attend to the bending of the human beyond what we normally prefer to think of as its limits, beyond its definition: *supraque fines moris humani*.[1] The Loeb translation of Atreus' words has 'beyond normal human limits', but that blurs the word *mori*, for *mos* means 'established practice, custom, civilized behaviour',[2] which is the work of human society; and what is it that lies beyond human society? Aristotle thought that he who could not live in society must

The Latin text and English translation are from *Seneca: Tragedies*, edited and translated by John G. Fitch, 2 vols., Loeb Classical Library (Cambridge, Mass., 2002–4). I have also used *Seneca's 'Thyestes'*, edited by R. J. Tarrant (Atlanta, 1985).

[1] Seneca, *Thyestes*, l. 268. See Charles Segal, 'Boundary Violation and the Landscape of the Self in Senecan Tragedy', in *Seneca*, edited by John G. Fitch, Oxford Readings in Classical Studies (Oxford, 2008), pp. 136–56.

[2] *OLD*, s.v.

be either a beast or a god,[3] but Atreus aims to surpass the gods, and no beast would calculate horror, and the increase of horror, in the way that Atreus does. What, then, is Atreus? What lies 'beyond the boundaries of human practice'? What do we accept as *mos humanus*? It is the tragic work of this play to place questioningly before us the commonplaces of 'human nature' or 'human custom' through a disconcertingly acute mapping of the human passions. The vocabulary which Seneca uses may be elementary, but the poetry presents these familiar terms to us in ways which test the limits of our imagination, and of our moral understanding.

Seneca figures the passions which animate his protagonist in two ways: as seated in or caused by certain specific parts of the body; and as abstractions which may be thought of as autonomous forces beyond the human, and therefore beyond our control.[4] Thus the play probes how we figure the body and its passions, the mind and its justifications, the security of such commonplace distinctions; it traverses inner and outer spaces, the spaces which the passions inhabit, the distinctions between inner and outer, repeatedly pushing at the boundary between the literal and the metaphorical. It unfolds the terrifying strangeness of our language for the human.

When preparing his crime Atreus is conscious of specific parts of his own body which seem to play a role in his decision-making—and this form of moral anatomy grimly prefigures the actual butchering of Thyestes' sons which will happen later. Atreus addresses himself, saying, *tandem incipe | animosque sume*: 'at long last rouse your heart and begin': rouse your *animos*.[5] What is it that is being roused

[3] Aristotle, *Politics*, 1253a 27–9.

[4] Fitch's Loeb edition (p. 12) has a good brief discussion of the problem of personification in Seneca, and the links between the human and natural worlds. See also John G. Fitch and Siobhan McElduff, 'Constructions of the Self in Senecan Drama', in *Seneca*, edited by Fitch, pp. 156–80.

[5] *Thyestes*, ll. 241–2. Tarrant notes that *anime* is a standard term of self-address in Senecan drama, often appearing in exhortations to action, especially to crime, 'perhaps because of his philosophical belief that voluntary acts require the assent of the soul' (p. 192). See also A. J. Boyle, *Tragic Seneca: An Essay in the Theatrical Tradition* (London, 1997), p. 157.

here? The word *animus* means the mind as the seat of consciousness and thought, as the originator of intentions; also as the seat of desires and emotions, and specifically of anger and pride.[6] In the plural, as it is here, *animi* denotes anger and animosity.[7] To rouse the *animos* is to direct the reason and the emotions into the shape of anger. Recalling his ancestors Tantalus and Pelops, Atreus says, *ad haec manus exempla poscuntur meae*,[8] 'my hands are called to follow their examples', as if his hands were autonomous of his will, responding of their own volition to the call. This is more than poetic synecdoche. Then he rebukes himself:

> non satis magno meum
> ardet furore pectus, impleri iuvat
> maiore monstro.[9]

> The madness firing my heart is not big enough, I want to be filled with some greater monstrosity.

But is this, precisely, an abstract 'monstrosity' with which he wants to be filled? The word *monstrum* denotes a monstrous or unnatural thing, creature, or act, so Atreus is saying that he wants to be filled (literally so: *impleri*) with a monster or a monstrous thing. The human fills itself with the non-human, and Seneca's language creates a disturbing combination of the physical and the abstract, evoking a form of space which is the inner space of the human body, but a space which is permeable to abstract entities. There is also another meaning which lurks in the shadows: *maior* ('greater') can also mean 'older', especially with reference to one's ancestors:[10] it is also, therefore, an 'ancestral monster' which Atreus embraces. His present and his future are extensions, even repetitions, of an ancestral past. The Latin language strains as it approaches the monstrous.

[6] seat of consciousness: *OLD* 4–7; of desires and emotions: 9–10; of anger and pride: 11, 12.

[7] *OLD* 11, citing Seneca's *Medea*, l. 175.

[8] *Thyestes*, l. 243.

[9] *Thyestes*, ll. 252–4.

[10] *OLD* 3.

When his assistant observes that Atreus' passion goes beyond anger, he admits it, and seeks a description of what is happening to him, or within him:

> tumultus pectora attonitus quatit
> penitusque volvit; rapior et quo nescio,
> sed rapior.—imo mugit e fundo solum,
> tonat dies serenus ac totis domus
> ut fracta tectis crepuit et moti Lares
> vertere vultum.[11]

A tumult of frenzy is shaking my breast, and churning it deep within. I am swept along, and know not where, but I am swept along.— The ground moans from its lowest depths, the sky thunders though cloudless, the house cracks throughout its structure as if shattered, and the household gods shake and avert their faces.

The 'tumult of frenzy' is *tumultus attonitus*, a tumult, a sudden attack, a turmoil; *tumultus* is often weakly applied to some mental disturbance, but here Seneca recalls it from cliché as the surrounding vocabulary evokes its fundamental meaning of an attack, a hostile crowd: the root *tum-* is ultimately the Sanskrit *túmraḥ* meaning 'swollen' and *tumulaḥ*, uproar;[12] it is a tumult which is *attonitus*, thunderstruck, stunned, frenzied,[13] so the tumult which shakes him is, with a transferred epithet, itself frenzied, not just the cause of frenzy in him. The physical imagery of the depths of his breast figures the depths of what we might call the psyche, but it is so tangibly, so physically imagined here that a word such as 'psyche' would draw us away from the bodily experience which Seneca is mapping. In a passive verb, *rapior*, Atreus is seized, carried off, swept away—but by no named force. He is made a prisoner and loses his independence of will and motion. These images all map the complexity of Atreus' feeling: it is not simply a matter of some passion, some 'overwhelming' passion (as we might say, picking up one aspect of the metaphor in *tumultus*) welling up from inside him, but of something from outside working deep down into him, something carrying him

[11] *Thyestes*, ll. 260–5. [12] *OLD, s.v.* [13] *OLD, s.v.*

away. This seems to be both an interior and exterior force, but, unlike the vocabulary of Aeschylus or Sophocles, the language which maps this will not allow us to denominate this as some god or *daimon*, and the 'I' which is apparently carried away is still the 'I' which is sufficiently rational to know and explain this.[14]

When the world around him—the ground, the sky, the house, the gods—all revolt in horror,[15] this is both a sign that the natural and supernatural worlds recoil from his unnatural plans, and also an extended metaphor for Atreus' complex human self: the ground being the physical, the sky being the intellectual parts of him, the house representing the body as the lodging of the soul, the gods representing the divine faculty in man. Though he feels something moving within him (which grimly anticipates Thyestes' response to his meal after he has eaten his own sons), he does not know what it is, and cannot name it:

> Nescioquid animo maius et solito amplius
> supraque fines moris humani tumet
> instatque pigris manibus. haud quid sit scio,
> sed grande quiddam est![16]

> Something greater, larger than usual, beyond normal human limits, is swelling in my spirit and jolting my sluggish hands. What it is I do not know, but it is something mighty!

Nescioquid ... haud quid sit scio: 'I do not know what ... I do not know what it is'. The rational mind which seeks to know phenomena is baffled by what it is that is swelling up (*tumet*: the *tum-* root again). And here is Atreus imagining the exact nature of his vengeance:

> tota iam ante oculos meos
> imago caedis errat, ingesta orbitas

[14] Cp. Seneca's *Oedipus*, l. 27, where Oedipus says *meque non credo mihi* ('and I do not believe in [or trust] myself'; my translation).

[15] *Thyestes*, ll. 262–5.

[16] *Thyestes*, ll. 267–70. Tarrant (p. 129) notes that Shakespeare borrowed this phrasing (though turning it in a different direction) in *King Lear*: 'I will do such things— | What they are yet, I know not, but they shalbe | The terrors of the earth?' (II ii 469–71).

in ora patris—anime, quid rursus times
et ante rem subsidis?[17]

Now the whole picture of the carnage hovers before my eyes—childlessness stuffed down the father's throat! Why take fright again, my spirit, and slacken before the event?

The image of the slaughter hovers in front of his eyes, accorded a semi-autonomous existence, not quite part of his own imagination; *errat* is 'floats, drifts', with its basic meaning 'wanders' used also for a derangement of the mind and for moral deviance.[18] In a Shakespearean combination of the abstract and the concrete, childlessness (*orbitas*) is said to be stuffed (*ingesta*) into Thyestes' mouth; *ingesta* carries an undertow of excess, of greed, or of compulsion.

When describing Thyestes, too, Seneca makes us attend to the body and its parts. Atreus wonders how to kill that *dirum caput*,[19] 'fearsome head', but in such a text *caput* cannot simply be read as a commonplace synecdoche, the head standing for the whole man, since Atreus is one who dismembers bodies. His imagination is already dismembering Thyestes; it seems as if, at some level, in some time scheme which we cannot quite comprehend, the act is already done.[20] Thyestes himself feels dismembered as he doubts the wisdom of accepting Atreus' invitation:

animus haeret ac retro cupit
corpus referre, moveo nolentem gradum.[21]

my spirit falters and wants to turn my body back, my steps are forced and reluctant.

This is more than the familiar antithesis of body and soul: the *animus* (perhaps 'mind', or 'reason' here) wishes, desires even (*cupit*), to draw the body back, while *moveo nolentem gradum*, literally, 'I move an

[17] *Thyestes*, ll. 282–4. [18] *OLD*, *s.v.* [19] *Thyestes*, l. 244.

[20] Cp. Seneca's *Oedipus*, ll. 347–83, where the details of the sacrificial victim portend Oedipus' blinding and the war of the Seven against Thebes: the future is already present in these signs. See also the discussions of *Choephori*, p. 58 above, and *Macbeth*, pp. 134–5 below.

[21] *Thyestes*, ll. 419–20.

unwilling step': there is threefold agency here, split between the *animus*, the first person in the verb *moveo*, and the step (*gradum*) which is itself unwilling.[22] His reaction to the banquet in which he unknowingly eats his own sons is similarly figured in terms of the disjunction of his own body:

> crinis...
> inter subitos stetit horrores,
> imber vultu nolente cadit,
> venit in medias voces gemitus.[23]

> my hair...bristles in sudden shivering fits, teardrops fall from my eyes unbidden, amidst my words there comes a groan.

Each part of his body reacts in horror, yet the man himself—in so far as such a coherent entity still exists at this point—is ignorant of what he has done, does not understand the movements of his own hair, tears, or voice. His hands will not obey when he raises the cup containing his sons' blood.[24] There is a dividing of the individual, but this individual will soon also be multiplied into a new monster which is composed of a father and his sons fused into one body but speaking with more than one voice. Soon he says, 'my breast groans with groaning not my own' (*meumque gemitu non meo pectus gemit*[25]): for his breast now contains his sons. The paradoxical *meum... non meo* signals the decomposition of self.

As well as exhibiting that passion which dissociates the whole man into ruined parts, Seneca's language deploys a series of possible abstractions which appear to be influencing Atreus.[26] He says of himself and Thyestes that 'crime is set between us, for the one who seizes it first' (*in medio est scelus | positum occupanti*[27]), as if crime were not a way of describing an individual's act but a thing out there

[22] Cp. ll. 423–8, where Thyestes addresses his *animus* and urges it: *reflecte gressum, dum licet, teque eripe* ('Turn back while you may, and rescue yourself').

[23] *Thyestes*, ll. 948–51. [24] *Thyestes*, ll. 985–6. [25] *Thyestes*, l. 1001.

[26] For a discussion of *furor, dolor*, and *nefas* in Seneca and his contemporaries see Florence Dupont, *Les Monstres de Sénèque: Pour une dramaturgie de la tragédie romaine* (Paris, 1995), pp. 57–90.

[27] *Thyestes*, ll. 203–4.

in the external world, a pre-existing event waiting to be seized as if it were a prize. There are a number of abstractions which could be read either as personifications—as superhuman, supernatural forces which weigh upon Atreus—or as aspects of his own psychology which are thus analysed and externalized in order to be better understood, but which are still aspects of his own will for which he carries responsibility. Atreus banishes *pietas*, and resolves to replace it with the band of Furies, and with some greater monster:

SATELLES. Nulla te pietas movet?
ATREUS. Excede, Pietas, si modo in nostra domo
umquam fuisti. dira Furiarum cohors
discorsque Erinys veniat et geminas faces
Megaera quatiens: non satis magno meum
ardet furore pectus, impleri iuvat
maiore monstro.
SATELLES. Quid novi rabidus struis?
ATREUS. Nil quod doloris capiat assueti modum.[28]

Does no affection move you?—Begone, Affection, if ever you existed at all in our house! Let the dread band of Furies come, and the Erinyes of strife and Megaera brandishing her twin torches. The madness firing my heart is not big enough, I want to be filled with some greater monstrosity.—What new scheme is your rage devising?—Nothing conforming to the limits of ordinary bitterness.

Like Greek, classical Latin could not distinguish typographically between abstract nouns and personifications, between *pietas* and *Pietas*, affection and Affection. Personification, especially the uncertain personification which we have here, is a mode of the uncanny, for we find it hard to know whether what is being referred to is some force outside of the man, or a feeling within him. 'Affection' is, in any case, not a sufficient translation for *pietas*, since this is a term which combines feelings of dutiful reverence towards the gods, the state, and the family:[29] *pietas* is therefore not simply an emotion which one

[28] *Thyestes*, ll. 248–55.
[29] See James D. Garrison, '*Pietas' from Vergil to Dryden* (University Park, 1992).

might or might not feel, it is a duty which—with social and divine sanction—constitutes one's relationships within and beyond the household. 'Reverent obligation' might be a better way of rendering *pietas*. When the Assistant asks Atreus whether he is not moved by any *pietas*, he replies by addressing *pietas* as he expels it (or *her*, for the noun is feminine) from his breast, while wondering if it had ever truly lodged there, or anywhere in the house of Atreus. He turns it into a personification in order to distance himself from its claims. In its place he summons the Furies, but they do not appear: they seem here to be a literary gesture, a trope of excess, rather than the embodied forces of cultural value which had policed the boundaries of Athenian family life. Atreus seeks to achieve something beyond 'the limits of ordinary bitterness'. In his reply, the Assistant takes up Atreus' word *dolor*, which the Loeb translates as 'bitterness',[30] and asks, *Quonam ergo telo tantus utetur dolor?*, 'what will such bitterness use as its weapons?'[31] This image moves *dolor* from being an emotion into being an agent capable of wielding a weapon, capable of being the killer; indeed, it translates Atreus himself into *dolor*,[32] at the same time as Thyestes is being translated into the instrument of his own destruction, for Atreus' reply to the Assistant's question is: *Ipso Thyeste*, 'Thyestes himself'. This handling of *pietas* and *dolor* is not an allegory so much as a way of indicating how completely Atreus is metamorphosing himself into something other than human—or something other than what we are willing to recognize as humanity. The Assistant's reaction to this is *Maius hoc ira est malum*:[33] 'this evil goes beyond anger', goes beyond it into terrain which cannot be named.

As Atreus shapes his plot, he uses and perverts some foundational words. He says that Thyestes 'desires' his kingdom; the Latin here is

[30] *OLD* offers: 'pain, distress, resentment, indignation'. [31] *Thyestes*, l. 258.

[32] Cp. Seneca, *De Ira*, I viii 2: *Neque enim sepositus est animus et extrinsecus speculatur adfectus...sed in adfectum ipse mutatur* ('For neither is the mind set apart, seeing the passions from outside...but itself changes into the passion' (my translation)).

[33] *Thyestes*, l. 259.

sperat, which would normally be translated 'hope', but the Loeb editor rightly understands that what Seneca has in sight here is something more visceral: it is Thyestes' *desire* for power which will lead him into Atreus' trap, and Atreus' multiple repetition of the word (*sperat . . . spe . . . spe . . . spe . . . spes*[34]) shows that this is not hope as the Stoic philosopher would understand it, but a selfish—and (therefore) ultimately self-destructive—passion. For, as he says, 'greedy desire trusts readily' (*credula est spes improba*). Greedy (*improba*: unprincipled, selfish, greedy, immoderate) desire will be duly rewarded when it (that is, Thyestes reduced to an incarnate emblem of *spes improba*) feasts on his own sons.

The dire slippage in the meaning of *spes* is a process of deformation which Thyestes himself almost recognizes. For although Thyestes says that it is best to desire nothing, and, in ostensibly Stoic fashion, claims that 'it is a vast kingdom to be able to cope without a kingdom',[35] his son Tantalus is in thrall to abstract nouns without really understanding their significance: he praises power (as *potestas*, and again as *imperium*[36]), and naïvely thinks that family feeling and brotherly love (*pietas* and *amor*[37]) can return when they have been banished. But such terms as *pietas* and *amor* are without purchase and substance here, and Tantalus has no notion of what visceral force there can be in the desire to grasp or to keep *potestas* and *imperium*. Thyestes himself warns his son that *falsis magna nominibus placent* ('great things please through false names').[38] Indeed, stronger abstract nouns than *pietas* are in play, for as he listens to his brother and his nephew arguing themselves into trusting the abstract principles of brotherly affection, Atreus says to himself, 'my hatred (*odia*) is on a firm footing'. This is the Loeb translation of *iam tuto in loco* | *versantur odia*,[39] but there is no word for 'my' in the Latin, which more literally means 'now hatred operates in a safe place'. One should not elide the verb *versantur*, 'operates',[40] which helps to give a degree

[34] *Thyestes*, ll. 289–95.
[35] *Thyestes*, l. 470.
[36] *Thyestes*, ll. 443, 471.
[37] *Thyestes*, ll. 474–5.
[38] *Thyestes*, l. 446; my translation.
[39] *Thyestes*, ll. 493–4.
[40] *OLD* 11, a middle sense of the passive voice.

of independence to *odia*. And since *verso* is often used for turning something over in the mind, there is the additional implication that this safe place is both within Atreus' mind and outside it. The lack of any equivalent for 'my' in the Latin maintains the autonomy of *odia*: not 'my hatred', but 'hatred' *tout court*, or even 'Hatred'. Abstractions take on a vigorously physical autonomy. Atreus can hardly restrain his *animus*, scarcely reign in his rancour (*dolor*) as if it were some headstrong hunting-dog; and when anger (*ira*) senses (*sperat*, ironically: 'hopes for') blood, it cannot be concealed.[41] From this day, he says to his brother, blood and family ties (*sanguis ac pietas*) must be cultivated;[42] but we know what he means by 'blood': *sanguis* is not an abstract noun but a bloodily literal one.

In some places, these abstractions appear to be thought of as personifications, as forces which have some mode of existence outside the human being, and act upon him from outside. While the Greeks often thought of anger or desire, say, as forces outside the individual which might take him over at moments of stress, the Senecan abstractions appear to have a different ontological status. They seem to be socially recognized principles, and socially condemned rages, as if this realm were the realm, in short, of the civilized, conforming to *mos humanus*. But it is a strange form of the social that we find in Seneca, since his plays in general have little sense of a shared milieu, and lack that intense and grounded evocation of a long-inhabited place which is so striking in Greek theatre. There the drama takes place in a recognizable house, on the edges of a grove which one could visit, in a city whose history is well known; and the texture of the play, its imaginative framework, is woven through shared myth, common assumptions about values and boundaries. Its ground is deeply inhabited, is the subject of memory, and can be made sacred or polluted. The Senecan world is, by contrast, populated only by the protagonists and their generally insignificant associates with whom they maintain a minimal dialogue; there is no richly woven texture of shared histories and communal spaces. Senecan spaces are the spaces of

[41] *Thyestes*, ll. 493–505. [42] *Thyestes*, ll. 510–11.

the individual mind, contoured by extreme desire, into which other characters are drawn.

In such a conceptual space, the abstract nouns—*pietas, crimen, ira, dolor*—are more isolated, more visible, and presented more forcefully to the reader's imagination as terms which require to be examined. When Atreus says *fas est in illo quidquid in fratre est nefas*[43] ('All that is wrong in dealing with a brother is right in dealing with him'), this almost palindromic sentence shows that he assumes the capacity to reverse the meaning of *fas*, which the translation cannot quite bring out: for *fas* is divine law, and also the natural law which provides the moral basis for our actions: so when Atreus uses the word *fas* for the way he is about to harm his brother, he is appropriating to his own purposes both the divine law and the rhetoric which defines the human. The unsettlingly neat rhetorical patterning not only brings *fas* and *nefas* into sharp conflict and redefinition, it separates *illo* from *fratre*, 'him', 'that one', from the idea of 'brother'; and pivots the line on the ominously vague *quidquid*, 'whatever'. In such a milieu, what could *fas* and *nefas* mean? They have already been contaminated by the Fury who spoke of *fas* and *nefas* when urging Tantalus to destroy his descendants: Atreus is possessed by the Fury to the extent that he is using her perverted vocabulary.[44]

Linguistic and conceptual boundaries are troubled, 'solicited' in Derrida's sense of the term (subjected to a questioning, troubling agitation),[45] and this crossing of boundaries between once stable categories is dramatized in the emergence of the ghost of Tantalus which has been compelled by the Fury to leave the underworld and come up into the world of humans. What is this Fury? Is it an external agent pressing him to destruction? Is it a personification of his own *furia*, madness, rage, lust for revenge? Once again, it is not

43 *Thyestes*, l. 220.

44 *Thyestes*, ll. 28, 47, 56. Alessandro Schiesaro notes that Atreus echoes the Fury's *abunde* ('amply': l. 105) in his *abunde* (l. 279) (Alessandro Schiesaro, *The Passions in Play: 'Thyestes' and the Dynamics of Senecan Drama* (Cambridge, 2003), p. 179). Cp. Lady Macbeth's use of the witches' vocabulary: see p. 127 n.19 below.

45 Jacques Derrida, *Marges de la philosophie* (Paris, 1972), p. 22.

the same as the Greek Erinys which punishes those crimes which the society has agreed to be the most heinous, though it is in some respects a translation of that dramatic figure, albeit not a translation of the concept which it represented: it is a figure of psychological obsession, not of collective value. It stands, perhaps, as a dramatic realization of Seneca's analysis in *De Ira* that a passion's 'first movement is not voluntary, but is as it were the preparation of passion and a sort of menacing'.[46] Tantalus had transgressed by serving the flesh of his son to the gods, and is punished by being forever denied the food and water which remain just out of reach. The ghost is goaded by the Fury to stir the house to terrible crimes, and when he objects, not wishing to afflict his descendants, the Fury punishes him by rousing in him intolerable hunger and thirst: *quid famem infixam intimis | agitas medullis?* he asks, 'why do you rouse the hunger set in my bones' marrow?'[47] Hunger is felt right down into the marrow. He is commanded to spread frenzy through the house, for his descendants must be driven to thirst for the blood of their own kin.

Much of the dialogue between the ghost and the Fury is cast in the future tense, as both see what will or may happen in Tantalus' family, though this is a passage composed largely of jussive subjunctives, of instructions rather than descriptions, so implying the direct influence of the Fury upon events; but then—in the present indicative tense—the house actually receives the madness of Tantalus:

sentit introitus tuos
domus et nefando tota contactu horruit.
actum est abunde.[48]

The house feels you entering, and shuddered throughout at this accursed contact. It is done, and amply!

[46] *De Ira*, II iv 1: *est primus motus non voluntarius, quasi praeparatio adfectus et quaedam comminatio* (my translation).

[47] *Thyestes*, ll. 97–9.

[48] *Thyestes*, ll. 103–5. I have altered the Loeb translation from 'shudders' to 'shuddered'.

The slippage from the present tense of *sentit* (feels) to the perfect tense of *horruit* (shuddered) denotes the all-too-rapidly completed action: *actum est*, it is done. The house, *domus*, is not the social, familial *oikos* of Greek theatre with its servants, its history, its entrances, and shrines. It seems to be a more restricted term, standing for the family as a set of individuals, linked—indeed, linked fatally—but receiving this fury individually (though *domus* is singular, *introitus* is plural: 'the house feels your entrances'). The *domus* also signifies the moral fabric of Atreus himself, the perverted version of what the good Stoic would regard as the interior citadel.[49] The ghost has crossed over the boundaries between the upper and the lower worlds, which suggests that Atreus himself is crossing the boundary between the civilized and—but what could the antithesis be here? Not 'wild' in the sense of the animal, since no animal plots revenge: rather Atreus crosses into what we are compelled to acknowledge as another aspect of the human—calculated cruelty. Is this an aspect of 'natural' man which the work of civilization attempts to hold in check? Perhaps; but Seneca's language suggests ways in which Atreus' revenge depends deliberately upon—is plotted as a careful perversion of—those modes of life which make up civilization. And Atreus seems to be crossing an inner boundary: our habitual antithesis between the conscious and unconscious mind will not quite serve here either, though the irruption of Tantalus from the underworld points to (but do we mean 'symbolizes' or do we mean 'causes'?) the irruption of some primitive feeling, perhaps some primitive code of vengeance which shadows the world which we like to regard as civilized.

Here and elsewhere in the play, the external natural world is used as a metaphor for what we would want to call the physiological or psychological or moral disturbance of the protagonist. But in such a text the status of the metaphorical is unclear. Metaphor expresses one thing in terms of another from which it is separate (rage, say, is imagined in terms of boiling water) while metonymy expresses

[49] I take the phrase from Pierre Hadot, *La Citadelle intérieure: Introduction aux Pensées de Marc Aurèle* (Paris, 1992).

something in terms of one of its components or aspects (the head figures the whole person). But when Seneca explores the ways in which the passions work, we are led into territory in which we cannot quite read the relations between such elements, cannot be sure whether the literal and the physical are so indeed, or are components of metaphor. Is the relationship between Fury and Atreus' anger one of cause and effect—the allegorical character being taken as a supernatural force which causes his passion—or is it an image which expresses the power of that passion? When the ghost of Tantalus comes up from the underworld, does some force from outside come to act upon Atreus, or is this a symbol of the inner welling up of anger from some previously unglimpsed region of Atreus' psyche? Both ideas seem to be held together.

For the spaces of the external world are not simply external. 'The underworld and its passions,' says Alessandro Schiesaro, 'alluring and disconcerting alike, are always lurking beneath the surface of the text, just as in the most sacred part of the Roman *forum* a small opening, the mundus, permitted a ritualized and strictly controlled contact with the realm below'.[50] But not really 'just as': in Seneca's text the half-submerged passions are not accessed through controlled, ritualized contact between two forms of space; instead, they shape the inner space of Atreus and erupt into the outer space of his victims, and they have a possible origin in the underworld. Space is layered, but the layers are not discrete. When the Messenger arrives to narrate the butchery of Thyestes' sons, he begins with the question, *Quaenam ista regio est?*:[51] 'What is this region?' Is it, he goes on to ask, civilized Greece or barbarian Scythia? So far, this is just a rhetorical question which supplies its own answer, but there is in it a deeper question: what, or how, does space signify? The Messenger's speech relates that within the deepest recesses of the palace there is an inner space which is populated by dark trees associated with death (yew, cypress) and hung with trophies of defeated enemies. It is not the kind of space to

[50] Schiesaro, p. 2. [51] *Thyestes*, l. 627.

which ordinary mortals have access: it is the space in which the rulers of the house commune with the gods and receive oracular replies. Its darkness is repeatedly stressed, and it has a night of its own even in daytime. There is a dark stream which is likened to the river Styx of the underworld, and one hears the groans of the gods associated with death (*ferales deos*[52]). Here are things more monstrous than any which are known (*maiora notis monstra*[53]). What kind of space is this? It is part of the built human world, but populated by the denizens of the underworld; it is night folded within day. It is the external and internal space which Atreus enters in his fury, *furens*.[54] And in it he proceeds not simply to kill the boys, but to butcher them according to the correct sacrificial procedures: *nulla pars sacri perit*: 'no part of the ritual is forgotten'.[55] In response, the natural world around him (if 'natural' is the right word here) recoils, as the grove trembles, the earth shakes, and the wine changes to blood as it is poured in libation.[56] But perhaps the most awful, and profound, detail in the catalogue of horrors is an ostensibly unhorrific word: when Atreus hesitates as to which of the boys he will kill first, Seneca says: *nec interest, sed dubitat et saevum scelus | iuvat ordinare*:[57] 'it makes no difference, yet he hesitates and takes pleasure in ordering the savage crime'. The crucial word here is *ordinare*: 'to set out in due order'. What could be due or orderly about such a perversion of sacrifice into—again, the antithesis hangs incomplete, for there seems to be no term which could describe a sacrifice when it is performed with such deliberate intent to destroy. The actual formula of civilization is employed specifically to make the atrocity more awful, it is civilization which enables the acme of barbarity, and in such a context an antithesis such as civilized/barbaric, or human/inhuman, blurs before our eyes.

52 *Thyestes*, l. 668.
53 *Thyestes*, l. 673.
54 *Thyestes*, l. 682.
55 *Thyestes*, l. 695.
56 'Atreus is at the same time the *sacerdos* and the addressee of the sacrifice, as he makes clear that he is offering the victims to himself... collapsing two roles which normal religious practice obviously kept apart' (Schiesaro, p. 151).
57 *Thyestes*, ll. 715–16.

Here we see Seneca's understanding of the question raised, according to Plato, by Socrates, who thought that no man does evil willingly, knowing it to be evil, but instead presents it to his mind as a good.[58] Atreus, on the contrary, knows that what he is doing is evil; deliberately and deliberatively he calls *nefas* '*fas*', seeks to make his vengeance more and more terrible, and at the end regrets only that he has missed certain opportunities to increase Thyestes' suffering. In this liminal tragedy, it would be comfortable to say that we are brought to the boundaries of the human, the limits of *mos humanus*. But no: this play shows us that, awfully, the human has no limits.

[58] Plato, *Laws*, 731c.

7

SHAKESPEARE

Macbeth

The three witches who open the play initiate an *unheimlich* interruption into the attendant space of the stage: attendant, rather than empty, since even before the action begins the stage space is filled with the audience's expectations about time, space, and causality, what they assume to be their common knowledge about the physical and moral contours of the human world. The witches themselves are strange enough in their theatrical manifestation, but more strange is the deformation of time and of space which they inaugurate; the decomposition of any stable form of individual agency which occurs as Macbeth follows the path which they have pointed out; and the fall of language into paradox and tautology. The question which forces itself upon readers of *Thyestes—quis hic locus?* what are the boundaries of the human *Heimat*?—returns in new ways in *Macbeth*.[1]

Macbeth is quoted from *The Complete Works of William Shakespeare*, edited by Herbert Farjeon, The Nonesuch Shakespeare, 4 vols. (London, 1953), which reprints the First Folio text verbatim. I have also consulted the editions by Kenneth Muir, The Arden Shakespeare, second series (London, 1951, revised 1972); A. R. Braunmuller, The New Cambridge Shakespeare (Cambridge, 1997); and Nicholas Brooke, The Oxford Shakespeare (Oxford, 1990).

[1] For the motif of self-dramatization and its origins in Seneca see T. S. Eliot, 'Shakespeare and the Stoicism of Seneca', in *Selected Essays* (London, 1932, revised 1951), pp. 129–31. For the wider Senecan influences on *Macbeth*, especially from *Medea* and *Agamemnon*, particularly via the translations by John Studley in *Seneca His Tenne Tragedies*, edited by Thomas Newton (London, 1581; reprinted in 2 vols.,

Those who meet the witches cannot place them securely in either physical or metaphysical terms. They 'looke not like th'Inhabitants o' th' Earth, | And yet are on't', says Banquo. 'Live you, or are you aught | That man may question?', he asks.[2] Are they alive, or are they any *thing* ('aught' is used for things not people) which may be engaged through a man's language. They look like women, but have beards. Are they 'fantasticall', that is, existing only in the imagination,[3] or 'that indeed | Which outwardly ye shew?'[4] And when they have vanished, Banquo asks,

> Were such things here, as we doe speake about?
> Or have we eaten on the insane[5] Root,
> That takes the Reason Prisoner?[6]

There are no answers to these questions.[7] It has been observed that one of the ways in which Shakespeare thinks of evil is that 'evil can produce a state of affairs in which a given entity is both one thing and its opposite',[8] and such unresolved antitheses characterize the conceptual world of the play to the point that, seemingly 'nothing is, but what is not'.[9] Banquo's uncertainty resonates through the play as neither Macbeth nor the audience is entirely sure who or what they are, or, more importantly, what their powers are. There are three of

London, 1927), see Muir's edition; Inga-Stina Ewbank, 'The Fiend-like Queen', *Shakespeare Survey*, 19 (1966), 82–94; Kenneth Muir, *The Sources of Shakespeare's Plays* (London, 1977), pp. 211–14; Robert S. Miola, *Shakespeare and Classical Tragedy: The Influence of Seneca* (Oxford, 1992), pp. 92–122; and Yves Peyré, '"Confusion now hath made his masterpiece": Senecan Resonances in *Macbeth*', in *Shakespeare and the Classics*, edited by Charles Martindale and A. B. Taylor (Cambridge, 2004), pp. 141–55.

2 Shakespeare, *Macbeth*, I iii 42–3.

3 *OED s.v.* fantastic 1a. Shakespeare took the word from Holinshead: see note 10 below.

4 *Macbeth*, I iii 53–4.

5 'insane' is unusually and emphatically stressed here on the first syllable, and this is the *OED*'s only example of the word in the sense 'causing insanity' (*OED s.v.* insane 3), which is a sense of the Latin *insanus* (*OLD s.v.* insanus 5), 'causing madness'.

6 *Macbeth*, I iii 81–3.

7 The play bristles with unanswered questions, as G. Wilson Knight points out (*The Wheel of Fire* (London, 1972; first published 1930), pp. 141–2).

8 G. I. Duthie, 'Antithesis in "Macbeth"', *Shakespeare Survey*, 19 (1966), 25–33, at p. 25.

9 *Macbeth*, I iii 141.

them, recalling the three Fates or Moirai of Greek myth, and they call themselves the 'weyward Sisters' (the term also used by Macbeth and Banquo), implicitly claiming the power to affect human destiny or 'weird'.[10] But whatever their powers of foresight, or of suggestion, they are visible dramatic manifestations (and perhaps instigators) of the terrain of the *unheimlich*, which becomes the terrain of Macbeth's imagination. For the strange way in which the witches relate to space and time (they are on the earth but do not seem to be like earth's inhabitants, and they seem able to 'looke into the Seedes of Time, | And say, which Graine will grow, and which will not'[11]) prefigures—if it does not actually create—Macbeth's own disturbed relationship to space and time.

[10] *OED s.v.* weird 1. The word occurs six times in the play, variously spelt *weyward* and *weyard* depending on which compositor set the passage in the First Folio. The word is normally modernized by editors to 'weïrd'. See Braunmuller pp. 239–40 for a discussion of the word. Shakespeare's principal source, Raphael Holinshead's *The Chronicles of England, Scotlande, and Ireland* (1587), demonstrates a repeated uncertainty as to the status and nomenclature of these figures, saying that as Macbeth and Banquo were travelling through a clearing in a wood ('laund') 'there met them three women in strange and wild apparell, resembling creatures of elder world'; the marginal note here calls them 'three women supposing to be the weird sisters or feiries'. The main text continues: 'This was reputed at the first but some vaine fantasticall illusion by Mackbeth and Banquho . . . But afterwards the common opinion was, that these women were either the weird sisters, that is (as ye would say) the goddesses of destinie, or else some nymphs or feiries, indued with knowledge of prophesie by their necromanticall science' (Geoffrey Bullough, *Narrative and Dramatic Sources of Shakespeare*, 8 vols. (London, 1957–75), vii 494–5). John Leslie, a possible source for Shakespeare, says that Macbeth met *quarundam mulierum, seu potius Dæmonum, qui mulierum personas ementiti* (*De Origine, Moribus & Rebus Gestis Scotorum Libri Decem* (Rome, 1578), p. 245): 'some women—or rather Demons who assumed the likeness of women' (translated by Bullough, vii 519). Andrew Wyntoun in his chronicle, probably an analogue rather than a source, says that Macbeth saw the three figures 'in his dremyng' (Bullough, vii 475). This range of explanations for the 'witches' (so called in the stage directions in the Folio, but not by any of the characters) is likely to have occurred to members of the audience. For other contemporary connotations of the figures see Arthur R. McGee, '"Macbeth" and the Furies', *Shakespeare Survey*, 19 (1966), 55–67. The most thorough recent treatment of the complex conceptual structures around early-modern witchcraft is Stuart Clark, *Thinking with Demons: The Idea of Witchcraft in Early Modern Europe* (Oxford, 1997). There may also be echoes of the Erinyes in the *Oresteia*, transmitted via Seneca's *Agamemnon*: see Miola, pp. 98–9.

[11] *Macbeth*, I iii 58–9; though this is uncertain: Macbeth says, '*If* you can looke . . . '.

The idea that Macbeth may one day be king, the method by which he seeks to bring that about, and the desire to control the consequences of Duncan's murder, are all formulated within the weirdly contoured spaces of Macbeth's imagination: these are conceptual spaces which are generated not only while Macbeth is alone and voicing a conventional soliloquy, but also in those singularities[12] which he creates around himself in scenes where there are actually other characters on stage. At several moments Macbeth withdraws from the conversation around him and retreats into his own thoughts, occupying for a while a form of stage space to which the other characters do not have access, for it is shaped by his own imagination. And often, within this enclosed world, Macbeth enters a peculiarly distorted or uncertain time scheme, where past, present, and future become present to his mind in new configurations, disturbing the quotidian logic of cause and effect. In Act I scene v, when Macbeth and his wife meet for the first time after the witches' prophecy, Lady Macbeth speaks twenty lines to him, but he is more reserved, and speaks only four to her; his only response to her resolution that she will manage 'This Nights great Businesse' is to say evasively, 'We will speake further':[13] even this oppressively intimate couple do not speak the same language or meet on the same ground. Later, in a conversation with her before the killing of Banquo, he suddenly turns to say 'Come, seeling Night',[14] and moves into a self-enclosed, eight-line meditation on light and darkness, addressing a personified Night in an inset monologue which amazes Lady Macbeth: 'Thou marvell'st at my words', he notices, when he emerges from this near-trance. She is standing next to him, but for these moments she no longer shares his space. When Banquo's ghost appears at the banquet, invisible to everyone else, Macbeth is once

[12] *singularity*: the condition of being apart from others (*OED s.v.* singularity 4a); but also, 'a region in which space and time have become so locally distorted that the present laws of physics are no longer applicable' (*OED* 9e, quoting the journal *Nature*).

[13] *Macbeth*, I v 68, 71.

[14] *Macbeth*, III ii 46–53.

again drawn into the singularity of an unrequited dialogue, and rejoins the social space only with difficulty.[15]

The first of these parenthetical spaces had occurred when the witches had hailed Macbeth as Thane of Cawdor and future King: there he began to be drawn apart into a new dimension, into a narrative which he will rapidly develop out of their bare statement. He reacts with surprise and fear, according to the stage direction which is implicit in Banquo's speech:

> Good Sir, why doe you start, and seeme to feare
> Things that doe sound so faire?[16]

Why indeed, unless the witches have spoken aloud Macbeth's own unspoken thoughts? 'My dull Braine was wrought with things forgotten'[17] he says to excuse his abstraction, inadvertently implying that the witches' words have stirred memory and not just desire. The near-homophone 'feare'/'faire' reminds us that the witches have already undermined the meaning of 'faire' in their maxim 'faire is foule and foule is faire', eerily and unconsciously echoed by Macbeth in his first words in the play, 'So foule and faire a day I have not seene'.[18] A strong but indecipherable link is established between the witches and Macbeth right from the start, and as he speaks their language without knowing it we must wonder about his autonomy—wonder, but remain unable to answer our own questions.[19] He drifts away from those around him and stands absorbed in his own contemplation: to

[15] Brooke notes that Macbeth's speech after the discovery of the murder of Duncan, 'Had I but dy'd an houre before this chance, | I had liv'd a blessed time ...' (II iii 84–9), is also in the language of the soliloquies, and Braunmuller suggests that there are different ways of speaking it, as a public address (with or without irony), or as a private aside; in any case, its meditative language places its speaker temporarily in his own space.

[16] *Macbeth*, I iii 49–50. [17] *Macbeth*, I iii 150–1.

[18] *Macbeth*, I i 12; I iii 36.

[19] Later, Lady Macbeth uncannily uses some of the witches' language without having heard them speak herself: their greeting, 'All haile *Macbeth*, that shalt be King hereafter' (I iii 50) is echoed in her greeting to him, 'Greater then both, by the all-haile hereafter' (I v 55). For the significant repetition of language between characters in this play see George Walton Williams, ' "Time for such a word": Verbal Echoing in

Banquo he seems 'wrapt' or 'rapt'—Banquo uses both words. While both mean 'deeply engaged in thought', 'rapt' essentially means 'carried away in spirit while remaining in the body', while 'wrapt' or 'wrapped' means 'hidden, enclosed'.[20] This second set of homophones suggests images of Macbeth being transported in spirit into a different world from that which his body inhabits, or Macbeth wrapped around by the thoughts which have been generated by the witches, this wrapping insulating him from his companions. The imagery of wrapping is congruent with other images of borrowed or new clothes which sit uncomfortably on the wearer, clothes which do not fit.[21]

Engrossed in his thoughts, Macbeth tells himself that 'This supernaturall solliciting | Cannot be ill; cannot be good';[22] it seems that the witches, 'imperfect Speakers'[23] as Macbeth calls them, have started to damage the perfection of speech, have solicited Macbeth into a world in which the terms 'ill' and 'good' cannot be applied with any confidence. The very word 'solliciting' means not only to urge, beg, incite, entice, or allure someone (especially to an unlawful action), it also means, in early-modern English, to disturb, disquiet, trouble.[24] The Latin root of the word in *sollicitare* means to disturb, harass, molest.[25] What the witches have done in soliciting him with 'All haile *Macbeth*, that shalt be King hereafter'[26] is not only to entice and incite

Macbeth', *Shakespeare Survey*, 47 (1994), 153–9. Another possible connection between Lady Macbeth and the witches is that iconographically witches were represented as carrying torches or tapers (see Frederick Kiefer, *Shakespeare's Visual Theatre: Staging the Personified Characters* (Cambridge, 2003) p. 109), and Lady Macbeth carries a taper in her sleepwalking scene. If the witches were so represented on stage, there would be a striking visual echo between the characters.

[20] *OED s.vv.* rapt, wrapped. Brooke and Braunmuller lose the nuances by modernizing both words to 'rapt'.

[21] *Macbeth*, I iii 106–7 ('Why doe you dresse me in borrowed Robes?') and 143–5 ('New Honors come upon him | Like our strange Garments, cleave not to their mould, | But with the aid of use'). Noted by Braunmuller p. 117, citing M. M. Mahood, *Shakespeare's Wordplay* (London, 1957), p. 165. The imagery of ill-fitting clothes was first pointed out by Caroline Spurgeon, *Shakespeare's Imagery and What It Tells Us* (Cambridge, 1935), pp. 324–7.

[22] *Macbeth*, I iii 129–30. [23] *Macbeth*, I iii 68. [24] *OED s.v.* solicit *v.* 1–4.

[25] *OLD s.v.* [26] *Macbeth*, I iii 50.

him, but to disturb both Macbeth's tranquillity and his bodily composition—together with his grasp of the distinction between present and future:

> This supernaturall solliciting
> Cannot be ill; cannot be good.
> If ill? why hath it given me earnest of successe,
> Commencing in a Truth? I am *Thane* of Cawdor.
> If good? why doe I yeeld to that suggestion,
> Whose horrid Image doth unfixe my Heire,
> And make my seated Heart knock at my Ribbes,
> Against the use of Nature? Present Feares
> Are lesse then horrible Imaginings:
> My thought, whose Murther yet is but fantasticall,
> Shakes so my single state of Man,
> That Function is smother'd in surmise,
> And nothing is, but what is not.[27]

Linguistic links continue to bind Macbeth to the witches: 'Cannot be ill; cannot be good' reworks their paradox 'Faire is foule, and foule is faire', and another form of bond is emerging too.[28] An 'earnest' is a pledge, instalment, or down payment,[29] especially one made for the purpose of securing a bargain or legal contract, so folded within this image is the possibility that Macbeth is making (or perhaps has in some sense already made[30]) a Faustian bargain with the witches, who have just delivered the first instalment of their promise—the Thaneship of Cawdor. Shakespeare has also packed multiple senses into the word 'successe': the upshot or outcome of events; the fortune, good or bad, which befalls someone; the attainment of one's desire; and, specifically, succession to the throne.[31] Like other key words in this

[27] *Macbeth*, I iii 129–41.

[28] See T. McAlindon, *Shakespeare's Tragic Cosmos* (Cambridge, 1991), pp. 213–14 for a discussion of Macbeth's bonds.

[29] *OED s.v.* earnest *n.*[2].

[30] 'Cause and effect do not work in *Macbeth* ... it is almost impossible to find the source of any idea in *Macbeth*; every new idea seems already there when it is presented to us' (Stephen Booth, '*King Lear*', '*Macbeth*', *Indefinition, and Tragedy* (New Haven, 1983), p. 94).

[31] *OED s.v.* success 1, 2, 3, 5; Mahood, p. 139.

play,[32] it is at once richly suggestive and evasive; and because its semantic field is so wide, some elements of its signification are deniable even within the speaker's own dialogue with himself: the meaning 'succession' could be shielded from Macbeth's conscious mind. And 'suggestion' is more than the offering of an idea, for it is specifically a well-established word for a prompting to evil, a temptation from the devil.[33] The witches' prophecy—or his elaboration of it—has disjointed Macbeth's body. When he says that 'Function is smother'd in surmise', 'Function' could mean either activity in general (Macbeth cannot make any movement because he is transfixed by his imagination) or the performance of a particular action (the performance of the murder is veiled by guesswork about its circumstances and methods).[34] The two abstract nouns are connected by the physical verb 'smother'd', which ominously suggests a particular mode of killing Duncan. And the little word 'yet' in 'Murther yet is but fantasticall' implies that the murder is as yet, so far, only imaginary, but will not always remain imaginary. Even the word 'fantasticall' associates Macbeth with the witches, since it was the word which Banquo had used of them. The last line of the speech, 'And nothing is, but what is not',[35] is paradoxical in complex ways, implying that nothing is now securely one thing or another, for instance securely good or ill, fair or foul; or that now nothing is truly real and present to him except for the one thing which is not yet a reality, Duncan's murder. In contrast to the theological notion that evil is the absence or the privation of good,[36] we see here evil taking on a possibly autonomous shape, neither quite substantial nor quite fantastical. The bodily revolt of Macbeth against his own imagination reworks Seneca's tropes of the physicality with which Atreus embraces his

[32] Braunmuller (p. 53) notes the importance of other terms, such as 'nature', 'perfect', 'present', 'security', and 'strange'.

[33] *OED s.v.* suggestion 1.

[34] *OED s.v.* function 1, 2.

[35] Cp. Iago's 'I am not what I am' (*Othello*, I i 64) which similarly opens up a profound existential challenge, and is incomparably more unsettling than 'I am not what I seem' would have been.

[36] Augustine, *Enchiridion*, 11; *De Civitate Dei*, xii 1–3; Thomas Aquinas, *De Malo*, q. 1.

crime, though Macbeth has a moral sense (which he perhaps never loses) which clearly identifies evil as evil.[37] Yet his standing as an autonomous agent is already precarious, for in this speech Macbeth's solid understanding of the distinction between past, present, and future, between what is and what is not, is shown to be fragmenting. And the language which he uses is becoming a repertoire of evasions and paradoxes, of blurred and multiple definitions. As Stephen Booth observes, in this play 'no kind of closed category will stay closed around any object'.[38]

Later soliloquies develop this unsettlement. In Act I scene vii Macbeth leaves the banquet which is in progress for Duncan, and communes with himself:

> If it were done, when 'tis done, then 'twer well,
> It were done quickly: If th' Assassination
> Could trammell up the Consequence, and catch
> With his surcease, Successe: that but this blow
> Might be the be all, and the end all. Heere,
> But heere, upon this Banke and Schoole of time,
> Wee'ld jumpe the life to come. But in these Cases,
> We still have judgement heere, that we but teach
> Bloody Instructions, which being taught, returne
> To plague th'Inventer.[39]

The truly unsettling thought here is that the killing of Duncan might actually not be 'done, when 'tis done': it might unwind and stretch its consequences out beyond the moment of the murder.[40] The repeated 'if' emphasizes Macbeth's uncertainty. The word 'Assassination' is new to English,[41] and this strange word stretches out to the end of the line to

[37] Thus challenging Socrates' idea that no man does evil knowing it to be evil: see p. 122 above. But Miola's claim (p. 93) that *Macbeth* shares the 'hierophantic elevation of *scelus*' which is seen in some of Seneca's protagonists seems overstated, as it ignores the moral sense which at times draws Macbeth back from his crimes.

[38] Booth, p. 96.

[39] *Macbeth*, I vii 1–10. Booth (pp. 104–5) has a perceptive analysis of this speech.

[40] Spurgeon (pp. 327–9) notes the repeated use in *Macbeth* of images of sound reverberating over a vast region.

[41] *OED s.v.* assassination records this as Shakespeare's coinage. The verb 'assassinate' postdates *Macbeth*, but there is a noun 'assassinate' (= 'assassination'

cover up for more basic English synonyms such as 'murder'. Macbeth wonders whether the assassination 'Could trammell up the Consequence', again linking two abstract nouns with a vividly physical verb: 'trammell' here is a multiply loaded verb,[42] meaning to entangle or catch as in a trammel (a long, narrow fishing net, also used for catching birds), but also, to bind a corpse. Could the killing wrap up the consequences as safely as a corpse is shrouded? Or would the act and the victim alike remain unburied? The lines use the word 'heere' three times, as Macbeth's imagination oscillates between an awareness of the present place and time, which is anxiously revisited and reconfigured, and an attempt to imagine the consequences of the assassination; this leads him into a weird form of space in which, he thinks, 'heere, upon this Banke and Schoole of time, | Wee'ld jumpe the life to come'. Editors have puzzled over 'Banke and Schoole', which is probably an image of a river bank and a sandbank in shallow water,[43] so creating a picture of Macbeth preparing to leap over the afterlife.[44] But his spatial imagination is significantly confused, as his image allows no place where the speaker will land after his jump; so too with the spatial imagery in his final lines:

I have no Spurre
To pricke the sides of my intent, but onely
Vaulting Ambition, which ore-leapes it selfe,
And falles on th'other.[45]

Characteristically, agency and moral responsibility are displaced onto a personified Ambition, and this Ambition overleaps itself (leaps over

and sometimes 'assassin') which appears in English in a translation of Gentillet's tract against Machiavelli in 1602, which might have been Shakespeare's inspiration. Its context there is a discussion of whether the use of murder for political ends could ever be justified (Innocent Gentillet, *A Discourse upon the Meanes of Wel Governing and Maintaining in Good Peace, a Kingdome, or other Principalitie... Against Nicholas Machiavell the Florentine*, translated by Simon Patericke (London, 1602), p. 228).

[42] As Braunmuller notes. *OED s.v.* trammel 1 (wrap corpse, last example 1558), 2 (use net), 4 (figurative use of sense 3, citing this instance as the first).

[43] *OED s.v.* shoal *n.*[1] 1a, citing this example.

[44] *OED s.v.* jump 11, citing only this example and one from *Cymbeline* for the sense 'hazard'.

[45] *Macbeth*, I vii 25–8.

itself? overreaches itself?) and 'falles on th'other': what this 'other' might be is left vague (the other side—but of what?): there is nowhere to land. Macbeth's imagination shapes spaces which are full of abstract nouns in violent movement, but they are not inhabitable spaces; they are moral and imaginative evasions of the screened scenario of Duncan's murder. Duncan's virtues, now personified,

> Will pleade like Angels, Trumpet-tongu'd against
> The deepe damnation of his taking off:
> And Pitty, like a naked New-borne-Babe,
> Striding the blast, or Heavens Cherubin, hors'd
> Upon the sightlesse Curriors of the Ayre,
> Shall blow the horrid deed in every eye,
> That teares shall drowne the winde.[46]

This is a strongly visualized scene of judgement, though a strange one, with heaven's (singular) cherubin riding (plural) horses; the word 'sightlesse' is also disconcerting in its multiple, and incompatible, possibilities, as it could mean that the cherubin's horses are either blind, or invisible, or appalling to see.[47] Like the consequences of Duncan's murder, the meanings of Macbeth's words will not be confined.

An apocalyptic scenario also inhabits the soliloquy which Macbeth speaks on his way to carry out the murder of Duncan, and once again the problem of agency emerges, since in Renaissance narratives demonic powers sometimes provided a potential murderer or suicide with the necessary weapons.[48] Who provides Macbeth with this dagger? Is he his own diabolical self-seducer, or is some external agency intervening?

> Is this a Dagger, which I see before me,
> The Handle toward my Hand? Come, let me clutch thee:
> I have thee not, and yet I see thee still.
> Art thou not fatall Vision, sensible

[46] *Macbeth*, I vii 19–25.

[47] *OED s.v.* sightless 1, 2, 3. Lady Macbeth had earlier invoked 'you murth'ring Ministers, | Where-ever, in your sightlesse substances, | You wait on Natures Mischiefe' (I v 48–50). Are these ministers blind, or invisible, or terrible to look upon?

[48] Braunmuller, pp. 139–40.

To feeling, as to sight? or art thou but
A Dagger of the Minde, a false Creation,
Proceeding from the heat-oppressed Braine?
I see thee yet, in forme as palpable,
As this which now I draw.
Thou marshall'st me the way that I was going,
And such an Instrument I was to use.[49]

The relationship between Macbeth and the dagger which he thinks he sees is one which implicates him in a play of tenses through which the murder (as yet undone) is seen as a deed which is already complete.[50] The two verbs 'was' in the last lines of the extract momentarily place his intention to kill Duncan in the past: to have said, 'Thou marshall'st me the way that I *am* going, | And such an Instrument I *am* to use', would have kept his intention present and active, whereas 'was' places it as a past (and perhaps even temporarily abandoned) intent. Yet in this imagined space which has been brought into being by the dagger, the murder seems to have been played out already, for drops of blood suddenly appear on the blade and haft of the knife, implying that in the seconds which have elapsed since the speech began, the murder has been carried out: 'I see thee still; | And on thy Blade, and Dudgeon, Gouts of Blood, | Which was not so before'.[51] Then yet another parallel narrative unfolds, as Macbeth imagines Murder, personified, moving towards Duncan's chamber:

wither'd Murther,
Alarum'd by his Centinell, the Wolfe,
Whose howle's his Watch, thus with his stealthy pace,
With *Tarquins* ravishing strides, towards his designe
Moves like a Ghost.[52]

Both the dagger and Murther seem to be acting autonomously of Macbeth, and in these parallel narratives the murder of Duncan is

[49] *Macbeth*, II i 33–43.

[50] For the complex way in which time is imagined in this play see Mahood, pp. 131–6.

[51] *Macbeth*, II i 45–7.

[52] *Macbeth*, II i 52–6; 'strides' is the commonly accepted emendation (proposed by Pope) for 'sides' in the First Folio.

already accomplished without his agency. Murther 'Moves like a Ghost', as if Murther is itself the avenging spirit of a dead man. In this way Macbeth's imagination tries to distance himself from the act; and yet it is simultaneously figuring him as Murther—the complex human being contracted into the allegorical noun, redefined as the deed's creature—and as a dead man's ghost, the man of flesh and blood already turned into a displaced, haunting wraith. When a bell rings, Macbeth exclaims:

> I goe, and it is done: the Bell invites me.
> Heare it not, *Duncan*, for it is a Knell,
> That summons thee to Heaven, or to Hell.[53]

Although the use of the present tense for the future is a common idiom, especially for emphasizing a dramatic sequence of events (as when Hamlet, about to kill Claudius, says: 'And now Ile doo't, and so he goes to Heaven, | And so am I reveng'd'[54]), here the clause 'it is done' implies, because of the temporal disturbances which we have just been hearing, that the murder is already a *fait accompli*. The idea that the bell invites him is another displacement of his responsibility onto an external force, another solicitation. And the sound becomes a knell, which is properly the sound which announces that a man has died—not that he is about to be killed. Time is out of joint once again.[55]

Strange though all this is, perhaps the most disturbing word in both these passages is 'done': 'If it were done, when 'tis done'; 'I goe, and it is done'.[56] In both speeches the existential status of the act is uncertain: in the first of these soliloquies, Macbeth doubts whether the killing will ever be done, in the sense of completed, over and done with, without

[53] *Macbeth*, II i 62–4. [54] *Hamlet*, III iii 73–4.

[55] Glynne Wickham, 'Hell-Castle and its Door-Keeper', *Shakespeare Survey*, 19 (1966), 68–74, and Bullough (vii 461–2) note that the Porter scene which follows echoes the medieval mystery plays of the harrowing of hell, so that Macbeth's castle is seen as a form of hell awaiting redemption, which locates Dunsinane in symbolic forms of time and space.

[56] Mahood (pp. 137–8) briefly notes the importance of 'done' in this play, and McAlindon (pp. 213–14) of 'deed'. There are 35 occurrences of 'done', 14 of 'deed', three of 'undone', and three of 'dont' ([T. H. Howard-Hill], *Macbeth: A Concordance to the Text of the First Folio*, Oxford Shakespeare Concordances (Oxford, 1971)). Miola (pp. 106–7) compares the insistent repetition of parts of the verb *facere* in Seneca's *Medea*.

ramifications; in the second, he imagines the murder already carried out, when it is yet to be attempted. The simple word 'done' and its cognates such as 'do', 'deed', and 'undone', echo through the play in a complex conjugation. Often 'do' and 'done' are used euphemistically to screen the fact of murder, in 'I goe, and it is done', or 'Had he not resembled | My Father as he slept, I had don't'.[57] Macbeth asserts to his wife: 'I dare do all that may become a man, | Who dares do more, is none.'[58] This repeated 'do' evades naming or defining the killing as killing, and Macbeth seems implicitly to be recoiling from the extravagant excess of Atreus, who persistently pursued 'more' in his violation of what becomes a man.[59] Another example of his inability to give things their full and proper name is when he tells her: 'I have done the deed',[60] or again, 'I am afraid, to thinke what I have done',[61] or again when he warns (or boasts):

> MACB. There shall be done a deed of dreadfull note.
> LADY. What's to be done?
> MACB. Be innocent of the knowledge, dearest Chuck,
> Till thou applaud the deed.[62]

She too uses the same vocabulary: 'These deeds must not be thought | After these wayes',[63] and 'A little Water cleares us of this deed'.[64] The murderers use the same terms: 'Well, let's away, and say how much is done'.[65] And the witches:

> MACB. How now you secret, black, & midnight Hags?
> What is't you do?
> ALL. A deed without a name.[66]

[57] *Macbeth*, II ii 12–13. Similarly evasive is Macbeth's 'Had I but dy'd an houre before this chance' (II iii 89), where 'chance' is his word for Duncan's death, and another denial of his own agency. Lady Macbeth is not immune from such evasions: 'Nor time, nor place | Did then adhere, and yet you would make both: | They have made themselves' (I vii 51–3).

[58] *Macbeth*, I vii 46–7.The second 'do' here is Rowe's emendation for 'no' in the Folio.

[59] It is unclear whether Macbeth is thinking of what is proper to a male or what is proper to a human being, but Lady Macbeth's rejoinder ('What Beast was't then | That made you breake this enterprize to me?') shows that she understands the latter sense.

[60] *Macbeth*, II ii 14.

[61] *Macbeth*, II ii 50.

[62] *Macbeth*, III ii 43–6.

[63] *Macbeth*, II ii 32–3.

[64] *Macbeth*, II ii 66.

[65] *Macbeth*, III iii 21–2.

[66] *Macbeth*, IV i 48–9.

Language backs away from naming whatever this is. Around the usages of 'do' by Macbeth and Lady Macbeth there gathers a fear of knowing such deeds: 'I am afraid, to thinke what I have done'; 'Be innocent of the knowledge'; 'These deeds must not be thought'. But such attempts to screen themselves from the actuality of the murder fail: blood sticks; and the words 'do' and 'deed' acquire a precise meaning within the idiolect fashioned by the couple.

In many of these instances our attention—and their fear—is drawn to the status of the act: when is a deed actually 'done'? Is it contained or containable? Will it spread, has it already spread, to contaminate time and space beyond its original moment? Who is responsible for an action? Can a deed be undone? Lady Macbeth tries to persuade her husband that 'things without all remedie | Should be without regard: what's done, is done',[67] a formula that she repeats with a different inflection in her sleepwalking scene, where what was previously offered as reassurance now reappears as a terrible realization: 'What's done, cannot be undone'.[68] Sometimes Macbeth shrinks from confronting what he has done: just after he has killed Duncan, he seems to be once more lost in his thoughts and oblivious to his wife who tries to draw him back into a shared space: 'be not lost | So poorely[69] in your thoughts', she says, to which he replies, 'To know my deed, | 'Twere best not know my selfe'.[70] This elusive formulation sets his 'deed' and his 'selfe' in an antithetical construction: in order to understand fully what it is that he has done, he would have to forget who he is. This is one example amongst many of the play's use of antithetical constructions which bring terms together into a relationship which seems to hover between oxymoron and tautology, so that one word undermines the semantic stability of the other without actually replacing it: 'faire is foule, and foule is faire'; 'Cannot be ill; cannot be good'; 'Blood will have blood'; 'What's done, cannot be undone'.

[67] *Macbeth*, III ii 11–12. [68] *Macbeth*, V i 64.

[69] 'in a way unworthy of your position'; 'mean-spiritedly, without courage' (*OED s.v.* 3, 4).

[70] *Macbeth*, II ii 70–2.

All this creates an instability around the very concepts of action and agency. Who actually did kill Duncan? Macbeth, certainly, but in other alternative scenarios which the speeches conjure up he is killed by an aerial dagger, or by Murther, by a second Tarquin; Lady Macbeth would have killed him if he had not resembled her father. And when we say 'Macbeth' we name someone whose integrity decomposes, whose mind produces hyper-physical scenarios, and parts of whose body seem to exist in uncanny detachment or autonomy. For the play also holds before us—in particular, holds before Macbeth's imagination—the unstable ontological footing on which things are founded. It is not only deeds which may or may not be done; a dagger may or may not be a dagger; witches may or may not be physical, as what 'seem'd corporall, | Melted, as breath into the Winde'.[71] The vocabulary of the play resonates with words prefixed by *un-*, which denote departures from the natural order of things, or from customary civilized behaviour: unbecoming, undeeded, unfelt, unfix, unjust, unkindness, unknown, unlineal, unmake, unmanned, unmannerly, unreal, unruly, unsafe, unsanctified, unsex, unspeak, unsure, untimely, untitled, unusual, unwelcome, unwiped.[72] A world of order is negated, and this sense of loss, of the privation of good, is quite as sickening as any overt manifestations of bloody actions: we are made to enter a dimension in which man and his actions are not becoming or mannerly or usual; not sanctified, just, or kind; not safe, not sure, not fixed, not real; a world not known.

And within this dimension what we call inanimate nature becomes animated; not only does Birnam wood move against Dunsinane, but 'The Earth hath bubbles, as the Water ha's'.[73] Solid, immovable

[71] *Macbeth*, I iii 81–2.

[72] Of these words, several are Shakespeare's coinages (according to the evidence in the *OED*) and therefore mark out the deviation from nature or custom all the more sharply: these are 'undeeded', 'unfix', 'unsex', 'unspeak', 'untitled'.

[73] *Macbeth*, I iii 79. *OED s.v.* bubble 3 lists a figurative sense, something unsubstantial, a mere show, but while this metaphorical sense is present in Banquo's word, the literal, physical meaning is primary, and creates the strange idea of bubbles of earth. Spurgeon (pp. 332–3) notes the prominence of images of unnatural occurrences in the natural world. The word 'nature[s]' occurs 26 times in the play, 'natural' twice, 'unnatural' three times.

elements are imagined to listen and speak: as Macbeth approaches the murder of Duncan he recoils from his mental scenario of Murther treading like a ghost and turns to apostrophize the reassuringly solid earth; but the earth and its stones may be animate, may be listening and speaking: 'sowre [i.e. sure] and firme-set Earth | Heare not my steps...for feare | The very stones prate of my whereabout'.[74] Light and dark, day and night, become animated through the adjectives, attributes, and verbs which Shakespeare attaches to them:

> darke Night strangles the travailing Lampe:[75]
>
> Darknesse does the face of Earth intombe,
> When living Light should kisse it[76]
>
> Come, seeling[77] Night,
> Skarfe up the tender Eye of pittifull Day,
> And with thy bloodie and invisible Hand
> Cancell and teare to pieces that great Bond,
> Which keepes me pale. Light thickens[78]
> ....
> Good things of Day begin to droope, and drowse,
> Whiles Nights black Agents to their Prey's doe rowse.[79]

Light and dark, night and day, become agents which act their play around Macbeth, creating a world in which his deed cannot be seen.

[74] *Macbeth*, II i 56–8.

[75] *Macbeth*, II iv 7. In this period the modern words 'travel' and 'travail' shared the same spelling: so this is a lamp used by travellers, but also a light which is struggling against the encroaching darkness.

[76] *Macbeth*, II iv 9–10.

[77] 'seel': to sew up the eyelids of a hawk (*OED s.v.* seel *v.*[2] 1).

[78] And so light which 'thickens' becomes associated with 'thick Night' (I v 50). The *OED* lists this as the first example of 'thicken' in sense 2, 'to become dark, obscure, or opaque', but it is possible that Shakespeare took the word from James I's account of witches moving through the air: 'For if the deuill may forme what kinde of impressions he pleases in the aire...why may hee not farre easilier thicken and obscure so the aire, that is next about them, by contracting it straite together, that the beames of any other mans eyes cannot pierce thorow the same, to see them?' (*Dæmonologie*, Book II Chapter iiii (first published 1597); from *The Workes of the Most High and Mighty Prince, Iames* (London, 1616), p. 114).

[79] *Macbeth*, III ii 46–53.

Meanwhile, Macbeth's own body is subjected to a form of decomposition. His repeated use of the word 'hand', a simple enough word in isolation, builds into a dissociation of himself from the part of his body which will carry out, or has carried out, the killing.[80] He tells himself, let

> The Eye winke at the Hand; yet let that bee,
> Which the Eye feares, when it is done to see.[81]

The eye must close itself[82] when the hand operates: there is a disjunction between two parts of Macbeth's body. And the eye has the capacity to feel fear. The wording in 'let that bee' and 'when it is done' is evasively passive, refusing to acknowledge his own agency, the work of his own hand. The phantom dagger appears with 'The Handle toward my Hand';[83] implicitly, the joining of hand and dagger will not be the result of his own will. Macbeth returns from Duncan's chamber with 'Hangmans hands';[84] Lady Macbeth urges him to 'wash this filthie Witnesse from your Hand';[85] but Macbeth can only focus with horror on his hands:

> What Hands are here? hah: they pluck out mine Eyes.
> Will all great *Neptunes* Ocean wash this blood
> Cleane from my Hand? no: this my Hand will rather
> The multitudinous Seas incarnardine,
> Making the Greene one, Red.[86]

Every word but four here comes from Old English or Germanic roots; the four exceptions which derive from Latin or romance roots are '*Neptunes* Ocean', 'multitudinous', and 'incarnardine', the last two also being Shakespeare's coinages.[87] The play's language has fashioned strong semantic fields around Old English words such as 'do',

[80] Miola (pp. 111–17) traces Senecan precedents for the emphasis on hands.

[81] *Macbeth*, I iv 51–3.

[82] *OED s.v.* wink *v.*[1] 1b; also 'connive at', 6a. The two meanings exist awkwardly together: does the eye not know because it is closed, or does it see and connive?

[83] *Macbeth*, II i 34. [84] *Macbeth*, II ii 27. [85] *Macbeth*, II ii 46.

[86] *Macbeth*, II ii 58–62. For the Senecan origins of this speech see Miola, pp. 113–14.

[87] For Shakespeare's use of Germanic and Latinate vocabularies see Jürgen Schäfer, *Shakespeares Stil: Germanisches und romanisches Vokabular* (Frankfurt am Main, 1973).

'hand', 'know', 'think', 'man', so that now the polysyllabic romance vocabulary seems to accentuate the enormity of the ocean and its awful powerlessness to remove the blood on Macbeth's hand. Lady Macbeth then enters, and says:

> LADY. My Hands are of your colour: but I shame
> To weare a Heart so white.[88]

'To *weare* a Heart'? To Lady Macbeth, the heart is something which is worn, displayed on the outside. But in the world of this play inside and outside often change their proper places. Seeing Banquo's blood on the face of his murderer, Macbeth comments, ''Tis better thee without, then he within',[89] and confronted by the ghost of Banquo which usurps his place at table, he exclaims:

> The times has bene,
> That when the Braines were out, the man would dye,
> And there an end: But now they rise againe
> With twenty mortall murthers on their crownes,
> And push us from our stooles. This is more strange
> Then such a murther is.[90]

The dead are out of their proper place: but so too is Macbeth's grammar. The only plural antecedent for 'they rise againe' is 'Braines': of course we understand a slippage from 'the man' to an understood plural 'men' (his victims are implicitly multiplying) but the grotesque scenario of brains rising, momentarily conjured by the syntax, remains to haunt us.

So it is that the most familiar objects—a stool, a wood, a man's own hand—are co-opted into an *unheimlich*, unnatural drama. Sometimes objects seem deracinated from the physical world, to have an autonomy and to act in a scenario of their own; meanwhile, Macbeth's own independence and agency are subjected to the suggestive (or perhaps determinative) power of the witches, and of his own wife—for, as Freud noted,[91] there is a sense in which Macbeth and Lady Macbeth

[88] *Macbeth*, II ii 63–4.
[89] *Macbeth*, III iv 13–14.
[90] *Macbeth*, III iv 7–82.
[91] See p. 37 above.

are two parts of one character. In the inset spaces of his soliloquies, abstractions take on a physical life and play out a drama of which he seems at once author and victim. He comes to live in a world populated by uncannily animate nature and threatening personifications, a world in which the normal temporal sequence of cause and effect seems not to apply: Duncan's murder is present before it is accomplished, and remains stubbornly present to haunt him with its consequences. Lady Macbeth too, in her sleepwalking scene, inhabits her own time and space in which her hand is for ever bloody. Her death is untimely: 'She should have dy'de heereafter; | There would have beene a time for such a word.'[92] But only in some vague, now unimaginable 'heereafter' would there be time for such an announcement. For Macbeth there is no hereafter, just a succession of tomorrows which represent an endless deferral, and an endless repetition of the same:

> To morrow, and to morrow, and to morrow,
> Creepes in this petty pace from day to day,
> To the last Syllable of Recorded time:
> And all our yesterdayes, have lighted Fooles
> The way to dusty death.[93]

This is Macbeth's time.

And through the dislocation of time, and the perplexing of agency, a persistent decomposition is occurring around the notion *is*, as the fundamental verb *to be* takes on a weird urgency and unsteadiness in a Shakespearean equivalent to the theologians' anxious debate over whether evil is an entity or only the privation of good, whether evil *is*.[94] In the world of *Macbeth*, 'faire is foule'; 'what are these'; 'what are you?'; 'that shalt be King hereafter'. Nothing is, but what is not.

[92] *Macbeth*, V v 17–18.

[93] *Macbeth*, V v 19–23.

[94] Aquinas begins *De Malo* by asking whether evil is an entity (q. 1, art. 1).

8

SHAKESPEARE
Othello

The superficial strangeness of Othello is evident from the start of the play; his deeper estrangement is brought about in the course of the tragedy; indeed, this is his tragedy. *Othello* is a drama of displacement, in which first Othello and then Desdemona are translated into a fictionalized time and space, estranged from and unreachable by the other characters. Gradually he is drawn by Iago, and draws himself (the agency is hard to determine in places, so closely are the two men linked) into an imagined world in which his wife Desdemona is adulterous. He starts as an outsider to Venice, as a highly respected foreign mercenary, and a Moor.[1] He is, according to Rodorigo, 'an extravagant, and wheeling Stranger, | Of here, and

Othello is quoted from the Nonesuch Shakespeare, which follows the Folio text of 1623, though at some points I have substituted readings from the Quarto text of 1622: *The Tragœdy of Othello, The Moore of Venice* (London, 1622), taken from *Shakespeare's Plays in Quarto: A Facsimile Edition of Copies Primarily from the Henry E. Huntington Library*, edited by Michael J. B. Allen and Kenneth Muir (Berkeley, 1981). The relationship between the two texts of *Othello* is complex: there are many small variants between them, and there appears to be no consensus amongst recent editors on how to explain their origins or judge the status of their readings. For this chapter I have also consulted the editions by E. A. J. Honigmann, The Arden Shakespeare, third series (Walton-on-Thames, 1997), and Michael Neill, The Oxford Shakespeare (Oxford, 2006).

[1] For the much-debated question of Othello's race and its significance, see the introductions to the editions by Honigmann and Neill, and Nabil Matar and Rudolph Stoeckel, 'Europe's Mediterranean Frontier: The Moor', in *Shakespeare and Renaissance Europe*, edited by Andrew Hadfield and Paul Hammond (London, 2004), pp. 220–52.

every where',[2] and the word 'extravagant', meaning not only 'vagrant' but 'wandering beyond bounds',[3] immediately places Othello beyond the boundaries of the Venetian world, while 'wheeling' implies that he reels giddily, turns suddenly, or deviates.[4] His place is not, or is only temporarily, in Venice, and he is liable to turn unpredictably.[5] This facile slander turns out to be true, though not in the way that Rodorigo implies, or could ever imagine. Iago tells Brabantio that an 'old blacke Ram | Is tupping your white Ewe', that his daughter is being 'cover'd with a Barbary horse', and that Othello and Desdemona 'are making the Beast with two backs'.[6] A simple and easily legible, easily refutable, form of the monstrous is being summoned up by Othello's enemies. But the tragedy which is about to unfold entails the more profound separation of Othello from the world around him, and his own self-estrangement, as he is drawn by Iago into the creation of a narrative which wheels himself and Desdemona into monstrous new forms.[7] Othello's true *Heimat* lies in his imagination, and this imagination becomes estranged and corrupted—'extravagant'. Step by step, Othello becomes trapped within the stories which he tells himself about Desdemona, and his habitual grammar, compounded so often of hypotheses, conditionals, and rhetorical questions, prevents him from grasping the outside world. He has an imaginative but not an analytical intelligence. Everyone—Desdemona and Cassio, but also

[2] *Othello*, I i 134–5.

[3] *OED s.v.* extravagant 1; its first citation is from *Hamlet*, I i 154, applied to the Ghost.

[4] *OED s.v.* wheel *v.* 1c, 4.

[5] For the significance of 'place' in *Othello* (meaning not only geographical location but also office and role) see Neill, pp. 147–58, drawing upon his earlier article 'Changing Places in *Othello*', *Shakespeare Survey*, 37 (1984), 115–31.

[6] *Othello*, I i 87–8, 110, 115.

[7] On Othello's self-dramatization see T. S. Eliot, 'Shakespeare and the Stoicism of Seneca', in *Selected Essays* (London, 1932, revised 1951), pp. 129–31. Stephen Greenblatt discusses 'the process of fictionalization that transforms a fixed symbolic structure into a flexible construct ripe for improvisational entry', which he further defines as '*submission to narrative self-fashioning*' (*Renaissance Self-Fashioning: From More to Shakespeare* (Chicago, 1980), p. 234; there is a full discussion of *Othello* on pp. 222–54).

Iago, and Othello himself—becomes translated into new roles in this hypothetical narrative; objects too, such as the handkerchief, become signs of adultery; words such as 'honest', or 'committed', take on new senses as Othello remakes language, recasting the world into an incontestable syntax.[8]

In the speech which he makes to the Duke and the Venetian senators explaining how he came to woo Desdemona, Othello recounts his story: he had told her of his life as a soldier,

> And portance in my Travellours historie.
> Wherein of Antars vast, and Desarts idle,
> Rough Quarries, Rocks, and Hills, whose heads touch heaven,
> It was my hint to speake. Such was my Processe,
> And of the Canibals that each other eate,
> The *Antropophague*, and men whose heads
> Doe grow beneath their shoulders.[9]

The textual problems in this short passage[10] indicate the difficulty which the printer (and perhaps before him the scribe and the actor) had with Othello's language. Some of the words are rare: 'portance' (bearing, carriage) is previously attested by the *OED* only in Spenser. 'Travellours' has been thought by recent editors to be an error for the rarer word 'travellous' or 'travailous' (meaning 'hard, labouring').[11] 'Antars' (spelt 'Antrees' in the Quarto) are caves, from the Latin *antrum* probably via the French *antre*; this is the first recorded use of the word in English (and the last before Keats reused Othello's term), so it is not surprising that the compositors of the Folio and Quarto texts stumbled over its spelling. The deserts are 'idle', which probably means 'empty', though the *OED* records no example of that sense

[8] For 'honest' see William Empson, *The Structure of Complex Words*, third edition (London, 1977), pp. 218–49, and for 'committed' see p. 151 below.

[9] *Othello*, I iii 140–6.

[10] I have emended several Folio readings from the Quarto: and Hills *Quarto* ['hils'], Hills *Folio*; heads *Quarto*, head *Folio*; other *Quarto*, others *Folio*; Doe grow *Quarto*, Grew *Folio*.

[11] The Folio reads 'Travellours', as printed here, while the Quarto simplifies the line to 'And with it all my travells Historie'. Honigmann, following Richard Proudfoot, emends to 'travailous'; the *OED*'s only Renaissance example of this is from 1565.

after 1450. Othello has encountered cannibals and anthropophagi, which both Quarto and Folio printers have trouble spelling.[12] The language of the passage (part of the 'Othello music'[13]) is strange, but the speaker is in control of the strangeness, presenting it as part of his carefully wrought persona. These traveller's tales distance Othello from the savagery which he describes, placing him squarely in the position of the intelligent and civilized observer, the confident narrator. The verb which he uses for presenting his story to the outside world, 'provulgate'—which separates the speaker from the vulgar to whom he tells his story—is itself unusual.[14] This is a self-dramatizing fiction, though not necessarily a lie.

When Iago begins to work on Othello, planting in his mind the idea of Desdemona's unfaithfulness, he does so linguistically in a way which manipulates Othello's predisposition for fiction. Grammatically, Othello is inclined to conditional utterances, which transpose life out of the indicative mood and the present tense, as when he greets Desdemona in Cyprus after their separation at sea:

> Oh my Soules Joy:
> If after every Tempest, come such Calmes,
> May the windes blow, till they have waken'd death:
> And let the labouring Barke climbe hills of Seas
> *Olympus* high: and duck againe as low,
> As hell's from Heaven. If it were now to dye,
> 'Twere now to be most happy. For I feare,
> My Soule hath her content so absolute,
> That not another comfort like to this,
> Succeedes in unknowne Fate.[15]

Othello's celebration of absolute contentment wheels through a grammar of conditionals—'If after every Tempest'; 'If it were now

[12] The Quarto spelling is 'Anthropophagie'.

[13] See G. Wilson Knight, *The Wheel of Fire* (Oxford, 1930; revised edition, London, 1972), pp. 97–119.

[14] *Othello*, I ii 21. 'provulgate' is the Quarto reading; the Folio has 'promulgate' which is probably a simplification of the rarer word. The *OED* has just two examples of 'provulgate', not including this one.

[15] *Othello*, II i 182–91.

to dye'; 'I feare . . . That'—so that while the principal thrust of the passage is an extravagant affirmation of happiness, the imaginative power is invested in scenarios of storm and death and fear. What emerges most forcefully is the foreboding rather than his content, and he is, as it turns out, right in thinking that 'not another comfort like to this, | Succeedes in unknowne Fate'. He is a fatally imaginative storyteller. The fertility of his mind is revealed again when he says of Desdemona, immediately before Iago begins his temptation scene:

> Excellent wretch: Perdition catch my Soule
> But I do love thee: and when I love thee not,
> Chaos is come againe.[16]

The grammar here is puzzling. 'Perdition catch my Soule | But I do love thee' may be intended as no more than an elegant version of the colloquial asseveration, 'I love you—damn me if I don't', but the longer and more vivid phrasing in 'Perdition catch my Soule' creates a brief possible narrative (and, again, one which will be fulfilled). The word 'when' in 'when I love thee not, | Chaos is come againe' hovers unsettlingly between meaning 'when' or 'whenever' and meaning 'if'.[17] The uncertainty as to whether he means 'whenever I do not love you' or 'if I were not to love you' is compounded by the verb 'is come' (present tense,[18] like the earlier 'Succeedes') rather than 'will come' (future): this is a hypothetical future made present. It is a scenario which runs parallel to that form of the present which we see enacted on the stage. In both these passages there is a miniature narrative of future disaster which will actually come about, as if he is, at some level, living in an alternative time scheme, already unsettled, already damned.

Notoriously, Iago works on Othello by making him construct the narrative of Desdemona's adultery himself out of hints which Iago

[16] *Othello*, III iii 90–2.

[17] For the sense 'if' see *OED s.v.* when 8; Honigmann. Cp. Othello's use of 'when' in 'Ile see before I doubt; when I doubt, prove; | And on the proofe, there is no more but this, | Away at once with Love, or Jealousie' (III iii 193–5), where 'when' might mean 'if', but seems ominously definitive.

[18] Or perhaps a form of the perfect tense, equivalent to 'has come'.

supplies. At each step Iago entices Othello further into his trap by stalling on a significant word which Othello then repeats in order to understand what it is that Iago is concealing:

IAGO. Did *Michael Cassio*
When you[19] woo'd my Lady, know of your love?
OTH. He did, from first to last:
Why dost thou aske?
IAGO. But for a satisfaction of my Thought,
No further harme.
OTH. Why of thy thought, *Iago*?
IAGO. I did not thinke he had bin acquainted with hir.
OTH. O yes, and went betweene us very oft.
IAGO. Indeed?
OTH. Indeed? I indeed. Discern'st thou ought in that?
Is he not honest?
IAGO. Honest, my Lord?
OTH. Honest? I, Honest.
IAGO. My Lord, for ought I know.
OTH. What do'st thou thinke?
IAGO. Thinke, my Lord?
OTH. Thinke, my Lord? Alas, thou ecchos't me;
As if there were some Monster in thy thought
Too hideous to be shewne.[20]

Othello is drawn into speaking Iago's language. He is made to take 'thought', 'indeed', and 'honest' as fragments of a narrative which is being withheld and which demands to be uncovered. But there are variant readings in the Quarto text for the last three lines which create an important alternative possibility for the way in which the dialogue is being conducted:

OTH. Thinke, my Lord? By heauen he ecchoes me.
As if there were some monster in his thought:
Too hideous to be shewne.[21]

[19] My emendation, following Honigmann and Neill: you *Quarto*, he *Folio*.
[20] *Othello*, III iii 94–111.
[21] *The Tragœdy of Othello, The Moore of Venice* (London, 1622), p. 44.

This Quarto text ('he ecchoes... in his thought' rather than the Folio's 'thou eccho'st... in thy thought') has Othello turn aside from Iago, speaking of him in the third person; so the idea that there is some monster in Iago's thought arises first within the private space of Othello's imagination, within the temporary private stage space of the aside. This is the first time that Othello has spoken such an aside, has inhabited such a singular self-enclosed theatrical space, and it is ominously the moment when the monster first appears, albeit one which is not yet defined or named. Iago asks him not to 'build your selfe a trouble | Out of his scattering, and unsure observance',[22] but this is exactly what he does. He builds his own prison, and its materials are linguistic: his preference for the hypothetical and the fictional, his inability to test evidence; in short, his conceptual estrangement from the world around him.

The soliloquy which Othello speaks after Iago has left him moves queasily between statement and hypothesis, indicative and subjunctive:

> If I do prove her Haggard,
> Though that her Jesses were my deere heart-strings,
> I'ld whistle her off, and let her downe the winde
> To prey at Fortune. Haply, for I am blacke,
> And have not those soft parts of Conversation
> That Chamberers have: Or for I am declin'd
> Into the vale of yeares (yet that's not much)
> Shee's gone. I am abus'd, and my releefe
> Must be to loath her. Oh Curse of Marriage!
> That we can call these delicate Creatures ours,
> And not their Appetites?[23]

The extract begins with a narrative which is grammatically hypothetical—'If...'—but the imagery of a hawk which reverts to its wild state[24] is so vivid that its imaginative energy seems to override the tentative grammar and constitute Desdemona's wildness as fact rather than as possibility. The next sentence begins with 'Haply' (meaning

[22] *Othello*, III iii 153–4. [23] *Othello*, III iii 264–74.

[24] 'Haggard': wild female hawk; 'jesses': straps attached to the legs of a hawk.

'perhaps'), which introduces a number of possible explanations for her supposed infidelity before ending on 'Shee's gone', which is emphatically placed at the beginning of a line. Those two words sound like an inescapable statement, yet grammatically they still depend on 'Haply', and the intervening thoughts about the possible reasons for her defection form a parenthesis: the bare syntactical frame of the sentence is 'Haply... Shee's gone'. But the 'Haply' fails to control the energy with which Othello's imagination explores his presumed betrayal, so that the final 'Shee's gone' becomes more fact than possibility. Othello's imagination once again drives hypothesis into statement. The uncertain relation between statement and hypothesis is apparent in a tiny textual variant which creates two contrasting ways of performing this speech. The Folio's full stop after 'Shee's gone' makes the subsequent 'I am abused' a statement of fact, whereas the Quarto's punctuation keeps in play the supposition launched by 'Haply': it reads, 'Shee's gone, I am abus'd, and my releife | Must be to lothe her', which creates the sense, 'Perhaps she is gone, perhaps I am abused...'. Such is the power of Othello's habitual recourse to imagined narratives that even his momentary exclamation of trust in Desdemona, when she enters and he is struck by her physical presence rather than her imagined form, is couched in hypothetical terms: 'Looke where she comes: | If she be false, Heaven mock'd it selfe: | Ile not beleeve't'.[25]

Fatally, Othello becomes addicted to rhetorical questions. Unlike a genuine question, the work of an inquisitor who wishes to get at the truth, the rhetorical question closes off any response, fails to recognize the autonomous existence of the external world, and prefers the foregone conclusion[26] which is already present in the questioner's mind. In early seventeenth-century printing, question marks often

[25] *Othello*, III iii 281–3.

[26] The phrase comes from Othello's reaction to Iago's account of Cassio's dream; Cassio's erotic fantasy about Desdemona implies, says Othello, a 'foregone conclusion' (III iii 430), so the dream is construed as a narrative of the past in which Cassio's relationship with Desdemona is already consummated.

have the function of the modern exclamation mark, and in Othello's speeches his questions tend to be exclamations of (supposed) fact rather than genuine enquiries. When he says, 'Ha, ha, false to mee?',[27] is that a question (is the case still open?) or is it already a statement? When he says, 'Cuckold me?...With mine Officer?'[28] is that an incredulous question or a credulous exclamation? Othello's habit of uttering questions which are really only rhetorical questions prevents him from engaging with Desdemona's genuine questions as she tries to understand what it is that has enraged him, perhaps because he hears them as disingenuous exclamations, a pretence of innocence behind which guilt shelters. Her real, urgent question, 'Alas, what ignorant sin have I committed?'[29] is thrown back at her by Othello as a series of rhetorical questions which are actually exclamations of outrage:

What commited,
Committed? Oh, thou publicke Commoner,
I should make very Forges of my cheekes,
That would to Cynders burne up Modestie,
Did I but speake thy deedes. What commited?
Heaven stoppes the Nose at it, and the Moone winks:
The baudy winde that kisses all it meetes,
Is hush'd within the hollow Myne of Earth
And will not hear't. What commited?[30]

Instead of any actual allegation, any charge relating to specific times, places, and people, Othello deploys a rhetoric which enlists heaven, moon, and wind as players in his fiction. The act of explaining what she is supposed to have done is consigned to an impossible conditional tense ('I should make very Forges...Did I but speake thy deedes'),

[27] *Othello*, III iii 336. [28] *Othello*, IV i 197, 199.

[29] Unluckily, Desdemona has chosen a verb which is specially associated with adultery, because 'commit' without any further specification can simply mean 'commit adultery' (*OED s.v.* commit 6c), as when Poor Tom says, 'commit not, with mans sworne Spouse' (*King Lear*, III iv 79–80); see Gordon Williams, *A Glossary of Shakespeare's Sexual Language* (London, 1997), pp. 76–7.

[30] *Othello*, IV ii 73–81.

while the indicative mood is reserved for the horrified reaction of heaven. And this she cannot refute.

Othello's rhetorical questions generate powerful (and false) scenarios as they close off alternative answers from outside:

> What sense had I, of[31] her stolne houres of Lust?
> I saw't not, thought it not: it harm'd not me:
> I slept the next night well, fed well, was free, and merrie.
> I found not *Cassio's* kisses on her Lippes:
> ....
> I had beene happy, if the generall Campe,
> Pyoners and all, had tasted her sweet Body,
> So I had nothing knowne.[32]

The rhetorical question draws his mind to dwell upon a succession of sexual encounters between Cassio and Desdemona, while the 'if...' opens out a gross scenario of the whole army having Desdemona. Such stories take on a life of their own. Though the first lines occupy a past indicative tense, and the second group a past conditional, there seems now to be little distinction between event and surmise in Othello's mind.

This is one of the moments when the play opens out into what has been called 'long time'.[33] Although the action of the play, once the characters have reached Cyprus, is virtually continuous, and takes only two days (the first day is the day of their arrival, the first night is the night of the brawl; the second day sees Othello's mind poisoned by Iago, and the second night is the night when Desdemona is killed), the suggestion is repeatedly made that events—and specifically Desdemona's supposed affair with Cassio—have stretched out over a longer period. Othello's accusation that Desdemona 'with *Cassio*, hath the Act of shame | A thousand times committed'[34] is the most extravagant example of this imagined long time, but it is

[31] of *Quarto*, in *Folio*. [32] *Othello*, III iii 341–50.

[33] For recent discussions of the double time scheme see Honigmann, pp. 68–72, and Neill, pp. 33–6.

[34] *Othello*, V ii 209–10.

evoked also in Iago's account of Cassio's erotic dream, which cannot have taken place on any night which the play actually encompasses.[35] The crucial point about the 'long time' is that it lodges stubbornly and creatively in Othello's imagination, and as the play progresses the alternative times and spaces which his imagination fashions come to be more compelling for him than those which the other characters are shown to inhabit. Whereas Cinthio's novella which formed his principal source[36] deploys a leisurely time-scheme, Shakespeare has concentrated the action in a way which prevents the processes of the outside world—argument, refutation, discovery—from intervening in Othello's private chronology. Fatally, Desdemona and Cassio are transposed into this alternative time frame, and these alternative spaces, which have substance only in Othello's mind.

So powerfully does his imagination work that Iago's hesitant 'lye' generates a linguistic tirade which ends with Othello collapsing into a retreat from consciousness:

OTH. What hath he said?
IAGO. Why, that he did: I know not what he did.[37]
OTH. What? What?
IAGO. Lye.
OTH. With her?
IAGO. With her? On her: what you will.
OTH. Lye with her? lye on her? We say lye on her, when they be-lye-her. Lye with her: that's fullsome: Handkerchiefe: Confessions: Handkerchiefe. To confesse, and be hang'd for his labour. First, to be hang'd, and then to confesse: I tremble at it. Nature would not invest her selfe in such

[35] And cp. Emilia saying of the handkerchief, 'My wayward Husband hath a hundred times | Woo'd me to steale it' (III iii 296–7). 'Hundred' and 'thousand' are of course rhetorical flourishes, but nevertheless contribute to a sense of repeated events over an extended period.

[36] Giovanni Battista Giraldi Cinthio, *Gli Hecatommithi* (1566), apparently available to Shakespeare only in Italian; translated in Geoffrey Bullough, *Narrative and Dramatic Sources of Shakespeare*, 8 vols. (London, 1957–75), vii 239–52.

[37] Even the word 'did' has sexual connotations (Williams, pp. 101–2).

> shadowing passion, without some Instruction. It is not words that shakes me thus, (pish) Noses, Eares, and Lippes: is't possible. Confesse? Handkerchiefe? O divell.
>
> *Falls in a Traunce.*[38]

'What you will': make up your own interpretation, draw whatever picture you want. Othello's mind, working around the implications of 'lye', alights momentarily on the idea that Desdemona is being belied, slandered. His mind still entertains some doubts, for 'is't possible' hovers between question and exclamation, but he no longer has the syntax for rational examination of the external world. The time scheme of his own internal world is disturbed ('First, to be hang'd, and then to confesse'[39]). The fragmentary 'Noses, Eares, and Lippes' may be shards of retrospective or prospective narratives, of an erotic scenario, or even of a fantasy of the barbaric dismemberment of the lovers.[40] He tries to convince himself that there is some solid, factual basis for his agitation, for 'Nature would not invest her selfe in such shadowing passion, without some Instruction. It is not words that shakes me thus': that is, 'my nature would not dress itself in such an ominous passion without some real prior knowledge other than mere words'. The word 'shadowing' may mean 'enfolding',[41] since the passion wraps him round and insulates him from the rest of the world, from reality: he is wrapt, like Macbeth.[42] Or it may mean 'prefiguring',[43] since this present passion prefigures the greater passion in which he will kill Desdemona. But the word also carries the implication that this passion is indeed false: a 'shadow' in Elizabethan English was a delusive image, and specifically an actor.[44] Thus Othello half recognizes that Desdemona is belied, that his passion has no basis in fact, that he is acting a part, but these glimpsed possibilities are part of a syntax which is already disintegrating, and are glimpsed by a mind which is no longer its own place. Nor are his

[38] *Othello*, IV i 31–43.
[39] A formula which was also used to accuse someone of lying (Honigmann).
[40] Honigmann and Neill, *ad loc.* [41] *OED s.v.* shadow *v.* 6b.
[42] See p. 128 above. [43] *OED s.v.* shadowing 2a.
[44] *OED s.v.* shadow *n.* 6a, b.

words his own: his question, 'is't possible', simply repeats Iago's earlier phrase.[45] Finally he collapses into a private space beyond words, beyond reason.

In Act I Othello had been in control of strangeness, presenting the Venetian council with a carefully crafted story of the strangeness of others; now he lives more and more in the estranged world of his own devising. He returns in his memory to his own past, perhaps to a memory of lost stability, as he tells Desdemona that the missing handkerchief had been a precious present from his mother. It had magical powers to keep a spouse faithful, and, if lost, to induce faithlessness:

> There's Magicke in the web of it:
> A *Sybill* that had numbred in the world
> The Sun to course, two hundred compasses,
> In her Prophetticke furie sow'd the Worke:
> The Wormes were hallowed, that did breede the Silke,
> And it was dyde in Mummey, which the Skilfull
> Conserv'd of Maidens hearts.[46]

Like the traveller's tales of the Anthropophagi with which he had wooed her, this story astonishes Desdemona: 'Is't possible?', she exclaims, and 'Indeed? Is't true?', which are real, not rhetorical questions, and tentatively ward off Othello's story as a mere fiction. Like Alonzo's finger,[47] the handkerchief becomes an object which draws the protagonists into new forms of time and space. The extravagant narrative, which is ostensibly autobiographical, and so subject to no external control, is wielded by Othello as a means of co-opting Desdemona into a text which has already been woven by strange powers beyond her Venetian world.

When Othello prepares to kill Desdemona, he retreats into a complex world in which several new fictions meet. The bed which had been kept teasingly out of view through all the play's references to

[45] *Othello*, III iii 361; Othello repeats his question at IV ii 89.

[46] *Othello*, III iv 71–7. [47] See pp. 25–6 above.

marital and adulterous love-making now appears on stage,[48] but (like the handkerchief) this object forms another inset space onto which Othello projects his own fictions:

Enter Othello with a light, and Desdemona in her bed.
OTH. It is the Cause, it is the Cause (my Soule)
Let me not name it to you, you chaste Starres,
It is the Cause.[49]

What is the cause? What is the reason or motive for action, or the object or purpose of the action, or the legal case or accusation, or the side in a dispute which is adhered to?[50] There are too many meanings for 'cause', and too little definition. The cause cannot be named because it would pollute the chaste stars, but also because 'it is something he cannot bring himself to name, either because he fears to confront it, or because the true "cause" of his actions remains in some deep sense obscure to him'.[51] There is no cause outside his own imagination, outside of Iago's machinations. He continues:

Yet Ile not shed her blood,
Nor scarre that whiter skin of hers, then Snow,
And smooth as Monumentall Alablaster:[52]

Desdemona already appears like a funeral monument; already, in some alternative time-scheme, dead, buried, and turned into a memorial. 'Put out the Light, and then put out the Light', he says, reflecting that he can rekindle the torch which he is holding, but once he has killed her 'I know not where is that *Promethæan* heate | That can thy Light re-Lume'. The verb 'relume' is Shakespeare's coinage, its novelty falling on the ear as a reminder of the strangeness of what he is proposing. Her breath as he bends to kiss her almost persuades

[48] See Neill, pp. 130–8.
[49] *Othello*, V ii 1–3. I have added 'with a light' from the stage direction in *Quarto*.
[50] Respectively, *OED s.v.* cause *n.* 3; 4; 7–9; 11. 'What was thy cause? Adultery?', asks Lear (*King Lear*, IV vi 108–9).
[51] Neill, p. 372.
[52] *Othello*, V ii 3–5.

'Justice to breake her Sword', an image which casts him momentarily in this allegorical role. He is carefully scripting the scene.

The space between Othello and the sleeping Desdemona is one which he seeks to control, as his fictions begin to issue in action. The shifting pronouns which he uses for her reveal some uncertainty in his approach. After initial lines spoken about her in the third person as he approaches her ('Yet Ile not shed her blood') he starts to use the familiar pronouns 'thou' or 'thee' ('Be thus when thou art dead, and I will kill thee, | And love thee after'). These forms are used between intimates, or from a social superior to an inferior, or as an insult in moments of anger: the register of 'thou' tends to be more intense than that of the 'you' forms.[53] But as she awakes he switches to the cooler 'you' ('Have you pray'd to night, *Desdemon*?'), distancing himself from her, using the formal mode of address as a way of warding off the dangerously loving, indeed, erotic, intimacy, which has come close to undoing his purpose. But he cannot maintain 'you' for more than a few lines, and as soon as he speaks of killing her, the familiar pronoun returns ('I would not kill thy unprepared Spirit... I would not kill thy Soule'); now the intensity has changed from erotic intimacy to a weird mixture of compassion for her and dedication to the approaching killing. The two feelings meet in words such as: 'Sweete Soule, take heed, take heed of Perjury, | Thou art on thy death-bed'. An alternative scenario appears briefly when he warns her

[53] For the distinction between 'you' and 'thou' see Charles Barber, *Early Modern English* (London, 1976; second edition, Edinburgh, 1997), pp. 152–7; Jonathan Hope, *Shakespeare's Grammar* (London, 2003), pp. 72–81. In Act I, for example, Iago and Rodorigo use 'you' to the senator Brabantio; enraged at being disturbed by his social inferiors in the middle of the night, he replies with 'thou', until he has to enlist Rodorigo's help in finding Desdemona, when he switches to the polite 'you'. When handing his daughter over to Othello he insultingly calls Othello 'thee' (I iii 194–6, 293–4). Othello sometimes uses 'thee' to Desdemona in moments of intimacy (his first words directly addressed to her are 'Come *Desdemona*, I have but an houre | Of Love, of wordly matter, and direction | To spend with thee' (I iii 299–301)), but after he has begun to suspect her he uses the formal, distancing pronoun 'you' ('This hand of yours requires | A sequester from Liberty' (III iv 39–40)), or 'thou' in speeches of anger or contempt: 'Heaven truely knowes, that thou art false as hell' (IV ii 40). She calls him 'you' throughout: as her husband, he is her superior.

that a denial cannot prevent him from killing her, since her denial cannot strangle his intention to strangle her:

> For to deny each Article with Oath,
> Cannot remove, nor choake the strong Conception
> That I do grone withall.[54]

This creates an image of Desdemona's denial strangling the idea with which Othello is pregnant and in labour. Has his mind already moved the fictional narrative of her adultery forward to the stages of her conception, pregnancy, and birth pangs? Her denial, he says, 'do'st stone my heart'—turns it to stone, but also kills it by stoning, as in the punishment for adultery.[55] Both images momentarily transfer to Othello traces of the crime of which he accuses her, a most uncanny testimony to the power of their intimacy, and the power of his imagination both to multiply and to fragment himself—and her.

At the end of Cinthio's story, the Moor is sent into exile;[56] in Shakespeare's play, Othello retreats to his own *Heimat*, which is the story of his career. His final speech is his final transposition of himself, first into rhetorically turned exemplum ('one that lov'd not wisely, but too well'); then into exotic narrative ('one, whose hand, | (Like the base Indian[57]) threw a Pearle away | Richer then all his Tribe'); and then into autobiography:

> in *Aleppo* once,
> Where a malignant and a Turbond-Turke
> Beate a Venetian, and traduc'd the State,
> I tooke by th'throat the circumcised Dogge,
> And smoate him, thus.[58]

[54] *Othello*, V ii 54–6.

[55] This is the *OED*'s first example of the verb 'stone' meaning 'turn to stone' (*OED s.v.* stone *v.* 2); the meaning 'kill by stoning' (*OED* 1) is attested from the middle ages. For stoning as a punishment for sexual transgression see Deuteronomy xxii 21–4, John viii 7.

[56] Bullough, vii 252.

[57] I emend the Folio's 'Iudean' to the Quarto's 'Indian', following Honigmann and Neill.

[58] *Othello*, V ii 350–4.

On 'thus' he stabs himself, superimposing past and present, and in so doing casting himself as a second malignant Turk being killed by a second Othello. Multiplied and divided: both Venetian Christian and circumcised Turk; divided, at the end, between belonging to Venice and belonging to her enemies, fractured precisely along the lines of strangeness which Rodorigo had announced and Iago had exploited.

This is an appropriately troubled form of agency and selfhood with which to conclude Othello's story, for his tragedy has entailed the blurring of the boundaries between his self and Iago. As Othello plots revenge, we ask, 'Who acts?', as we ask 'Who acts?' when Macbeth plots the murder of Duncan. As Iago's scheme began to take root in Othello's mind, the two men grew together in such an intimate relationship that Othello's capacity for thought and action seemed to have been usurped by Iago, and yet it was always Othello's mind which constructed the story. So intense is this intimacy that at the end of Act III scene iii, when Iago has succeeded *ex nihilo* in convincing him of Desdemona's adultery, Othello and Iago kneel and swear common purpose in his revenge. When Othello says to Iago 'I am bound to thee for ever', and Iago ends the scene by echoing 'I am your owne for ever', these ominous lines sound like a parodic marriage vow.[59] As he is drawn into this bond with Iago, he is drawn into his own singularity of time and space where no one but Iago—his author—can reach him.

[59] *Othello*, III iii 217, 482. For the modern stage tradition which gives Iago suppressed homosexual feelings for Othello see Neill, pp. 85–9.

9

SHAKESPEARE
King Lear

In *King Lear* characters exist in an uncertain, displaced, relationship to language. They use it to serve their own ends, and yet it never seems quite to be theirs. The play is built from commonplaces and proverbs and rhetorical formulae, and from quotations of fable and song, as if many voices, many generations of experience inhabit each

This chapter adapts some material from my essay 'The Play of Quotation and Commonplace in *King Lear*', in *Toward a Definition of Topos: Approaches to Analogical Reasoning*, edited by Lynette Hunter (London, 1991), pp. 78–129. The play is quoted from the Nonesuch edition, which follows the Folio text (1623); some readings are also quoted from the Quarto (1608): *M. William Shak-speare: His True Chronicle Historie of the life and death of King Lear and his three Daughters* (London, 1608), taken from *Shakespeare's Plays in Quarto: A Facsimile Edition of Copies Primarily from the Henry E. Huntington Library*, edited by Michael J. B. Allen and Kenneth Muir (Berkeley, 1981). There has been much debate over the status and relationship of the two texts. Until the 1980s, editors generally produced a conflated text by moving eclectically between the two versions, e.g. *King Lear*, edited by Kenneth Muir, The Arden Shakespeare, second series (London, 1964; revised edition, 1972). Then scholars began to see the Quarto and Folio as representing two distinct states of the play, the Quarto preserving the original version (albeit in a badly printed text: see Peter W. M. Blayney: *The Texts of 'King Lear' and their Origins: Volume I: Nicholas Okes and the First Quarto* (Cambridge, 1982)) and the Folio a revised text (see *The Division of the Kingdoms: Shakespeare's Two Versions of 'King Lear'*, edited by Gary Taylor and Michael Warren (Oxford, 1983)). This led to the view that the two texts should be offered to readers as distinct plays, so that the one-volume Oxford Shakespeare of 1986 provides both *The History of King Lear* (based on the Quarto) and *The Tragedy of King Lear* (based on the Folio). Subsequently Jay L. Halio's edition of *The Tragedy of King Lear*, The New Cambridge Shakespeare (Cambridge, 1992) follows the Folio, while Stanley Wells's *The History of King Lear*, The Oxford Shakespeare (Oxford, 2000), follows the Quarto. Recent studies have cast doubt on the case for there having

phrase.[1] In other texts, such ghostly presences in the utterances might lend them authority, for we customarily cite precedents in order to give stability and persuasiveness to our own words. But instead of giving such speech solidity, the play of quotation and commonplace in *King Lear* dissolves coherence, displaces the individual characters, prising apart the relationship between self and utterance. Who are these speakers? Whom do they become as they speak? What are they made into as they are quoted? A decomposition of language decomposes its speakers.

Characters' words are quoted by others,[2] often unconsciously, so that weird echoes are set up across the play, making unsure the boundaries of the self, the relationship of speaker to language, and the significance of the words themselves. Macbeth's voice spoke the words of the witches, Othello's voice the words of Iago; in this play Shakespeare's exploration of the dissociation between voice and self reaches more deeply. Cordelia's 'Nothing' sounds also in the mouths of Lear, Edmond, Gloster, and the Fool. Characters put on forms of speech which are disguises, but these disguises solidify, or they metamorphose into yet other shapes, as Edgar becomes Poor Tom, a peasant, a stage yokel, and a knight whose 'name is lost'.[3] New kinds of self are generated and decay through speech as it proliferates.

It is Lear who begins to make language the subject as well as the medium of the tragedy. In the first scene he conscripts everyone into the

been a really substantial revision of the play, and R. A. Foakes's *King Lear*, The Arden Shakespeare, third series (Walton-on-Thames, 1997) presents a conflated text with a bias towards the Folio.

[1] For the centrality of commonplaces and proverbs in Renaissance thought see Ann Moss, *Printed Commonplace-Books and the Structuring of Renaissance Thought* (Oxford, 1996); the principal literary example of the use of proverbs is the *Adagia* of Erasmus (first published 1500, but repeatedly expanded and reprinted). Brian Vickers relates the play to the tradition of paradox in '"King Lear" and Renaissance Paradoxes', *Modern Language Review*, 63 (1968), 305–14. See also Joel B. Altman, *The Tudor Play of Mind* (Berkeley, 1978).

[2] Stephen Booth notes that characters in *King Lear* sometimes sound disconcertingly like other characters with whom they have no connection (*'King Lear', 'Macbeth', Indefinition, and Tragedy* (New Haven, 1983), p. 22).

[3] *King Lear*, V iii 119.

text of his own will, a text which he shapes through his rhetorical power. He commands presence and absence, demands speech, and refuses to accept silence. His first words are imperatives: 'Attend the Lords of France & Burgundy...Give me the Map there.[4] Know, that we have divided | In three our Kingdome'.[5] But when he turns to ask his daughters to tell him how much they love him, he initiates a language game whose rules are uncertain and whose outcome unpredictable:

Tell me my daughters
(Since now we will divest us both of Rule,
Interest of Territory, Cares of State)
Which of you shall we say doth love us most,
That we, our largest bountie may extend
Where Nature doth with merit challenge. *Gonerill,*
Our eldest borne, speake first.[6]

Lear's 'we' in 'Which of you shall we say doth love us most' slips between being the assertive royal plural and the wheedling 'we' of a parent playing a game with his child, but though the daughters are made to speak, it is Lear who will ultimately 'say' who loves him most. Goneril realizes that a performance is expected of her, and she performs an oration on the topic 'love':

Sir, I love you more then word can weild the matter,
Deerer then eye-sight, space, and libertie,
Beyond what can be valewed, rich or rare,
No lesse then life, with grace, health, beauty, honor:
As much as Childe ere lov'd, or Father found.
A love that makes breath poore, and speech unable,
Beyond all manner of so much I love you.[7]

A Renaissance audience trained in the arts of rhetoric would have recognized Goneril's devices: hyperbole (*passim*), asyndeton (the emphatic suppression of conjunctions in her list 'grace, health, beauty, honor'), auxesis (moving from one idea, 'Deerer then eye-sight', to a bigger, grander claim, 'No lesse then life'), ploce (the

[4] Or in the Quarto, more brusquely, just 'The Map there'.
[5] *King Lear*, I i 33–7. [6] *King Lear*, I i 48–54. [7] *King Lear*, I i 55–61.

insistent repetition of 'love'), the alliterative linking of 'rich or rare' and 'word can weild', and epanalepsis, which begins and ends the passage with the same phrase, 'I love you'. In addition, she makes the double assertion, framing this performance, that her love is so strong that it disables her speech. Regan cannot match Goneril's rhetoric, so she caps it in the only way she can, outdoing Goneril's hyperbole: 'I professe | My selfe an enemy to all other joyes'.[8]

Then Lear turns to Cordelia:

> Now our Joy,
> Although our last and least; to whose yong love,
> The Vines of France, and Milke of Burgundie,
> Strive to be interest. What can you say, to draw
> A third, more opilent then your Sisters? speake.
> COR. Nothing my lord.
> LEAR. Nothing?
> COR. Nothing.
> LEAR. Nothing will come of nothing, speake againe.[9]

The play on 'last and least' and the imaging of the two suitors in terms of the products of their countries keep Cordelia within Lear's domain, an object in the game in which he and the suitors are 'interest'. But Cordelia's reply moves the two of them into a parenthetical space within this staged game, a tense semi-privacy where their words are neither wholly intimate nor wholly public, but partake of both idioms.[10] When Cordelia says 'Nothing', Lear's command is broken, and for the moment he is helplessly reduced to quoting her reply. He then manages to turn it into a proverbial commonplace, 'Nothing will come of nothing',[11] whose impersonality momentarily protects them both from the breach which has opened, but the proverb also tries to draw her back into the world of consensus, of communal wisdom, which is additionally, here, the realm of rewards, of speech which has

[8] *King Lear*, I i 72–3. [9] *King Lear*, I i 82–90.

[10] Stanley Cavell discusses the possible degrees of the public and the private in this exchange (*Disowning Knowledge in Six Plays of Shakespeare* (Cambridge, 1987), p. 64).

[11] Morris Palmer Tilley, *A Dictionary of the Proverbs in England in the Sixteenth and Seventeenth Centuries* (Ann Arbor, 1950), N 285.

material results. Cordelia tries to avoid the inflation of rhetoric, tries to make her words fit what she feels:

> I love your Majesty
> According to my bond, no more nor lesse.[12]

Her sisters have spoken both more and less than they feel. She appeals to her 'bond' with her father, or rather with her King. Unhappily, 'bond' is an ambiguous word, meaning not only 'uniting force' but also cold 'duty' and, more coldly still, 'shackle'.[13] Lear, made to interpret Cordelia's 'bond', and no doubt hearing its unexpected steeliness, tries to woo (or threaten) her by reminding her of another bond, that between speech and material fortune: 'Mend your speech a little, | Least you may marre your Fortunes'.[14] Her reply attempts to mend not her own speech but the inflated rhetoric—coercive on one side, dissembling on the other, in both cases grasping—which her father and her sisters have been using:

> Good my Lord,
> You have begot me, bred me, lov'd me.
> I returne those duties backe as are right fit,
> Obey you, Love you, and most Honour you.[15]

Even here too glib a rhetoric is avoided through the lack of a precise link between the two sets of terms, for there is no exact parallel between 'begot . . . bred . . . lov'd' and 'Obey . . . Love . . . Honour': they do not return term for term, measure for measure; they observe a discipline, while saying that love cannot itemize and account for itself so exactly. When Lear then exclaims, 'So young, and so untender?', Cordelia replies, 'So young my Lord, and true'. Lear resorts to a neologism, for 'untender' is apparently Shakespeare's coinage here,[16] as Lear reverses the commonplace link between 'youth' and 'tender'.[17] Cordelia claims not tenderness but truth, and to be

[12] *King Lear*, I i 92–3.

[13] Respectively, *OED s.v.* bond 7; 6b; 1, 5. For 'bond' here see Leo Salingar, *Dramatic Form in Shakespeare and the Jacobeans* (Cambridge, 1986), pp. 96–8.

[14] *King Lear*, I i 94–5.

[15] *King Lear*, I i 95–8.

[16] *OED s.v.* untender 1.

[17] *OED s.v.* tender 4.

'true' can apply to both a person and a speech, so that through her revised proverb she is implicitly revealing the falsity of the exchanges, bound into a mercenary rhetoric, which have been taking place between her father and her sisters. The contrast between Goneril and Regan's hyperbole and Cordelia's 'Nothing' is the first indication that Lear has made language untrue, that the bond between signifier and signified will be strained, and, indeed, that the signifier will drift away into signifying nothing.[18] Lear wants to retain 'The name, and all th'addition to a King', without the 'Sway, | Revennew, Execution of the rest',[19] but he has not thought about what it means to have the word without the thing itself.

The scene in which Cordelia is banished enacts a form of ventriloquism, with Lear attempting to produce from his daughters words which are an echo of his, rather than their own. The next scene extends this idea, with Edmond, Gloster's bastard son, as the ventriloquist, for the play which had begun with Lear disinheriting Cordelia continues with Edmond's plot to oust Edgar from his inheritance. Like Cordelia, in this respect at least, Edmond immediately announces the bond which he recognizes:

BAST. Thou Nature art my Goddesse, to thy Law
My services are bound, wherefore should I
Stand in the plague of custome, and permit
The curiosity of Nations, to deprive me?
For that I am some twelve, or fourteene Moonshines
Lag of a Brother? Why Bastard? Wherefore base?
When my Dimensions are as well compact,
My minde as generous, and my shape as true
As honest Madams issue? Why brand they us
With Base? With basenes Barstadie? Base, Base?[20]

[18] Several images have suggested that love is weighty and speech light, insubstantial. Cordelia says, 'I am sure my love's | More ponderous then my tongue' (I i 77–8); and 'I cannot heave | My heart into my mouth' (I i 91–2). The Quarto's 'richer' makes the point more simply, but the Folio's 'ponderous' gives love a weight which is signalled also in the verb 'heave'.

[19] *King Lear*, I i 137–8.

[20] *King Lear*, I ii 1–10.

Edmond invokes 'Nature', as any Renaissance man might, as the basis for his actions.[21] But when appealing to 'Nature' he sets in motion a complex word, and this term will sound through the play. Edmond is Gloster's 'natural' son in the sense that he is illegitimate, but he proves not to be 'natural' in the sense of one who acts humanely in accordance with familial affection.[22] The law of nature prompts him first to self-advancement (rather than to self-defence, which is commonly regarded as the first law of nature[23]), and he helps dissolve natural bonds between Gloster and Edgar so as to place them in a state of nature, that is, a state of mutual war.[24] He defines Nature by contrast with 'the plague of custome' and 'the curiosity[25] of Nations', so that the structures of civilization are said to be founded not on nature but against nature. One hears the sarcastic quotation marks which he places around the terms 'base' and 'bastard', as he does later in the speech around their opposite, 'legitimate': 'fine word: Legitimate'. Here, to quote is to parody, to hold up a concept to sceptical view, to control its meaning, to drain a word of its customary, commonplace power.

When Gloster enters, Edmond manipulates his father in a dialogue which sounds like a quotation of Cordelia's exchange with Lear in the previous scene:

GLOU. What Paper were you reading?
BAST. Nothing my Lord.
GLOU. No? what needed then that terrible dispatch of it into your Pocket? The quality of nothing, hath not such neede to hide it selfe.[26]

Edmond himself becomes the ventriloquist now, providing Gloster with a letter supposedly written by his half-brother Edgar. As Gloster reads this letter aloud, Edgar is doubly displaced: we hear not Edgar's voice and Edgar's words, but Gloster's voice reading words attributed

[21] On the significance of the concept of 'nature' in this play see John F. Danby, *Shakespeare's Doctrine of Nature* (London, 1948); William R. Elton, *'King Lear' and the Gods* (San Marino, Calif., 1966); Salingar, pp. 119–23.

[22] *OED s.v.* natural 13c, 16a.

[23] Thomas Hobbes, *Leviathan* (London, 1651), p. 64.

[24] Hobbes, pp. 60–3.

[25] fancy, whim (*OED s.v.* curiosity 8).

[26] *King Lear*, I ii 31–5.

to Edgar but scripted by Edmond. Edgar himself has not yet appeared on stage. Gloster's own speech is a collection of commonplaces: he is thinking in terms borrowed from the Book of Homilies and similar conventional texts:[27]

> These late Eclipses in the Sun and Moone portend no good to us... Love cooles, friendship falls off, Brothers divide. In Cities, mutinies; in Countries, discord; in Pallaces, Treason; and the Bond crack'd, 'twixt Sonne and Father.[28]

The obtrusive rhetorical patterning of the speech alerts us to its secondhand quality; it is 'dull stale tyred', as Edmond described the marital bed.[29] Edmond subsequently quotes his father's philosophy, transposing the tired saws of legitimate discourse from his father's voice into his own ironic inflection:

> when we are sicke in fortune, often the surfets of our own behaviour, we make guilty of our disasters the Sun, the Moone, and Starres, as if we were villaines on necessitie, Fooles by heavenly compulsion, Knaves, Theeves, and Treachers by Sphericall predominance. Drunkards, Lyars, and Adulterers by an inforc'd obedience of Planatary influence; and all that we are evill in, by a divine thrusting on.[30]

Edmond is asserting his autonomy through this parody, but this scepticism is recognizably modish, just as Gloster's credulity is recognizable too. If Gloster has been listening to the Homilies, Edmond has been reading Montaigne.[31] We hear that both characters, in asserting their places, speak commonplaces.

Like Iago stage-managing Othello, Edmond prepares the entrance of his brother, and as Edgar enters, Edmond begins to play his new part, taking his cue, putting on the role of 'villainous Melancholly', and—anticipating the disguise which Edgar will soon be forced to adopt—beginning 'with a sighe like *Tom* o'Bedlam'. He is framing Edgar in more than one sense. Edmond ironically mimics their

[27] Wells, p. 120. [28] *King Lear*, I ii 103–9.
[29] *King Lear*, I ii 13. [30] *King Lear*, I ii 119–26.
[31] For Shakespeare's use of Montaigne (whose essay 'Des cannibales' explores the precarious antithesis between nature and custom) see Salingar, pp. 107–39.

father's concerns, so that Edgar at first seems to find it difficult to recognize his brother's voice:

Enter Edgar.

Pat: he comes like the Catastrophe of the old Comedie: my Cue is villainous Melancholly, with a sighe like *Tom* o'Bedlam.— O these Eclipses do portend these divisions. Fa, Sol, La, Me.

EDG. How now Brother *Edmond*, what serious contemplation are you in?

BAST. I am thinking Brother of a prediction I read this other day, what should follow these Eclipses.

EDG. Do you busie yourselfe with that?[32]

When Edgar leaves, Edmond comments, 'A Credulous Father, and a Brother Noble...on whose foolish honestie | My practises ride easie'.[33] The frame is complete, displacing Edgar into a different form of stage space from that which the others occupy; soon he will be an outcast, nearly naked, and seemingly without rational speech. While the characters are quoted, framed, exhibited, so too are their philosophies. But Edmond the puppeteer is not granted a privileged space, for in spite of his appeal to nature rather than custom, he is himself exhibiting the customary theatrical disaffection of the marginalized malcontent who seeks to displace those at the centre.

Characters in this play change voices and swap places. There are many uncanny links which suggest that characters may substitute one for another, that their roles are parallel, or form parts of the same mythic role.[34] Edmond echoes Cordelia, but in other respects it is Edgar and Cordelia who are paired, as the dutiful children unjustly banished. Cordelia and the Fool are paired as truth-tellers to Lear, to the extent that in his last moments Lear uses the endearment 'Foole' to apply to Cordelia when he says 'And my poore Foole is hang'd';[35] some editors have wondered whether the roles might be doubled in performance. Lear and Gloster are paired in being fathers who both mistake the true natures of their children. In his madness Lear sees

[32] *King Lear*, I ii 134–42. [33] *King Lear*, I ii 177–80.
[34] Cp. Freud's reading of *Macbeth*, p. 37 above. [35] *King Lear*, V iii 304.

Gloster as '*Gonerill* with a white beard'.[36] And Lear and the Fool are twinned (since the Fool's age is never specified, he might be either a brother or a son to Lear), in that the Fool provides a necessary if sometimes unwelcome voice which replaces the inner voice, of insight and love, which Lear has silenced.

In the margin of the play's plot, but central to its tragic work, the Fool contributes a disruptive commentary on Lear's actions. This is in part built up from parodic quotations of Lear's own words, and since the Fool's role was probably written for Robert Armin, a talented mimic, it is possible that on stage his parodic quotation of Lear included mimicry of Richard Burbage's voice and gestures. He soon makes a reference back to the play's opening scene, quoting Lear's actions:

> why this fellow ha's banished two on's Daughters, and did the third a blessing against his will.[37]

This re-presentation of the banishment of Cordelia unnerves us in that it reverses what we have seen on stage, yet at a deeper level it helps to confirm that we were right in interpreting the scene through the template of romance,[38] which told us that (as in the Cinderella story) it was the third child who would ultimately be blessed, and the two elder sisters punished. In Act I scene iv the Fool recapitulates the fatal exchange between Lear and Cordelia when Kent says of the Fool's song:

> KENT. This is nothing Foole.
> FOOLE. Then 'tis like the breath of an unfeed Lawyer, you gave me nothing for't, can you make no use of nothing Nuncle?
> LEAR. Why no Boy,
> Nothing can be made out of nothing.[39]

The Fool expects to be paid for his speech: so did Goneril and Regan. This reprise of the opening scene is developed when the Fool leads Lear back to Cordelia's word, 'Nothing', as if by asking 'can you make no use of nothing Nuncle?' he is gently suggesting that Lear might return to

36 *King Lear*, IV vi 96.
37 *King Lear*, I iv 100–2.
38 For the romance elements in the play see Salingar, pp. 91–106.
39 *King Lear*, I iv 126–30.

Cordelia's word and rethink its meaning, that he might actually make use of her 'nothing'. But Lear will only repeat, not revise, the past, and just reiterates what he had said to Cordelia: 'Nothing can be made out of nothing'. He stubbornly adheres to his proverb.

The Fool's speeches repeatedly quote the action, recapitulating it in miniature, fragmented forms, thus reproducing the division of the kingdom in a series of emblems. These are not the kind of emblems which come from the sophisticated, morally stable, didactic world of the Renaissance emblem book, but instead evoke the half-playful, half-educative world of the nursery:

FOOLE. Nunckle, give me an egge, and Ile give thee two Crownes.
LEAR. What two Crownes shall they be?
FOOLE. Why after I have cut the egge i'th'middle and eate up the meate, the two Crownes of the egge: when thou clovest thy crowne[40] i'th'middle, and gav'st away both parts, thou boar'st thine Asse on thy backe o're the durt, thou had'st little wit in thy bald crowne, when thou gav'st thy golden one away; if I speake like my selfe in this, let him be whipt that first findes it so.[41]

This quotes the moment in the first scene when Lear says to Albany and Cornwall, 'this Coronet part betweene you'.[42] The Fool has turned Lear's crown into two halves of an (empty) egg shell, and Lear himself into the foolish man who in the Aesopian fable carries his own ass on his back.[43] The Fool's emblems and fables are efforts at undoing what Lear has made too rigid, enlisting collective proverbial wisdom against Lear's egoism, an egoism which is itself entrenched in proverbial shorthand, thus warding off variety and *copia*, and any true ground of meeting.

Lear uses emblems to give himself stability and coherence at moments when his world seems to be dissolving. In the first scene he had pictured himself as a figure in an emblem of old age ('while we | Unburthen'd crawle toward death'), and later he will see himself as a

[40] crowne *Quarto*; Crownes *Folio*. [41] *King Lear*, I iv 148–57.
[42] *King Lear*, I i 140. [43] Foakes, p. 200.

damned soul 'bound | Upon a wheele of fire'.[44] After his first contretemps with Goneril, Lear invokes the emblem of Ingratitude:

> Ingratitude! thou Marble-hearted Fiend,
> More hideous when thou shew'st thee in a Child,
> Then the Sea-monster.[45]

And when Lear's understanding of Goneril is shown to be faulty he produces allegories of his own mental operations in an attempt to keep his grip on his own identity:

> Beate at this gate that let thy Folly in,
> And thy deere Judgement out.[46]

King Leir in the source play had also used emblems to describe his condition, but there the rhetoric is significantly different:

> I am as kind as is the Pelican,
> That kills it selfe, to save her young ones lives:
> And yet as jelous as the princely Eagle,
> That kils her young ones, if they do but dazell
> Upon the radiant splendour of the Sunne.[47]

Leir's commonplace comparisons are neatly worked-out similes, whereas Lear's are angry metaphorical fragments.

Lear's first moments of doubt take the form of incipient self-estrangement, as he switches between third- and first-person pronouns,[48] between an external and an internal perspective:

> LEAR. Are you our Daughter?
> GON. I would you would make use of your good wisedome
> (Whereof I know you are fraught), and put away

[44] *King Lear*, I i 39–40; IV vii 46–7. Wells p. 54 reproduces an illustration of a man bound on a wheel surrounded by flames from Giovanni Ferro, *Teatro d'imprese* (Venice, 1623).

[45] *King Lear*, I iv 251–3.

[46] *King Lear*, I iv 263–4.

[47] Anon, *The True Chronicle Historie of King Leir* (1605), in *Narrative and Dramatic Sources of Shakespeare*, edited by Geoffrey Bullough, 8 vols. (London, 1957–75), vii 349.

[48] Shakespeare uses similar illeism when Othello says, 'Man but a Rush against *Othello's* brest, | And he retires. Where should *Othello* go?' (*Othello*, V ii 268–9), in which the distanced self is made the subject of a despairing rhetorical question.

These dispositions, which of late transport you
From what you rightly are.
FOOLE. May not an Asse know, when the Cart drawes the Horse?
Whoop Jugge I love thee.
LEAR. Do's any here know me?
This is not *Lear*:
Do's *Lear* walke thus? Speake thus? Where are his eies?
Either his Notion weakens, his Discernings
Are Lethargied. Ha! Waking? 'Tis not so?
Who is it that can tell me who I am?
FOOLE. *Lears* shadow.[49]

This is the Folio text. Lear's speech runs thus in the Quarto:

LEAR. Doth any here know mee? why this is not *Lear*, doth *Lear* walke thus? speake thus? where are his eyes? either his notion, weaknes, or his discernings are lethergie, sleeping or wakeing; ha! sure tis not so, who is it that can tell me who I am? *Lears* shadow? I would learne that, for by the markes of souerainti e, knowledge, and reason, I should bee false perswaded I had daughters.[50]

The speech starts and ends in the Folio as forceful iambic verse, but loses its way metrically and grammatically in the middle ('Either his Notion weakens, his Discernings | Are Lethargied'); perhaps Lear momentarily loses his grip on his sentence when he begins to contemplate the possibility that his intellect is weakening.[51] His rhetorical questions are designed to remind Goneril that it is her father and her king whom she is treating in this way, but they take on a plangent life of their own, turning from rhetorical questions into real questions which need reassuring answers. The blurring of the grammar of mastery (which is how the rhetorical question normally sounds) into the grammar of

It contrasts with the egoistical confidence of Caesar's illeism in such declarations as '*Cæsar* shall forth', and 'Danger knowes full well | That *Cæsar* is more dangerous than he' (*Julius Caesar*, II ii 10, 44–5), though the self thus fashioned proves brittle through its over-confidence.

[49] *King Lear*, I iv 209–22. [50] *Quarto*, sig. D1^{v}.

[51] It is difficult to know whether the syntactical awkwardness is Shakespeare's representation of Lear's angry incoherence, or the printer's corruption of a grammatically correct text.

bewildered dependency (the real question) signals a fissure in Lear's mind: 'Do's any here know me? . . . Who is it that can tell me who I am?' The reply to that last question, '*Lears* shadow', is assigned to the Fool by the Folio, but to Lear himself in the Quarto. Spoken by the Fool, it is a statement; spoken by Lear, it could be another rhetorical question, or it could be an exclamation, a moment of recognition: '*Lears* shadow!'[52] That the words can so easily be reassigned indicates the way in which the Fool functions as the external voice of Lear, while Lear answers his own questions, engaged in an internal rather than an external dialogue.[53] '*Lears* shadow' reduces Lear to a mere image, or an actor, or a ghost; or to being his own constant companion, his own Fool.[54]

The Fool's running commentary on the action moves between text and margin. In some respects he is another voice for Lear, and in a morality play he might be Lear's good angel, but he is also a voice for the audience, articulating the protests and advice which we would wish to speak ourselves. His own direct exchanges with Lear are often cast in the form of riddles, their surrealism and indirection reflecting back to Lear his own lack of sense and logic, and his refusal to attend to logic or argument:

> FOOLE. . . . thou canst tell why ones nose stands i'th' middle on's face?
> LEAR. No.
> FOOLE. Why to keepe ones eyes of either side's nose, that what a man cannot smell out, he may spy into.[55]

This begins as a rather feeble schoolboy joke ('Why is your nose in the middle of your face? To keep your eyes apart.') but then metamorphoses into a proleptic version of Regan's savage command that the blinded Gloster 'smell | His way to Dover'.[56] The Fool's speeches never settle into

[52] In seventeenth-century typography the question mark was often used where modern punctuation would use an exclamation mark.

[53] Foakes (following Muir) patches together the two texts to form a dialogue which has no basis in either of the extant authorities: '*Lear*. Who is it that can tell me who I am? *Fool*. Lear's shadow. *Lear*. I would learn that . . .'.

[54] Respectively, *OED s.v.* shadow 6a, 6b, 7, 8. Cavell discusses the possible significance of 'Lear's shadow' on p. 79.

[55] *King Lear*, I v 19–23.

[56] *King Lear*, III vii 92–3.

a predictable pattern. Commonplace, proverb, and song are turned from being communal resources of experience and moral thought into being fragments; the Fool has no voice, but many quotations. Much of the Fool's language parodies the modes of educative enquiry: there are traces of the nursery in which children ask questions and adults answer. There are bizarre taxonomies, as when the Fool produces a catalogue of animals according to how they are tied, and a classification of forms of madness.[57] His songs quote literary sources (including *Twelfth Night*), and his prophecy is a prophecy of a prophecy: 'This prophecie *Merlin* shall make, for I live before his time'.[58] The Fool's many voices—fragments and parodies of rational discourse—provide the only sustained commentary which the play can muster on Lear's behaviour, but he abruptly disappears halfway through, his exit-line displacing him into an inverted time scheme: 'And Ile go to bed at noone'.[59]

The mode of speech adopted by Edgar in his disguise as the mad beggar Poor Tom likewise moves between different voices, and multiple quotations. He takes over the Fool's rhyming verses, and part of his function as Lear's interlocutor.[60] Poor Tom's first words are distracted and fragmentary ('Fathom, and halfe, Fathom and halfe; poore *Tom*') but his first substantial speech anthologizes different kinds of utterance. Lear asks him, 'Did'st thou give all to thy Daughters?' (for the world is now reduced to being a mirror of his own case), and he replies:

> Who gives any thing to poore *Tom*? Whom the foule fiend hath led through Fire, and through Flame, through foord,[61] and Whirle-Poole, o're Bog, and Quagmire, that hath laid Knives under his Pillow, and Halters in his Pue, set Rats-bane by his Porredge, made him Proud of heart, to ride on a Bay trotting Horse, over foure incht Bridges, to course his owne shadow for a Traitor. Blisse thy five Wits, *Toms* a cold. O do, de, do, de, do de, blisse thee from Whirle-Windes, Starre-blasting, and taking, do poore *Tom* some charitie, whom the foule Fiend vexes. There could I have him now, and there, and there againe, and there.[62]

[57] *King Lear*, II ii 198–200; III vi 9–19.
[58] *King Lear*, III ii 74–96.
[59] *King Lear*, III vi 82.
[60] Foakes, p. 277.
[61] foord *Quarto*; Sword *Folio*.
[62] *King Lear*, III iv 50–61.

Who speaks? This speech begins as an answer to Lear's question, so it is to that limited degree engaged with the world around him, and perhaps 'Blisse thy five Wits' is a compassionate address to Lear, though it could also be spoken to himself: we cannot be sure of the boundary between self and other. The second sentence is rhetorically elegant, but the sophistication breaks down into mere meaningless sounds, 'O do, de, do, de, do de'. In the final sentence, where is Tom's 'there'? Does he snatch at imaginary devils? Does he slap his own body?[63] The fiend has, he says, tempted him to suicide, and the speech itself is a form of suicide, dissolving the coherence of that selfhood which Edgar used to possess. The man whose voice was once usurped by Edmond now has no voice of his own. The sum of these different voices is Poor Tom.

'Tom' is a performance, and yet in this play performance is never ontologically simple, be it Goneril's first reply to Lear, Lear's irate rhetorical questions to Goneril demanding who he is, or the Fool's jests. Edgar's performance seems to stretch beyond what the role demands, so that we cannot say that Edgar is, in all untroubled sanity, simply adopting the persona of Poor Tom: he slides from voice to voice, and his speech fissures and multiplies him. His position as Gloster's cherished son is usurped by Edmond; his role as Poor Tom is elaborate and incoherent; as he leads the blinded Gloster to Dover the voice of Poor Tom slips away, as Gloster notices, and Edgar now speaks in a third voice as he describes (falsely) the view from the top of the cliff.[64] His fourth role is as the person who helps Gloster to his feet after he has supposedly fallen from the cliff; his fifth, the stage rustic who kills the steward; his sixth, the unknown knight who challenges Edmond; and finally he speaks the play's last words in his role as Edgar, Earl of Gloster, and the state's new ruler. And in between these assumed voices there are occasional asides when the voice reverts to the educated speech of Gloster's heir.[65] The metamorphoses of Edgar,

[63] Hunter ap. Foakes, p. 275.

[64] *King Lear*, IV vi 10–24. Foakes (p. 326) notes that in leading Gloster to suicide, Edgar is playing the traditional role of the devil, which adds yet another part to the list.

[65] e.g. *King Lear*, IV i 1–13.

multiplied beyond anything that the plot demands, play out weird displaced versions of himself which are at the same time versions of Lear, since on the heath Lear's incipient madness is externalized theatrically in the errant speech of the Fool and of Poor Tom.

Lear's madness takes him into strange new territory. *Quis hic locus?* Having given up his kingdom, and decided to live by turns in the houses of his two daughters (thereby surrendering his home, his *Heimat*), Lear is forced out onto the heath, to the no-man's-land of storm without shelter. Now the *heimlich* and the *unheimlich* exchange places. In a reversal or parody of the romance motif of the young man on a quest, the old man sets out on a pointless journey. What might have been a place of safety, Gloster's castle, becomes a place of danger even for Gloster himself, as it is there that he is blinded. The storm-swept heath, by contrast, becomes a place where Lear is cared for, and finds warmth and compassion. But tragedy detests sentimentality: this is also the terrain on which Lear is driven mad. Here the unlocalized stage of the Renaissance playhouse is important. We should disregard editorial fictions such as the stage directions 'Another part of the Heath' or 'A Room in Gloucester's Castle',[66] because such a literal concept of space is alien to the way in which the play uses location: the stage is a symbolic space, a space which maps the human potential for care or for cruelty; the heath and the castle are states of mind.[67] And as Lear's wits begin to turn, his language creates imagined spaces and narratives into which the other characters are translated. Poor Tom is supposed to have been reduced to beggary by his daughters; Goneril and Regan are put on trial in a courtroom of Lear's devising, with the Fool and Poor Tom as judges. Lear is self-enclosed in his madness.

Against such cruelty and such suffering we would bring some remedy. But wherever we turn, the vocabulary seems to have been used up. We might appeal to nature, but Edmond has usurped that

[66] Muir's settings for III ii and III iii. The Quarto and Folio do not specify locations.

[67] Cp. Alan C. Dessen, *Elizabethan Stage Conventions and Modern Interpreters* (Cambridge, 1984), pp. 103–4.

philosophy, and each time the play revisits the word it seems that we understand less and less about the nature of nature. Edmond and Gloster between them have destroyed the language of astrological influence, Edmond by his derision, Gloster by his credulity. Lear swears by a variety of supernatural powers, by the sun, by Hecate, by Apollo and Jupiter, but the play seems to have no settled theological framework. The Christian assumptions and references in the source play, *King Leir*, have been systematically removed.[68] From time to time characters voice philosophical remarks which appear attractive: Edgar says that his abject condition is not the worst possible state, because 'The lowest, and most dejected thing of Fortune, | Stands still in esperance'; but there is in fact a worse state still in store for him: just then his blinded father is led in. The words of philosophical acceptance have been mocked, and he has to rebuke his earlier self: 'O Gods! Who is't can say I am at the worst? | I am worse then ere I was'.[69] Gloster when being tortured appeals twice to the 'kinde Gods'—the gods who are both benevolent and the guardians of natural behaviour[70]—yet he later himself sees the gods as vicious, for 'As Flies to wanton Boyes, are we to th'Gods, | They kill us for their sport'.[71] This is another commonplace, with ancestry in Plautus, Montaigne, and Sidney.[72] When Gloster refuses to go any further, Edgar attempts to console him with a quasi-Stoic thought:

> Men must endure
> Their going hence, even as their coming hither,
> Ripenesse is all.[73]

To which Gloster replies, 'And that's true too'. *Too*: does he mean, 'yes, indeed, that's true', or 'yes, that's as true as any other platitude'? Both Edgar and Gloster exemplify the emptiness of philosophical language, for in their hands philosophy has come apart into easy

[68] See Elton. [69] *King Lear*, IV i 3–4, 27–8.

[70] *King Lear*, III vii 35, 91. *OED s.v.* kind 1 ('natural'), 5 ('benevolent'). Amongst the ironies of this word used here by Gloster is that it also means 'belonging to one by right of birth, descent, or inheritance' (*OED* 2), whereas Gloster, who used to invoke a trite sense of universal order, has disinherited his legitimate son.

[71] *King Lear*, IV i 38–9. [72] Muir, p. 140. [73] *King Lear*, V ii 9–11.

superstition, unearned sententiousness, or savage maxims: the pained, searching speech of terribly wounded humanity. What we are left with is a collection of quotations of old saws, names of gods, and gods without names. There are no complete signs, only stray signifiers; and because the philosophical speeches of individual characters are rarely accepted as meaningful by anyone else, these are signifiers without signifieds: there is no hope of a *signifié transcendantal*. In the old play of *King Leir*, thunder indicates divine disapproval when Leir and Perillus are threatened with death; in Shakespeare's *King Lear*, the storm images the psychological and social derangement of Lear and his world, but there seems to be nothing behind it.

As the play moves towards a conclusion, Shakespeare gives us several near-endings, too many near-closures: the romance ending in which Lear and Cordelia are reunited, the history-play ending in which Albany resigns the kingdom to Lear, and the tragic ending in which Lear dies. On the heath, language had been pushed close to meaninglessness, to mere sound: 'O do, de, do, de, do de'; 'alow: alow, loo, loo'.[74] Now theatrical genre itself follows the same path, as the play quotes a number of recognizable generic formulae for ending a play—quotes, only to break them. In the final scene the overthrow of Edmond by an unnamed challenger is a device from the world of romance, and through its generic allusion to the play's opening scene it offers the prospect of a courtly conclusion. Yet the episode feels awkwardly out of place, an attempt to summon heroic values into a play from which they have been banished; it is indeed an 'interlude' as Goneril calls it.[75] Ironically, she complains that in the single combat Edmond has not been fairly 'vanquish'd | But cozend, and beguild'.[76] But Goneril is not the only one to be clutching at fragments of abandoned moral and generic codes; Edgar tells Edmond:

> The Gods are just, and of our pleasant vices
> Make instruments to plague us:
> The darke and vitious place where thee he got,

[74] *King Lear*, III iv 56, 76.
[75] *King Lear*, V iii 90.
[76] *King Lear*, V iii 151–2.

Cost him his eyes.
BAST. Th'hast spoken right, 'tis true,
The Wheele is come full circle, I am heere.[77]

Edmond, the Machiavellian child of Fortune, recognizes that Fortune has turned her wheel and placed him back where he started, as the disregarded outsider. In contrast to the way he had parodied his father's beliefs and usurped his half-brother's voice in Act I, Edmond now echoes Edgar's philosophy with approval. But such an endorsement can only contaminate Edgar's own judgement, and reveals the cruelty in Edgar's view that his father's blinding was a just punishment for adultery. We recoil from the glib symbolism, the linking of the 'darke and vitious place' with the darkness of the blinded man. Recalling the violent way in which the blinding of Gloster had literalized a metaphor, tearing out the eyes of the father who could not see the true characters of his sons, this correspondence must outrage us, as it offers a form of equivalence which is aesthetically neat but morally abhorrent. Metaphor—an attempt to construct coherence—itself appals.

More staged symbolism is to come. The bodies of Regan and Goneril are brought on stage in order to assemble a visual quotation of the opening scene, and no doubt the characters should be arranged in order to reproduce their positions at the beginning of the play. Shakespeare is preparing the kind of symbolic tableau which would facilitate a morally legible ending, but in the event the fact that we glimpse such a symbolic order being re-assembled makes the terrible amorality of the ending all the more stark. The return to the beginning is completed when Lear enters with the body of Cordelia. His final speech over his dead daughter has a haunting half-quotation of the word 'nothing' which they had exchanged at the beginning:

no, no, no life?
. . . .
Thoul't come no more,
Never, never, never, never, never.[78]

[77] *King Lear*, V iii 168–71. [78] *King Lear*, V iii 304–7.

All the rhetorical games of the opening scene are reduced to the desolate ploce and asyndeton of that five-fold 'never', as father and daughter are once more held in parentheses in a semi-private space within the public sphere. But the painful play with quotations of the first scene is not yet over, for Albany attempts to divide the kingdom between Kent and Edgar.[79] When Kent declines, Edgar is left to provide the play's concluding commonplace:

> The waight of this sad time we must obey,
> Speake what we feele, not what we ought to say:
> The oldest hath borne most, we that are yong,
> Shall never see so much, nor live so long.[80]

The lines are inadequate, but their inadequacy is patent. Though Edgar says that 'we must... Speake what we feele', no one says anything after these lines. Language is exhausted.

[79] He says, 'Friends of my soule, you twaine, | Rule in this Realme, and the gor'd state sustaine' (*King Lear*, V iii 318–19). It is not clear whether he is inviting Kent and Edgar to share the rule with him, or to divide it between them.

[80] *King Lear*, V iii 322–5.

10

RACINE

Phèdre

In *Phèdre* Racine shows us a tragedy of double displacement. In prey to her passion for her stepson Hippolyte, Phèdre herself no longer inhabits space in the ways that other characters do; she moves in her own, strangely-contoured world, and her ventures into the spaces shared by others are catastrophic. She herself has become more and less than herself: her mind and body fragmented by, or into, passion, she is no longer simply Phèdre but she is the daughter of Pasiphaé, she is the victim of Vénus; she is part *veines*, part *flamme*, part *raison*, part *cœur*. The multiplication of influences and the play between abstract and physical nouns decompose her integrity.[1] This

Phèdre is quoted from the most recent Pléiade edition, Racine, *Œuvres complètes: I: Théâtre-Poésie*, edited by Georges Forestier (Paris, 1999), which calls the play *Phèdre et Hippolyte* following the first edition (1677); it was retitled *Phèdre* for the second edition in 1687. To avoid confusion I have used the customary, revised title. Other classical French plays on the myth of Phaedra and Hippolytus are Robert Garnier, *Hippolyte* (1573); Guérin de La Pinelière, *Hippolyte* (1635); Gabriel Gilbert, *Hypolite* (1647); Mathieu Bidar, *Hippolyte* (1675); Jacques Pradon, *Phèdre et Hippolyte* (1677). For Garnier see *Œuvres complètes de Robert Garnier: Marc Antoine, Hippolyte*, edited by Raymond Lebègue (Paris, 1974); the plays by La Pinelière, Gilbert, and Bidar are reprinted in *Le Mythe de Phèdre: Les Hippolyte français du dix-septième siècle*, edited by Allen G. Wood (Paris, 1996); and Pradon's play is reprinted in *Théâtre du XVIIe siècle: III*, edited by Jacques Truchet and André Blanc, Bibliothèque de la Pléiade (Paris, 1992). All translations in this chapter are my own.

[1] Roland Barthes suggestively calls *Phèdre* 'une tragédie nominaliste': *Sur Racine* (1963), in *Œuvres complètes*, edited by Éric Marty, 5 vols. (Paris, 2002), ii 148. In Seneca's *Phaedra* much use is made of the terms *amor* and *furor* to describe Phaedra's passion, nouns which (like the *furor* which impels Atreus) appear to denote a force which is at once within and without the character.

tragedy shows us something which ought to have remained hidden being brought to light, and this is much more than the revelation of a guilty passion: what is brought to light is the fragility of the *Heimat*, which in this case is the sense of self, its possession of space and its self-possession, its wholeness within secure boundaries.

Racine shows us the tragic isolation of Phèdre from the characters around her, but in the shaping of her tragedy it is also the unwelcome and inescapable connections which bring about her fate.[2] She is first referred to in the play not by her own name, but as the daughter of Minos and Pasiphaé,[3] and is thereby immediately linked to a mother who was notorious for her monstrous sexual desire for a bull. No mythical character can be properly identified without an account of their lineage, but here the mapping of Phèdre's ancestry is a preliminary mapping of the terrain of her actions, the limits of her will. Is Phèdre an autonomous and coherent individual with the power to free herself from such a link? Is she an *unheimlich* double of her mother, as the same crime of illicit passion is repeated from one generation to the next? Much is made of the ways in which characters are linked to others, or try to escape such links. Hippolyte, we are told, joins the ranks of the rest of mortals by falling in love with Aricie ('vous mettant au rang du reste des mortels', says Théramène, 'putting you on the same plane as the rest of the human race'[4]), and it is notable that Racine plays down the classical tradition of Euripides and Seneca, continued by Robert Garnier, which made Hippolytus a virginal devotee of Artemis and located him in the wild, natural spaces which symbolize a life untainted by desire or by the court.[5]

[2] Georges Poulet sees the continuity of the past with the present, and the repetition of the past in the present, as distinctive features of Racinian tragedy ('Notes sur le temps Racinien', in his *Études sur le temps humain: I* (Paris, 1952; reprinted 1997), pp. 148–65, esp. pp. 149–51).

[3] Racine, *Phèdre*, I i 36.

[4] *Phèdre*, I i 63.

[5] In Euripides (*Hippolytus*, ll. 73–87) Hippolytus offers Artemis a garland which has been plucked from a virgin meadow, the meadow being a metaphor for his own virginity; Seneca metamorphoses the space of Hippolytus into a terrain where he pursues a life free from the corruptions of the city and re-creates the golden age (*Phaedra*, ll. 1–84, 483–539).

Racine, comparatively, integrates him into the life of the court, and courtly notions of honour, even though he is always on the point of leaving. Phèdre, however, through her passion, becomes isolated from the world of the court and appears rather to join the ranks of her monstrous ancestors. Hippolyte, mindful of his father's history as a womanizer, is wary of being 'lié'[6] ('joined', 'linked', 'chained') in love or in sexual passion. Phèdre, by contrast, has, according to Œnone, cut herself off from her husband, her children, her servants, and from the gods:

> Vous offensez les Dieux auteurs de votre vie.
> Vous trahissez l'Époux à qui la foi vous lie.[7]

> You offend the gods, authors of your life; you betray the husband to whom your vow binds you.

Once again we have the verb *lier*. Racine often delicately italicizes his tragic ironies through his rhyme words; in Hippolyte's speech 'lié' had been rhymed with 'humilié', for he had seen an erotic link to another human being as a form of humiliation; here in Œnone's words to Phèdre 'lie' is ominously rhymed with 'vie'. Those bonds, she suggests, constitute life; we know that another, stronger, connection will bring death. Racine's rival Jacques Pradon, who staged his own *Phèdre et Hippolyte* a few days after Racine's, made Phèdre only the fiancée of Thésée, but Racine strengthens the bond of obligation by making her his wife. Yet for Phèdre, the marriage pledge which binds her to Thésée is as nothing compared with the involuntary bonds of ancestry and desire. Racine carefully does not make it simply a matter of inheritance, of an inherited guilt which might absolve her of moral responsibility, and leaves open the question of exactly how this ancestral connection constrains her. He gives us multiple maps of her psychology, and therefore of her responsibility for her passions and her actions. Moving between mythological and physical vocabularies, Phèdre says, 'Ce n'est plus une ardeur dans mes veines cachée. | C'est Vénus toute entière à sa proie attachée' ('It is no longer a desire

[6] *Phèdre*, I i 95. [7] *Phèdre*, I iii 197–8.

hidden within my veins, it is Venus completely attached to her prey').[8] Racine reworks the Greek double psychology whereby the same passion may be figured by external or internal causes, but his intricate movement between languages leaves us not knowing whether this is, on Phèdre's part, recognition or evasion.[9]

Phèdre's connections tie her to a world elsewhere, and provide a kind of space which she alone inhabits. In his preface to *Bajazet* Racine argued that the tragic protagonist should be distanced from the world of the audience;[10] in the case of Phèdre this distancing is extreme and intricate. The word *lieu* ('place') resonates through the play,[11] as we watch Phèdre's struggle to live in or to escape from a place—both Trézène and her own state of mind—which has become intolerable since the arrival of Hippolyte. Roland Barthes proposes that the Racinian tragic conflict is a crisis of space, in which characters cannot share space with a rival, but must either possess or destroy the other.[12] Yet in *Phèdre* the primary space which the protagonist occupies is a largely mental, largely mythic one, from which she is driven into an awkwardly conducted and only temporary use of shared stage spaces when she speaks to Œnone, Hippolyte, or Thésée. Hers is a space which excludes other mortals, but which is peopled by her own ancestors.[13] She is the descendant of the sun-god. One of Racine's predecessors, Guérin de La Pinelière, makes the Nurse tell Phèdre that her lofty social position exposes her to the gaze, and the judgement, of gods and men, and that the gods who are her ancestors

[8] *Phèdre*, I iv 305–6.

[9] For a discussion of Racine's treatment of Phèdre in the light of contemporary philosophical and religious thought see Lucien Goldmann, *Le Dieu caché: Étude sur la vision tragique dans les 'Pensées' de Pascal et dans le théâtre de Racine* (Paris, 1959, reprinted 1976), pp. 416–40. Subsequently there has been an extended debate over Racine's Jansenism, and the question of whether his characters are conceived through an Augustinian understanding of human corruption and lack of freewill: for an overview see John Campbell, *Questioning Racinian Tragedy* (Chapel Hill, 2005), pp. 205–44.

[10] 'On peut dire que le respect que l'on a pour les Héros augmente à mesure qu'ils s'éloignent de nous': Racine, *Œuvres complètes*, ed. Forestier, p. 625.

[11] It occurs seven times in the singular and seventeen times in the plural: see Bryant C. Freeman and Alan Batson, *Concordance du théâtre et des poésies de Jean Racine*, 2 vols. (Ithaca, NY, 1968), *s.v.* The concept is also important in Garnier's play.

[12] Barthes, ii 59–61, 78.

[13] *Phèdre*, IV vi 1273–6.

will see and punish her crime.[14] In this version, the Nurse thus acts as the external voice of moral conformity—one vigorously rejected by La Pinelière's Phèdre, who retorts that the gods themselves have pursued illicit affairs, and that queens like her are gods on earth. Racine's Phèdre, however, internalizes this ancestral judgement, largely through the imagery of light and dark. Light creates a particular kind of space for her.[15]

Under the pressure of Phèdre's passion, as the world becomes *unheimlich*, the various words for 'light' (*lumière*, *jour*, *clarté*) become unstable signifiers, since light does not mean the same for Phèdre as it does for the other characters. Since at this period the word *jour* means both 'day' and 'daylight', each occurrence of *jour* is liable to remind us that this special form of light exists only for the crucial single day which neo-classical tragedy occupies: this is light rethought *sous le signe* of tragedy. When she first appears, Phèdre cannot inhabit a single place: she both wants and does not want the light. Phèdre, according to Théramène, is 'Lasse enfin d'elle-même et du jour qui l'éclaire' ('weary finally of herself and of the day which lights her'), and yet Œnone says that Phèdre wishes to see the light, and orders the removal of others.[16] She thus creates a space within a space, a light which is for her alone. But it is oppressive. Her eyes are 'éblouis'[17] by this unaccustomed light: it means 'dazzled' or 'blinded', but the semantic field of this word in the seventeenth century also includes 'wronged', 'cheated', 'seduced'[18]—as if the ancestral light itself is her enemy and her seducer. As the descendant of the sun, there is nowhere for her to hide: 'Où me cacher?'[19] is a purely rhetorical

[14] *Le Mythe de Phèdre*, pp. 94, 92.

[15] Racine may have taken this imagery from Euripides, who repeatedly refers to light in his *Hippolytus*, though neither Euripides nor Seneca suggests that Phaedra experiences light and dark in a distinctively different way from the other characters; it is Racine's imagination which creates a particular form of light for her. For details of Racine's use of Euripides and Seneca, see the notes in the Pléiade edition.

[16] *Phèdre*, I i 46; I ii 149–50. [17] *Phèdre*, I iii 155.

[18] *Dictionnaire historique de la langue française*, edited by Alain Rey, 3 vols. (Paris, 1992, reissued 1998), *s.v.*

[19] *Phèdre*, IV vi 1277.

question. The character created by Robert Garnier brazenly invokes the ruler of the heavens, and the sun which sees into men's hearts, to witness that she has been outraged by Hippolyte.[20] But Racine's Phèdre, with a stronger moral awareness, feels the full weight of the ancestral light, and cannot summon it to endorse a lie. Being in the light, in that light, is painful. She is surprised that she can still sustain life, if it is life: 'Et je vis? Et je soutiens la vue | De ce sacré Soleil, dont je suis descendue?' ('And do I live? And do I endure the sight of this sacred Sun from which I am descended?').[21] It is the sun's gaze on her which is almost insupportable. In seventeenth-century French *soutenir* is a strong verb: not just 'sustain' but 'undergo the assault of', 'resist', 'endure'.[22] Again, the influence of the ancestors and the gods upon her seems to be a form of violence. But neither is there any escape to the darkness of the underworld, since her father Minos is judge there.[23] Once again a public space—in this case, the collectively mythologized darkness of Hades—has been turned into a singularity, a part of her own mythic space.

But other characters stand differently in the light: they seek enlightenment, they seek to bring matters to light. Thésée thinks that his (and anyone's) sight would be misled by the outward appearance of Hippolyte into thinking him virtuous; Hippolyte maintains that his heart is as clear as day: 'Le jour n'est plus pur que le fond de mon cœur'.[24] Thésée asks the gods to cast light on his trouble, but eventually laments that things have become all too clear.[25] Aricie implores Hippolyte to enlighten Thésée, but he refuses to 'mettre au jour' Phèdre's crime.[26] Aricie also asks Thésée why he cannot see Hippolyte's innocence, when it is so plain to other observers.[27] As used by this group of characters, these are familiar metaphors for the transparency or opacity of the human heart, for the ease or difficulty of reading character from appearance; but Phèdre stands apart from

[20] Garnier, IV 1715–26. [21] *Phèdre*, IV vi 1273–4.

[22] Jean Dubois et al., *Dictionnaire du français classique: Le XVIIe siècle* (Paris, 1992), *s.v.*

[23] *Phèdre*, IV iv 1277–88. [24] *Phèdre*, IV ii 1035–6; IV ii 1112.

[25] *Phèdre*, V vii 1647. [26] *Phèdre*, V i 1339–40.

[27] *Phèdre*, V iv 1430–2.

this group, enduring a mythologized light, inhabiting a singular conceptual space. So much of what is shown in this light is monstrous: Racine's vocabulary keeps insisting on the etymological connection between *montrer* and *monstre*.[28] Phèdre herself thinks of Hippolyte 'comme un Monstre effroyable à mes yeux' ('like a monster which is fearful to my eyes'), and Thésée also calls him 'monstre'.[29] Thésée asks the gods, 'éclairez mon trouble, et daignez à mes yeux | Montrer la vérité' ('clear away my doubt, and show the truth to my eyes').[30] Thésée has killed monsters, including Phèdre's half-brother the Minotaur, but fatally misrecognizes Hippolyte, and brings about his death through Neptune's sea-monster. This eruption of the uncanny which destroys Hippolyte is a metaphor for—or rather a metonymic manifestation of—the destructive power of Phèdre's desire.

Phèdre may move in and out of the spaces defined or occupied by others, but she is much preoccupied with, and mentally dwells in, imaginary spaces elsewhere. She torments herself by envisaging the times and places in which she imagines Hippolyte and Aricie to have met.[31] When Œnone explains that they are lovers, Phèdre exclaims 'Depuis quand? Dans quels lieux?' ('Since when? In what places?'), but this is more than a question about mundane arrangements, it is an exclamation of her own despair at being unable to possess Hippolyte in any time or place except that of her imagination. She thinks that 'Tous les jours se levaient clairs et sereins pour eux' ('Every day dawned clear and serene for them'), unlike the contaminated daylight in which she lives. Their days are imagined as plural, even though we know that they have only just declared their mutual love. In her eyes, they will always enjoy their love, even if they are physically separated. A train of reflexive verbs describing the love of Hippolyte and Aricie envisages a mutuality which Phèdre cannot attain, and these verbs—some

[28] The link goes back to the Latin *monstro* (to show) which derives from *monstrum* (monster, prodigy), which in turn is connected to *moneo* (to warn).

[29] *Phèdre*, III iii 884; IV ii 1045.

[30] *Phèdre*, V ii 1411.

[31] *Phèdre*, IV vi 1232–56.

in the imperfect tense of repeated and habitual action—create a series of metaphysical spaces and hypothetical times in which the love of the couple unites them in a dimension which is not defined by physical limitations:

> Ils s'aiment! . . .
> Comment se sont-ils vus? Depuis quand? Dans quels lieux?
> . . . .
> Les a-t-on vus souvent se parler, se chercher?
> Dans le fond des forêts allaient-ils se cacher?
> Hélas! Ils se voyaient avec pleine licence.[32]

> They love each other! . . . How did they see each other? Since when? In what places? Were they often seen talking together, looking for each other? Did they go to hide themselves in the depths of the forests? Alas! They were seeing each other with complete freedom.

Œnone assures Phèdre that 'Ils ne se verront plus' ('They will see each other no longer'), but Phèdre retorts, 'Ils s'aimeront toujours' ('They will love each other for ever'). This leads into her asking 'Où me cacher?' ('Where can I hide myself?')[33]—using the same verb which she had just used for the erotic meetings of Hippolyte and Aricie—and realizing that there is nowhere for her to hide in a universe which is peopled by her ancestors.

Quis hic locus? One spatial image is laminated upon another. She dreams of sitting in a forest or watching a chariot in the dust—in other words, of inhabiting spaces used by Hippolyte, yet not quite sharing these spaces with him, for these are spaces in which she could gaze unrestrainedly upon him.[34] This idea derives from Euripides,[35] where his Phaedra longs for the refreshment of pure water and the excitement of the hunt, and the insistence in Racine upon the work of the eye forms a remarkable contrast with Garnier's version, in which Phedre envies the forest streams for their erotic contact with the sweaty Hippolyte who kisses them when drinking after the hunt.[36] Racine's protagonist sees only an alternative space for another kind of

[32] *Phèdre*, IV vi 1232–7. [33] *Phèdre*, IV vi 1277. [34] *Phèdre*, I iii 176–8.
[35] Euripides, *Hippolytus*, l. 208. [36] Garnier, III 1025–46.

sight. Her sight is too creative. It doubles characters, or it reduces all signifiers to the one signified, for everything spells 'Hippolyte'. In the temple where she sacrificed to Venus, she had thought only of Hippolyte, seeing him continually even while standing in front of the altar.[37] She looked at Thésée, but saw only Hippolyte; looking at Hippolyte she sees a younger Thésée.[38] She imagines an alternative past in which she would have guided Hippolyte through the labyrinth instead of Ariadne guiding Thésée.[39] And this alternative myth of Hippolyte killing the Minotaur turns into a poignant image for Phèdre's passion:

> Et Phèdre au Labyrinthe avec vous descendue,
> Se serait avec vous retrouvée, ou perdue.

> And Phèdre, having descended into the labyrinth with you, would with you be recovered, or lost.[40]

Now we have moved from one kind of hypothetical space—part of a parallel mythological narrative—into another kind of space, the labyrinth of Phèdre's psyche, the dangerous and intricate space created by her desire. The maze is a place of unreason, of multiple deviations. To descend into this space with Hippolyte would lead, would have led, to her being either rescued or lost. 'Se serait retrouvée' here is richly suggestive: it means both that (if Hippolyte surrendered to her) she would find her way again after having lost it, and that she would be in possession of herself again. But such a recovery and repossession are cast into a conditional tense whose realization depends upon Hippolyte reciprocating her desire, and this labyrinth too will remain an unrealizable space which cannot be entered. A lamination or intercalation of spaces is at work: a privately imagined space overlaying and qualifying her apprehension of that commonly perceptible space in which others move. And as with space, so too with time: the present is repeatedly disturbed by her mind dwelling in alternative scenarios of the past, or parallel versions of the present.

[37] *Phèdre*, I iii 279–88.
[38] *Phèdre*, I iii 290; II v 628–9, 640.
[39] *Phèdre*, II v 645–62.
[40] *Phèdre*, II v 661–2.

Phèdre does not know where she is: 'Insensée, où suis-je? . . . Où laissé-je égarer mes vœux, et mon esprit?' ('Mad, where am I? Where have I let my vows and my spirit stray?').[41] In the 1677 edition of the play, 'laissé' is spelt 'laissay', which could be either present or past tense: [42] 'where *have* I let my desires and my spirit stray?' or 'where *do* I let my desires and my spirit stray'? The ambiguity of tense is productive, as Phèdre's 'je' inhabits past and present simultaneously—and so dwells in neither. Momentarily there is a fracturing of the self, as the form of self figured by the first-person pronoun imagines that its 'vœux' and its 'esprit' have strayed. 'Vœux' and 'esprit' seem briefly to be granted agency, acting autonomously from that 'je' which seeks to assert its control and so its stability. *Esprit* is one of Racine's multiply suggestive words: perhaps 'soul' or 'spirit', but also 'intelligence'. *Vœux* in this period has the particular sense of 'sexual desires', specifically, 'desires seeking to be reciprocated', but also retains the originary meaning of 'vows made to a god', 'votive prayer';[43] so even within the semantic field of the single word there is in Phèdre's speech a doubled field, a overlayering of sexual desires upon prayer. When Phèdre prays to Vénus for relief from the torments of love—'Par des vœux assidus je crus les détourner, | Je lui bâtis un Temple' ('By assiduous prayer I thought to turn them aside, I built her a temple')[44]—the word 'vœux' clearly means 'prayers' but carries within it the trace of another meaning, the desire for Hippolyte; so too, in 'Je lui bâtis un Temple' 'lui' could mean 'him' as well as 'her': she is building a temple to Vénus, but is it not rather a temple to Hippolyte?

If *lier* ('bind') is one of Racine's repeated motifs in this play, another is almost its opposite, *égarer* ('stray'): 'Où laissé-je égarer mes vœux, et mon esprit?' 'Que fais-je?', she says, 'Où ma raison se va-t-elle égarer?' ('What am I doing? Where will my reason stray?') with another unsettling switch of tenses from present to future. When

[41] *Phèdre*, I iii 179–80.

[42] As Forestier points out (Racine, *Œuvres complètes*, ed. Forestier, p. 1646).

[43] Dubois and Rey, *s.v.*

[44] *Phèdre*, I iii 279–80.

speaking to Hippolyte, she says that she seems to see Thésée: 'Je le vois, je lui parle, et mon cœur... Je m'égare, | Seigneur, ma folle ardeur malgré moi se déclare' ('I see him, I speak to him, and my heart... I wander, Sir, my mad desire in spite of myself declares itself').[45] The strain of speaking ostensibly about Thésée while thinking about and addressing Hippolyte is too much, and she breaks off. 'Je m'égare': she loses herself syntactically in her aposiopesis, but she is also straying morally in thus indirectly confessing her love for Hippolyte. Her 'folle ardeur' speaks in spite of herself, 'malgré moi'. But when it is 'ardeur' which speaks, who is this 'Je' who is wandering, who is the 'moi' in 'malgré moi'?[46] Who speaks? The self decomposes in this tense utterance. Ultimately, when she has taken the poison, her completely alienated eye, 'Son œil tout égaré',[47] no longer recognizes her servants. When hesitating where to begin the story of her own passion, she diverges into speaking of the 'égarements' into which lust led her mother.[48] She wanders in an eternal return, experiencing a 'doubling, dividing and interchanging of the self'[49] as she seems to be repeating the stories of her mother and her sister. When Œnone laments that they ever landed at Trézène, and Phèdre replies 'Mon mal vient de plus loin',[50] she is both locating the origin of her passion in another country and thinking spatially about its etiology. Her imagination seems to delve into a layered psyche, looking into the past, and in foreign places, for an explanation of the spaces of her own desiring self. The *heimlich* self is shown to be built upon an *unheimlich* foundation. As she sacrificed to Vénus,

> De victimes moi-même à toute heure entourée,
> Je cherchais dans leurs flancs ma raison égarée.

> Myself surrounded by victims at every moment, I sought in their entrails my strayed reason.[51]

[45] *Phèdre*, IV vi 1264; II v 629–30.
[46] Cp. Barthes on Racine's pronouns: ii 86.
[47] *Phèdre*, V v 1476.
[48] *Phèdre*, I iii 250.
[49] See Freud, quoted on p. 5 above.
[50] *Phèdre*, I iii 269.
[51] *Phèdre*, I iii 281–2.

She sought (imperfect tense: an incomplete or vainly repeated action) her strayed reason outside herself in the entrails of these sacrificial victims.

In startling images such as 'Je cherchais dans leurs flancs ma raison égarée' the decomposition of Phèdre's self-coherence is mapped as the boundaries keep shifting between the abstract and the physical, offering us multiple readings of this divided individual. She feels 'une flamme si noire',[52] and although 'flamme' is a conventional term for 'love' in this period,[53] and 'noire' is obviously 'black' in a moral sense, the visual image in 'noire' reawakens the literal meaning of 'flamme' to create a weird locution akin to Milton's 'darkness visible'[54] and to make desire conceptually estranged. Similarly in Hippolyte's 'Phèdre toujours en proie à sa fureur extrême' ('Phèdre still a prey to her extreme rage')[55] the routine phrase 'en proie à' is energized by a recollection of 'Vénus toute entière à sa proie attachée', so that the savagery of that image returns physicality to the dead metaphor, and existential force and a degree of personification to 'fureur'. 'Et l'espoir malgré moi s'est glissé dans mon cœur' ('And hope, in spite of myself, has slipped itself into my heart'),[56] she says, giving the abstract noun a physical verb, and once again signalling in 'malgré moi' the fissured self and the invasive power of desires which apparently have some external origin and are beyond her control. Or again:

> Je le vis, je rougis, je pâlis à sa vue.
> Un trouble s'éleva dans mon âme éperdue.
> Mes yeux ne voyaient plus, je ne pouvais parler,
> Je sentis tout mon corps et transir, et brûler.
> Je reconnus Vénus, et ses feux redoutables,
> D'un sang qu'elle poursuit tourments inévitables.[57]

> I saw him, I blushed, I grew pale at his sight. A disturbance arose in my deeply shaken soul. My eyes no longer saw, I could not speak, I felt my whole body both pierced and burning. I recognized Venus and her powerful fires, the inevitable torments of a blood which she pursues.

[52] *Phèdre*, I iii 310. [53] Dubois, *s.v.* [54] Milton, *Paradise Lost*, i 63.
[55] *Phèdre*, III vi 989. [56] *Phèdre*, III i 768. [57] *Phèdre*, I iii 273–8.

What coherence is now left, what power of agency, to that emphatically reiterated 'je' which is so split between 'trouble', 'âme', 'yeux', and 'corps', the 'feux' of Vénus, and the 'sang' which seems to oscillate between meaning 'blood', 'sexual passion', and 'family'? Through the multiple possibilities of that word Racine holds back from providing a single aetiology of passion. We see here Phèdre's unavailing struggle to understand her own self spatially, to map the physiology and psychology of desire; the result is a confession of radical tragic incoherence and powerlessness.[58]

Although Œnone laments that they ever came to Trézène and its 'Rivage malheureux' and 'bords dangereux' ('unhappy shore', 'dangerous coast'),[59] it is not the geographical place called Trézène which is the truly dangerous terrain. Repeatedly characters struggle with the boundaries of their world and what may lie beyond them. Phèdre's very first line says that she will go no further: 'N'allons point plus avant. Demeurons, chère Œnone' ('Let us go no further. Let us stay, dear Œnone').[60] She is referring at once to her inability to walk further in her enfeebled state, her desire to end her life, and, kept within the silence of her heart for a few minutes longer, her desire to go further and broach her love to Hippolyte. Phèdre's use of the first person plural creates a shared agency, but this cannot last. 'Demeurons': but where? The ground on which she stands is unstable, its boundaries labile. The word 'bord' and its cognates echo through this play.[61] Thésée is said to be unable to return across the frontiers ('bords') of the underworld; Hippolyte thought that he could watch safely from the shore ('bord') as other men experienced the storms of passion; Phèdre wants Thésée not to limit his vengeance on Hippolyte.[62] Phèdre recognizes that 'De

[58] Her uncertain state of mind is much more delicately figured by such semantic fluidity than in Pradon's clumsy list of the abstract nouns which his Phèdre says have torn her apart: 'Gloire, honte, dépit, douleur, rage, pitié, | Raison, haine, fureur, jalousie, amitié, | Tous déchirent mon âme en ce désordre extrême' (Pradon, IV iii 1241–3).

[59] *Phèdre*, I iii 267–8.

[60] *Phèdre*, I iii 153.

[61] The word 'bords' occurs 11 times, 'bornes' twice, and 'bornant', 'borne', and 'bornera' once each.

[62] *Phèdre*, II i 388; II ii 534; IV vi 1261.

l'austère pudeur les bornes sont passées' ('The boundaries of austere modesty have been crossed').[63] In speaking to Hippolyte, Phèdre herself has crossed a fatal Rubicon, for she cannot take back her speech, but throughout the play she crosses and recrosses the strange boundaries between her inner space (the terrain configured by her desire) and the outer space in which other characters move.

It is an estranged language that creates Phèdre's inner space and that separates her from the other characters. Within Phèdre's language there is an undertow of *différance*[64] which displaces her into a world elsewhere (or into a series of perhaps impossible worlds beyond the reach of others). Words such as *vœux* slide away from their intended meaning. Phèdre cannot name Hippolyte herself, but uses a circumlocution which makes Œnone produce his name, to which Phèdre replies, 'C'est toi qui l'as nommé' ('It is you who have named him'),[65] as if this shifts responsibility onto Œnone not only for speaking the name but for bringing Phèdre's passion into the outer world. Silence guards the inner world, and contributes significantly to the tragic plot, for it allows something from the unspoken world to be construed or misconstrued, while evading responsibility for such constructions. Silence creates a series of spaces in which fatal narratives can be generated. Much of the tragedy depends on untimely speech or on silence: Phèdre suppresses speech within her, and then speaks too soon, for her husband is not dead; her enigmatic words and ominous silence when Thésée returns foster in him an anxiety which Œnone exploits with her false story of Hippolyte's attempted rape of his stepmother; then, when Phèdre is about to acknowledge her guilt to Thésée, she learns of Hippolyte's love for Aricie, and keeps silent. Hippolyte refuses to denounce Phèdre, and so his father construes his silence as guilt. Thésée curses his son too soon, and cannot withdraw his words. Œnone dies without confessing her lie. When Phèdre finally speaks, it is too late.

[63] *Phèdre*, III i 766.

[64] Jacques Derrida, 'La différance', in his *Marges de la philosophie* (Paris, 1972), pp. 1–29.

[65] *Phèdre*, I iii 264.

Where does Phèdre end? In Euripides, after Phaedra has killed herself, her body is displayed along with a tablet on which she has written that she has been raped by Hippolytus. It is an extraordinary, uncanny moment. The dead woman speaks—lies—through writing, through a writing which Theseus pauses to read silently, so creating a space of private communion with the dead within the more public stage space. When he reads the words aloud, they are not spoken but sung, a most unusual dramatic italicization. Words which are physically dissociated from their author take on a new kind of substantiality. In Garnier's play, Phedre, the Nurse, and These all at various moments think that they are already feeling the punishments of Hades, as the space of the human world begins to turn, in their imagination, into the space of eternal punishment.[66] La Pinelière gives Phèdre a private scene in which she laments in her chamber over a casket into which the remains of Hippolyte have been gathered. Pradon grotesquely imagines a union in which Phèdre stabs herself so that her blood spurts out over the body of Hippolyte. All these dramatists think about how the special spaces of Phèdre might finally be integrated with, or separated from, the space occupied by the other characters. After a drama in which the self is multiplied or fissured, multiplied *and* fissured, and the words which define the sources of our identity become floating, even contradictory signifiers, Racine's conclusion moves towards the stabilization of time, space, and language. Racine brings Phèdre into the presence of Thésée at a point when she has already taken the poison, and so her words come from an *unheimlich* source, from one on the borders of death, a more unsettling form of speech even than the words on the tablet in Euripides. In a play which has been so much concerned with *bords* ('boundaries', 'limits', 'edges'), Phèdre's final speech is spoken on the ultimate boundary. At the beginning of the play she is, we are told, on the point of death; at the end of the play that death is accomplished: her life in the course of the play is therefore suspended in parentheses between death and death, between its announcement and its arrival,

[66] Garnier, IV 1891–8, V 2249–56, 2309–22.

between signifier and signified. In her final speech she speaks of having stained the daylight:

> Et la Mort, à mes yeux dérobant la clarté
> Rend au jour, qu'ils souillaient, toute sa pureté.[67]

> And Death, taking clear sight from my eyes, restores to the day, which they had stained, all its purity.

Here, as the clarity of physical vision fails her, death restores purity to the light (or the day) which she has contaminated simply by looking upon it. Three near synonyms—'clarté', 'jour', and 'pureté'—three kinds of light, are returned into normal usage, purged of their implication in the *unheimlich* spaces of Phèdre.

[67] *Phèdre*, V vii 1643–4.

Epilogue

Quisquis suos patimur manis.[1]

Rilke believed that each individual contains within himself his own death, peculiar to himself, which grows and matures as he grows and matures.[2] But this death may never come to maturity. For there are two kinds of death: the first is *der grosse Tod* or *der eigne Tod* (one's own death, that which is appropriate); and the second is *der kleine Tod* or *der fremde Tod* (death which is alien, foreign). The former is the distinctive, personal death which is the eventual fulfilment of an individual life; and a man should so mould his life that his death may come in a personal, not a mass or impersonal form. The latter is the anonymous death which comes to those who have not understood the meaning of life; it is an alien, alienating death.

In the tragedies discussed in this book, the characters eventually move into the singularity of their own death, which has been prepared long before. Agamemnon's murder, or sacrifice, was prepared by his own hand at Aulis when he sacrificed his daughter. Clytemnestra in her dream foresees her own death at the hands of the serpent who is her son, and the theatrical staging of her murder as an echo of the death of Agamemnon implies that her death is an outcrop of her

[1] Virgil, *Aeneid*, vi 743: 'each of us undergoes his own purgatory'.

[2] William Rose, 'Rilke and the Conception of Death' in *Rainer Maria Rilke: Aspects of his Mind and Poetry*, edited by William Rose and G. Craig Houston (London, 1938), pp. 41–84.

own earlier act. Cassandra's vision of the bloody house of Atreus makes her imminent killing a part of her intimate prophetic knowledge which is enclosed in a language which no one else can comprehend. Oedipus eventually attains the grace of a resting place at Colonus, which is a sign of his separation from other mortals—a separation which he had begun in the partial suicide of his self-blinding. And that blinding had been a way of enclosing himself against a death which would have led him into an unbearable proximity with his parents in the underworld. Antigone's death is the fulfilment of her path to the underworld on which she had set out before the play opened. Othello's suicide is staged in his final narrative as his only remaining mode of self-assertion, a transportation of himself into a time and place where no one else can reach him—'in *Aleppo* once'. Macbeth's actual death is a commonplace death in battle, but what more deeply characterizes his end is the self-knowledge which attends the long death of his moral awareness. Lear's death is prefaced by anguished protest at the wanton destruction of Cordelia, and when that has been voiced there is no more work for his voice to perform, and he dies within the enclosure which he has formed around himself and his daughter. Phèdre's death is announced at the beginning of the play and completed at the end; everything in between is held in parentheses, awaiting what must come. Indeed, there is a teleology attached to all mythic figures, in that we know their story in advance, and therefore death for the heroes occupies a pre-existing off-stage space into which they are summoned: a form of *Heimat*. These are all instances of *der eigne Tod*: completed tragedy.

Defining the *Heimat* as conceived by Hölderlin, Heidegger writes:

> Das verbirgt sich für Hölderlin im Heimischwerden des Menschen, welches Heimischwerden ein Durchgang durch die Fremde und eine Auseinandersetzung mit der Fremde ist. *Das* Fremde freilich, durch das hindurch die Heimkehr wandert, ist kein beliebiges Fremdes im Sinne des bloßen unbestimmten Nicht-Eigenen. Das auf die Heimkehr bezogene, d. h. mit ihr einige *Fremde*, ist die *Herkunft* der

> Heimkehr und ist das gewesene Anfängliche des Eigenen und Heimischen.[3]
>
> For Hölderlin, that essence [of history] is concealed in human beings' becoming homely, a becoming homely that is a passage through and encounter with the foreign. *That* foreign, of course, through which the return home journeys, is not some arbitrary 'foreign' in the sense of whatever is merely and indeterminately not one's own. The *foreign* that relates to the return home, that is, is one with it, is the *provenance* of such return and is that which has been at the commencement with regard to what is one's own and the homely.[4]

Quis hic locus? The journey which the tragic protagonist makes is one which takes him out of the shared *Heimat*, the common home with its agreed structures of thought, into a form of the *unheimlich* where the usual relations of time and space, signifier and signified, are deformed into strange shapes. In this dimension the individual may appear strong, may seem to have a Hegelian stature and solidity, but the work of tragedy is to estrange such a selfhood from the world around it, and from itself. That which impels the protagonist, and seems to be a source of strength—love, ambition, duty—turns against him to undo him, is seen as excess or as error, and is called by names such as *hubris*, *hamartia*, or *furor*. Values are deformed into strange parodic shapes. The foreign through which the tragic figure moves is, as Heidegger puts it, a foreign which relates to the return home. And the return home is a return to the dark.

[3] Martin Heidegger, *Hölderlins Hymne »Der Ister«*, Gesamtausgabe 35 (Frankfurt am Main, 1984), p. 67.

[4] Martin Heidegger, *Hölderlin's Hymn 'The Ister'*, translated by William McNeill and Julia Davis (Bloomington, 1996), p. 54.

Index